Split-Gut Song

Split-Gut Song

Jean Toomer and the Poetics of Modernity

KAREN JACKSON FORD

THE UNIVERSITY OF ALABAMA PRESS

Tuscaloosa

Copyright © 2005
The University of Alabama Press
Tuscaloosa, Alabama 35487-0380
All rights reserved
Manufactured in the United States of America

Typeface: Minion

∞

The paper on which this book is printed meets the minimum requirements of American
National Standard for Information Science—Permanence of Paper for Printed Library
Materials, ANSI Z39.48–1984.

Library of Congress Cataloging-in-Publication Data

Ford, Karen Jackson.
Split-gut song : Jean Toomer and the poetics of modernity / Karen Jackson Ford.
p. cm.
Includes bibliographical references and index.
ISBN 0-8173-1456-3 (cloth : alk. paper)
1. Toomer, Jean, 1894-1967—Criticism and interpretation. 2. Modernism (Literature)—
United States. 3. African Americans in literature. 4. Race in literature. I. Title.
PS3539.O478Z64 2005
813'.52—dc22

2004022371

Excerpts of the poems "And Pass," "As the Eagle Soars," and "To Gurdjieff Dying" by Jean
Toomer are reprinted by permission of Yale Collection of American Literature, Beinecke
Rare Book and Manuscript Library, Yale University.

To Donald Laird

Contents

Acknowledgments

I AM GRATEFUL TO many friends and colleagues who helped me with this book. Two research assistants gave careful attention to the project: Stephanie Callan did bibliographic searches as I was setting out, and Patrick Jackson proofread the manuscript, checked quotations, and located citation information as I was finishing. Louise Bishop, Gary Mar, Kathleen Karlyn, Paul Peppis, George Rowe, and Harry Wonham read and commented on parts of the manuscript, and I am grateful for their interest and rigor. John Gage has been talking to me about the ideas here since I interviewed at Oregon in 1992, and he made possible a sabbatical in 2001 during which I wrote most of the book. Cary Nelson generously offered advice and encouragement. I thank the staff of The University of Alabama Press, and I am also very grateful to Rebecca Johnson, whose scrupulous editing and good humor made even tidying up the manuscript an enjoyable task. I also want to thank Amber Pilar Ford, Anna Ford Cullifer, and Jamie Ford Valley for their moral support.

My two greatest debts are to Donald Laird and Shari Huhndorf. Donald Laird read the entire manuscript more than once; his suggestions for revision made it clearer and more to the point, and his belief in the work heartened me. He also located articles and books, tracked down incomplete citations, and spent many hours in the library and at the copying machine assuring that I had the materials I needed. Shari Huhndorf also read draft after draft of the entire manuscript, offering rigorous and productive criticism, astute suggestions for issues to develop, and steady encouragement. Her intellectual companionship was essential to my work, and her knowledge, good sense, wisdom, and patience are gifts I can never adequately acknowledge. I often felt I was writing this book for her, so crucial was her mind to its development.

Abbreviations

C: Cane. Edited by Darwin T. Turner. New York: Norton, 1988.

Reader: A Jean Toomer Reader: Selected Unpublished Writings. Edited by Frederik L. Rusch. New York: Oxford UP, 1993.

Wayward: selections from *The Wayward and the Seeking* as published in *The Lives of Jean Toomer: A Hunger for Wholeness,* edited by Cynthia Earl Kerman and Richard Eldridge. Baton Rouge: Louisiana State UP, 1987.

CP: The Collected Poems of Jean Toomer. Edited by Robert B. Jones and Margery Toomer Latimer. Chapel Hill: U of North Carolina P, 1988.

Split-Gut Song

1

The Scratching Choruses of Modernity

FROM THE OUTSET, Jean Toomer's *Cane* has been recognized as a pivotal work in American literature. When it appeared in a small edition in 1923, it was heralded as the first book to treat African American life *artistically* because it replaced Negro stereotypes with complex, impressionistic portraits; clichéd tales of racial tragedy or triumph with subtle explorations of black artistic development; and supposed African American literary forms with modernist experimental structures. Though *Cane* would not become a popular success for another forty years, contemporary reviewers and critics regarded it as an inaugural event in American letters. It was again accorded literary primacy upon its republication in 1969 during the Black Arts movement for its unconventional style and its celebration of African American origins. Since then "the book that launched the Harlem Renaissance" (Bell, *Afro-American Novel* 321), the "seminal text for the New Negro Renaissance of the twenties and for the New Black Poetry movement of the sixties" (Gates 202), "the most frequently studied, the most respected of all the books of the Harlem Renaissance" (Turner, *C* 122) has also been pronounced a key modernist text, ranking in significance and style with T. S. Eliot's *The Waste Land* (1922), James Joyce's *Ulysses* (1922), and William Carlos Williams's *Spring and All* (1923).[1]

Cane is a preeminent text for all these movements not simply because of its fresh treatment of African American subjects but because of its distinctive structure and style. The work gathers sonnets, ballads, free-verse poems, work songs, spirituals, popular songs, short stories, a quasi drama, and brief prose pieces into three separate sections in a rich collage of cultural forms, historical epochs, and national locales. Moreover,

Cane's prose is highly figurative and lyrical, contributing to many critics' sense that the volume is extending the limits of literary forms.[2] Readers have responded to *Cane*'s variety of forms differently at different moments, at first expressing bewilderment, then ignoring its heterogeneity by classifying the book as a novel or a collection of short stories, and recently, arguing that it self-consciously defies any generic categorization.[3]

At stake in earlier readings of *Cane* as a novel or collection of short stories is the conviction that prose can offer a realistic portrayal of African American life and culture. This is a poetics of depiction or representation. From Frederick Douglass to Toni Morrison, obviously in quite different ways, black narratives have witnessed and interpreted African American existence. Indeed, so important is the task of documenting the actuality of African American life that Toomer is most frequently compared to naturalist Richard Wright and praised for depicting "the earthy realities of a Black past" (Bradley 684). Even those who acknowledge that *Cane* is not a strictly realistic novel can claim that it offers a "higher realism of the emotions." Through lyricism and impressionism, Toomer achieves an accuracy of representation that exceeds realism. Either way the argument is made, realism or "higher" realism, *Cane* is valued for its authentic depiction of African America.[4]

Conversely, more recent critics have emphasized the antirealistic aspects of the text, its impressionism, lyricism, symbolism, and disjunction. Here is a poetics of disruption. *Cane* rejects the burden of representation, disrupting formal conventions as a means of shattering racial expectations. *Cane* still performs a political function but now through the indeterminacy, not the authenticity, of racial identity. The text registers resistance to rigid racial categorizations in the ambiguity of its formal structures, and what is "represented" is the impossibility of a stable racial portrayal.[5]

While these approaches have produced important and discerning readings, they have also devalued the poems in *Cane*—not simply by oversight but by necessity. To come to terms with the poems is to unsettle many established notions about the book, and about African American literature more generally, especially the claim that *Cane* invents new literary forms to articulate a radical conception of racial identity.[6] Moreover, guided through the text by the poems, our sense of the structural logic and thus the significance of the ending will change. For the poetry of *Cane* tells quite a different story from the one many readers have sought in its pages, a story not of awakening, reconciliation, or promise but one of nostalgia, fragmentation, defeat.[7] Toomer himself described the book in these terms to his publisher Horace Liveright when he sent in the readied manuscript:

> The book is done.
> I look at its complacency and wonder where on
> earth all my groans and grunts and damns have gone.
> It doesn't seem to contain them
> And when I look for the power and beauty
> I thought I'd caught, they too seem to thin out
> and and [sic] elude me.
> Next time, perhaps . . . (*C* 154)

The letter, which is distinctive among Toomer's published letters for being formatted as poetry, is clearly elegiac. In the context of the whole document, the opening sentence is dirgelike: "The book is done." The repeated "and" in the penultimate line sounds less accidental than deliberately evocative of the elusiveness he laments. The faint hope in the last line echoes the ending of *Cane*—both gestures attempt to summon future possibility as an epilogue to tragedy. As I will show, focusing on the poems in *Cane* produces a text that accords poignantly with Toomer's discouraged letter to Liveright. *Cane* records the impossibility of representing the "power and beauty" Toomer associates with his material. As he came more and more to insist in the months and years following *Cane*'s publication, "*Cane* was a swan-song. It was a song of an end" (*Wayward* 123). What's more, *Cane*'s song of an end regards the very end of song, the inability of the modern black poet to transform the last echoes of the spirituals into a new poetry.[8] The poems of *Cane* dramatize this failure, and it is in the poetry that the elegiac strains of the book are most evident.

Despite the fact that it is impossible to understand *Cane* without understanding the function of its poems, only one short article has focused on the poetry in the eighty years since *Cane* first appeared—and even there, only on the poetry of part 1.[9] Many studies of *Cane* analyze the prose without so much as a reference to the poems, and even those that do treat the prose and poems in equal detail still conceive of the poems as supplementary to the prose.[10] The poems fare even worse in studies of *Cane*'s formal hybridity. To argue for a breakup of old forms or the invention of new ones, critics point to the prose, where lyric outbursts, ellipses, apostrophes, and dense figuration seem to signal generic defiance. In such a reading, the actual poems in *Cane* are almost an embarrassment, vestiges of a traditional notion of literary form that the book as a whole questions.[11]

In fact, however, the poems in *Cane* are central to its structural logic; they do not simply round out the three sections, as even Toomer himself sometimes suggested, but rather define each section and give coherence to the whole volume. We must consider the poetry with these things in mind: how the poems relate to the prose, how the poems relate to each other, and how the poems relate to the three-part structure of the volume. That third issue, how the poems function in the larger structure of the book, was something even Toomer struggled to enunciate. When Toomer first conceived of the book, he planned to organize it by genre, with the poems occupying the middle section of the book. The completed volume, of course, is organized by region, with poems dispersed throughout. Yet the poems only gain force and meaning through their juxtaposition with other forms, and the tension between poetry and prose, and even among different kinds of poetry, functions as a figure for all the other conflicts in the book.

These other conflicts were initially elaborated by Waldo Frank in his introduction to the first edition: "Part One is the primitive and evanescent black world of Georgia. Part Two is the threshing and suffering brown world of Washington, lifted by opportunity and contact into the anguish of self-conscious struggle. Part Three is Georgia again . . . the invasion into this black womb of the ferment seed: the neurotic, educated, spiritually stirring Negro" (*C* 139). His abbreviation of this structure at the end of the introduction makes his interpretation even more explicit: "the simple slave Past, the shredding Negro Present, the iridescent passionate dream of Tomorrow" (140). Frank's thesis-antithesis-synthesis model for *Cane* suggests that the circular movement of the book—the southern past, the northern present, the northerner "returning" to the south—is at heart a forward journey: the future lies in a return to origins.[12] However, the poetry tells a different tale. Poetry, especially in the form of song, is associated with cultural origins in part 1, but the meaning of poetry shifts as the book proceeds northward and into the present. There are ten poems in part 1, only five in part 2, and no actual poems in part 3. Significantly, the part 1 poems are *Cane*'s greatest achievement; part 2 poems are, by design, weak and confused by comparison. That is, poetry flowers, falters, and ultimately falls silent in *Cane*, witnessing the impossibility of recovering one's roots, the failure of the "dream of Tomorrow" to take hold even in ancestral lands.

As Toomer sent the completed manuscript off, he described the structure of the book in contradictory terms that hint at the importance of poetry, emphasizing "form" at the expense of regional logic:

> From three angles, CANE'S design is a circle. Aesthetically, from simple forms to complex ones, and back to simple forms. Regionally from the South up into the North, and back into the South again. Or, From [sic] the North down into the South, and then a return North. From the point of view of the spiritual entity behind the work, the curve really starts with [the last story in part 2] Bona and Paul (awakening), plunges into [part 3] Kabnis, emerges in [the first story in part 1] Karintha etc. swings upward into [two stories midway through part 2] Theatre [sic] and Box Seat, and ends (pauses) in [the final poem of part 2 and of the book] Harvest Song. (*Reader* 26)

Toomer's inconsistent portrayal of the book as both angular and circular, indeed as angles that somehow sketch a circle, captures his urge to form a whole out of disparate parts—to forge those angles (South, North; rural, urban; simple, complex) into a circle through the architectonics of the volume. Yet the oppositions that make up the lines of his "angles" remain resistant to resolution. If the book goes "from simple forms to complex ones, and back to simple forms," we have assumed that these forms map onto the South, North, and South respectively. But he immediately offers not just an alternative reading, but a converse one—"*or*" North, South, and North. In one breath he associates simple forms with the South and complex ones with the North, but in the next breath he reverses those associations. And, in any case, what would those simple or complex forms be?[13] In the first scenario, we might assume that folk songs and spirituals are simple forms associated with the primitive South, while prose vignettes and prose-drama are complex forms associated with the modern North—a fairly obvious distinction between "old" and "new" modes. However, in Toomer's alternate scenario, the forms associated with the North would be simple and those with the South complex. Here narrative might be considered *simply* direct and representational, attentive to historical accuracy, while lyric might offer something subtler—indirection, evocation, and emotional accuracy (perhaps this sense of the book is a holdover from when Toomer planned to organize it by genre, with poetry making up the second, "complex" section). But neither poetry nor prose is limited to one section, and Toomer's description of *Cane* is difficult to square with the book we have.

The one form that does change from section to section, however, is poetry. Part 1, as is widely acknowledged, contains several poems in traditional forms (ballads, a sonnet, rhymed quatrains), while part 2 poems are all in free verse. Is this the development Toomer refers to as the move from simple to complex forms? Certainly the prose does not admit of such a pointed change. Toomer seems to have regarded poetry as simple when he associated it with "primitive" stages of culture and complex when he associated it with the regeneration or redemption of modern culture. That is, poetry originates in the primitive past as chants and songs that express and preserve the spiritual life of a people, but it has necessarily evolved into the arcane idiom of the modern poet-prophet. The poet's task is to listen to the originary voices while transmitting their wisdom to a world grown deaf to the simple truth. In this sense, Toomer's scheme suggests that the book moves from simple poetic forms (perhaps the spirituals, work songs, and ballads of part 1) to complex poetic forms (the free-verse imagistic poetry of part 2). Thus, the lyrical aspects of poetry (the euphony, rhyme, meter, assonance, repetition, and cadence for which part 1 is famous) recall the oral poetry of primitive singers, while antilyrical poetic devices (dissonance, disjunction, and visual imagery) comprise the instruments of the modern poet. Still, the terms "simple" and "complex" fall far short of distinguishing the poems from each other (the intricately structured sonnet "November Cotton Flower," for instance, would be a "simple" form because it appears in part 1), and Toomer's comment only suggests the importance of "form" without clarifying the form that form takes.

Another crucial detail of his comment, though, points to the special significance of the poems. The larger structural configuration, in which part 1 captures the African American past, part 2 records the destruction of that way of life in the move to the urban, industrial North, and part 3 attempts a reconciliation and return to the South, vies here with Toomer's assertion that *Cane* begins at the end of part 2 with Paul's awakening, descends into Kabnis's dark night of the soul, emerges at the rural past of Karintha's world, and journeys through history to the urban present of John and Dan; finally, *Cane* ends at "Harvest Song," the last poem in the volume, a poem that longs for the agrarian past but acknowledges its failure to recover that moment. It is striking that Toomer conceived of *Cane* pausing at "Harvest Song," as if for him the book ends where the poems end.

In fact, a generic hierarchy does organize the volume, and lyric poetry is quite conventionally at the top of this hierarchy. The lyric strain is the voice of memory, beauty, and cultural authority. Lyric poetry in traditional forms, moreover, constitutes the most persuasive and authoritative voice in the book, a powerful, idealizing discourse that the volume clearly prizes. Free-verse poetry carries some of the same cultural weight, but Toomer uses it to expose the vicious realities and bitter disappointments of racist America rather than to conjure an ideal time and place. Echoes and snippets of folk songs, on the other hand, erupt throughout the text to mark loss and cynicism but exert only a renegade, disruptive power over the text's meanings.[14] The short stories and prose portraits seem associated with realism, though *Cane*'s documentary impulse is always qualified by a nagging lyricism that insists on the inadequacies of a strictly realistic mode. Finally, a quasi-dramatic form uneasily delivers narrative as stage directions, conveying a sense not of action being narrated and character being developed but of puppets being pulled on their strings. Certainly, much twentieth-century drama would reduce realistic characters to modernist puppets, but Toomer's use of the method in a short story context only deepens the sense that something is amiss in the form of these stories. That is, the prose and drama in *Cane* work against the idealizing impulse of lyric. It should come as no surprise, then, that the most successful poems appear in part 1, the least successful poems in part 2, and that poetry is absent in part 3. The beauty and authority of lyric poetry belong to the idealized past that part 1 desires to represent; the corruption and loss of such cultural authority belong to part 2; and the fact that lyric poetry cannot be recovered even when the narrative returns to the South in part 3 points to the function of lyric in *Cane*: its function is to fail.

The priority of poetry is perhaps more immediately obvious in the thematics of *Cane* than in its structure. It is no coincidence that most of the men in the book fancy themselves poets since poetry is the volume's privileged mode. For instance, "Song of the Son," a poem in part 1, is typically understood to express the mission of the book: to capture the last echoes of the slave songs in contemporary poetry.[15] Through the poem's speaker, usually taken to be Toomer, the past becomes "[a]n everlasting song, a singing tree" perpetuated in the songs of the son (14). Numerous male characters in *Cane* share this ambition to be the poet of their people. The narrator of "Avey" recites his poems to her in the hopes of evoking "an art that would open the way for women the likes of her" (48), Dan Moore imagines himself a poet-prophet in "Box Seat" (66, 67), Paul in "Bona and Paul" is assumed to be a poet (79), and Kabnis, the title character of the third section, longs to interpret the South in poetry: "How my lips would sing for it, my songs being the lips of its soul" (84). Poetry and song are near-synonyms in *Cane,* their equivalence suggesting the evolution of folk songs and chants into literary poetry, and narrators or narrator-characters valorize song in "Karintha," "Carma," and "Fern"; the corruption of song is equally momentous in "Becky," "Esther," "Blood-Burning Moon," and "Rhobert." Poems like "Cotton Song," "Song of the Son," "Evening Song," and "Harvest Song" formalize an obsession with song evident even in the phrases of the prose: "supper-getting-ready songs" (3), "her body is a song" (12), "an evening folk-song" (17), "a Jewish cantor sing[ing]" (17), "[f]ragments of melodies" (23), "improvised songs" (30), "jazz songs" (41, 52), "a promise-song" (48), "discordant snatches" of song (53), "[s]inging walls" (55), "the life of coming song" (58), "street songs" (59), "forgotten song" (59), a "sentimental love song" (68), the night winds' song (83), a "sleep-song" (84), church singing (90–93), "a soft chorus" (98), a "womb-song" (105), and a "birth-song" (117). And spirituals, folk songs, and popular songs are referred or alluded to throughout *Cane*: "Roll, Jordan Roll" (11), "Deep River" (43, 83, 87, 105), "My Lord, What a Morning" (93), "Little Liza Jane" (77), "Dixie's Land" (89), "(What Did I Do to Be So) Black and Blue?" (108), "Swing Low, Sweet Chariot" (98), and "Rock-A-Bye, Baby" (84, 117).

So great is the emphasis on song in *Cane* that despite the preponderance of prose in the book and the fact that many readers have been inclined to read *Cane* as a prose work, Toomer himself is typically regarded first and foremost as a poet. Virtually every commentator on *Cane* refers to Toomer as such, and several argue that he is not merely the poet who wrote the book but a poetic force within *Cane* who interrupts narrators, especially at moments of crisis, and rescues the action from the prose. For instance, the third part of *Cane* is a portrait of an aspiring artist, "Kabnis." Kabnis longs to be a poet-prophet of his race, but racism has paralyzed him with fear and self-doubt, and he gives up his dream in the end. Still several readers claim that the story "Kabnis" succeeds even though Kabnis the character fails because the poet steps in as Kabnis trudges away in defeat and saves the ending with a lyrical affirmation of renewal in the famous description of sunrise that concludes the volume: "Lewis leaves, and Kabnis gives up teaching, but the poet remains to catch the 'birthsong' of a new day's sun and to create the 'Song of the Son' through *Cane*" (McKay 177).[16]

The notion that "the poet" can reverse Kabnis's decline, indeed can reverse an epoch's decline, as the "Song of the Son" promises, presupposes his tremendous power and importance. Toomer's repeated creation of characters who strive to be poet-prophets, and his own personal efforts to fulfill such a role, suggest something more than the cultural prestige that poetry has always enjoyed or even the supposed primacy of song in African American culture.[17] The prevailing sense of the poet's importance was heightened for Toomer by his interest in Peter Demianovich Ouspensky's *Tertium Organum*, a mystical treatise on consciousness, which Toomer was reading during the writing of *Cane*. Alice Poindexter Fisher has demonstrated that Toomer became familiar with Ouspensky's work sometime during 1922 (505). The relevance of Ouspensky's ideas to Toomer's conception of poetry is striking. Ouspensky claimed that knowledge of the noumenal world comes in mystical sensations, and these sensations must be translated for the uninitiated:

Ouspensky states that only a poet can communicate both the mystical, emotional feelings of an experience and the concepts inherent in that experience. Thus, "Poetry endeavors to express both music and thought together. The combination of feeling and thought of high tension leads to a higher form of psychic life. Thus in art we

have already the first experiments in a language of the future."
(Fisher 508)

Fisher attributes Toomer's radical language experiments to Ouspensky's
conception of the artist as prophet, one who must create a new idiom in
order to communicate the noumenal world to the masses (508), and
Toomer's valorization of the poet may originate here as well. In any case,
Toomer clearly linked poetry and spirituality, refusing to remove the
flawed poem "Prayer" from *Cane,* even when Frank, his trusted friend
and literary mentor, urged him to drop it, insisting "its *idea* is essential
to the spiritual phase of CANE" (qtd. in Scruggs and VanDemarr 130).
That a poem does "essential" work for the book despite its weakness—
moreover, work that the prose cannot do—suggests Toomer's conviction
that poetry is the genre of truth. Further, as we shall see, "Prayer"'s flaws
are precisely what make it true in the context of the part 2 poems.

Considering *Cane*'s exaltation of the poet and his poems, it is surprising
that the poems have always occupied an uneasy position in that most
poetical of volumes. Toomer himself was uncertain about the status the
poems would have in the book, assigning them changing roles as he composed *Cane.* When he first began to imagine collecting his work into a
single volume, in July of 1922, he envisioned *Cane* this way: "I've had the
impulse to collect my sketches and poems under the title perhaps of
Cane. Such pieces as K.C.A. ["Karintha," "Carma," "Avey"?] and Kabnis
(revised) coming under the sub head of Cane Stalks and Choruses [*sic*].
Poems under Leaves and Syrup Songs. Vignettes under Leaf Traceries in
Washington" (*Reader* 11). This design seems to suggest the centrality of
the prose pieces, especially those set in the South; they are the "stalks"
that will support the poems and vignettes, yet he refers to them with the
lyrical term "choruses," meaning not songs or poems *per se* apparently
but choral qualities related to both African American musical culture
and Greek drama. The actual poems in this scheme are peripheral to the
prose but nevertheless important, as the leaves of the cane stalk are integral to its proper functioning. Still, "leaves" indicates something less
substantial than the stalk. "Syrup Songs," in contrast to these organic
metaphors, regards the poems as the product of a human refining process, perhaps even suggesting that the poems are more finely wrought
than the prose pieces. Yet even here, "syrup" connotes something sweet

but insubstantial. Finally, "Leaf Traceries in Washington" takes the natural metaphor of the plant to the urban North, where the leaves, separated from the stalk or trunk, are desiccated. One imagines a fretwork of autumn leaves on the pavement of a city street, outlines of something once beautiful but no longer thriving. If "Leaves and Syrup Songs" are poems, then the "Leaf Traceries in Washington" suggests a withering of song in that setting.[18]

Three days later, in a letter to *Double Dealer* editor John McClure, Toomer had dropped "Syrup Songs" from his design, reducing the poems to mere leaves: "I think I shall call [the book] CANE. Having as subheads Cane Stalks and Choruses [*sic*] (Karintha, Fern, etc. and two longer pieces), Leaves (poems), and Leaf Traciers [*sic*] in Washington, under which I shall group such things as For M.W., and other sharp, brief vignettes of which I have any number" (*Reader* 12). Again, his organization for the projected volume assembles the pieces by genre and intimates, by virtue of the metaphor, that prose is the foundation of the book.[19]

In March 1923, when *Cane* was in press, Toomer still invoked the natural metaphor in a letter to Gorham Munson; however, the plant is now an unspecified tree, as though the structure of his book has been generalized to all literature: "I see the importance of form. The tree as symbol comes to mind. A tree in summer. Trunk, branches: structure. Leaves: the fillers-out, one might almost say the padding. The sap is carried in the trunk etc. From it the leaves get their sustenance, and from their arrangement comes their meaning, or at least, leaves upon the ground do not make a tree" (*Reader* 21). Though not necessarily referring only to *Cane,* the terms of Toomer's discussion here—"trunk," "leaves," "sap"— are plainly drawn from the structural metaphor he had worked out for that book. Now though, the figure explicitly devalues those parts of a book that would be its leaves, for *Cane,* the poems. Leaves only fill out the more substantial structures, provide "the padding" for the trunk and the branches. Their meaning derives solely from their relationship to those more basic structures. Toomer seems to be developing a theory of art that reduces poetry to mere embellishment. Yet in a series of contradictory amendments to this idea, he appears reluctant to forgo the leaves: "This symbol is wanting, of course, because a tree is stationary, because it has no progressions, no dynamic movements. A machine has these, but a machine is all form, it has no leaves. Its very abstraction is now the death of it" (*Reader* 21–22). Leaves, then, provide movement and life; though he conceives of them as extraneous to "form," form lacks something without these "fillers-out." Still, he concludes the letter with what sounds like a final repudiation of the leaves and a commitment of his artistic energies to prose: "The point is, from now on I'm going to shoot the sap into the trunk, where it belongs" (22).

The unnatural image of shooting sap, which derives from the trunk, back into the trunk introduces a telling ambiguity into Toomer's metaphor for literary form. The lifeblood of the plant, sap is also extracted to make syrup. That is, Toomer wants to shoot his artistic efforts into the foundational part of the work, the prose, but he also imagines the sap being refined into syrup, which he invariably associates with lyric. This double sense of "sap" may account for *Cane*'s apparent generic fluidity. In a sense, Toomer would shoot the *syrup* into the trunk to create *Cane*'s lyrical prose, a prose style that seems always on the verge of becoming poetry. He himself refers to several of the sketches in the volume as "prose poems," a form he was familiar with from reading Symbolist poetry, especially Baudelaire's *Petits poèmes en prose* (1869). Robert B. Jones argues that prose poems and "lyrical narratives" embody an internal contradiction (between poetry and prose) and thus give Toomer a structure in which he might reconcile his own internal divisions (48). Jones's sense that Toomer experimented with these hybrid forms in a modernist effort to defamiliarize language and renew literature is a useful way to regard pieces like "Seventh Street," "Rhobert," and "Calling Jesus," which Jones terms prose poems, or "Karintha," "Becky," "Carma," and "Fern," which he calls lyrical narratives (37). In this reading, Toomer seeks to overcome the alienation of body from soul, as in "Calling Jesus," for instance, by virtue of the hybrid form, which brings two antithetical modes together in a new structure.[20]

Yet I continue to insist that *Cane*'s lyrical prose is finally not a new structure and, above all, not poetry. Opposites are not reconciled in *Cane*'s lyrical prose, in fact, but thrown into starker relief by their often eerie proximity. The generic voices in *Cane* never constitute the idealized "chorus of the cane" (15) referred to in "Georgia Dusk," where disparate sounds are orchestrated into a harmonious choir of song; rather, the competing genres produce something more like the "[s]cratching choruses" (12, 13) of cacophonous sounds heard in "Carma." Thus, the ambivalence about form subtly resonating in Toomer's metaphor of sap does not result from the collapse of the two genres but from their contention. The issue of generic difference and the metaphor of sap are dramatized in "Fern" when Fernie May Rosen bursts violently into song: "Her body was tortured with something it could not let out. Like boiling sap it flooded her arms and fingers till she shook them as if they burned her. It found her throat, and spattered inarticulately in plaintive, convulsive sounds, mingled with calls to Christ Jesus. And then she sang, brokenly" (19). Fern's song is simultaneously imagined as the sap in a tree (flowing through her limbs) and the syrup in a refining pot (boiling out of her throat). Here, too, "sap" figures forth a lyricism that is both intrinsic and extrinsic, natural and cultivated. The question behind this uneasy figure for lyric is not whether poetry and prose can be distinguished but what is the proper place for poetry.

Indeed, Toomer's restless diagrams for *Cane* reveal his uncertainty about the significance of different genres, especially poetry. Though he has been credited from the beginning with creating new forms in *Cane*, forms above all that blur generic distinctions, his comments in these letters make clear that he was working with distinct genres, which he enumerated in yet another letter as "poems, prose poems, sketches, short stories, and dramas" (*Reader* 22), and wrestling to determine their relative values and meanings. This was not merely a question of what resources he thought each genre offered—poetry's musicality and emotion, prose's narration and realism, drama's dynamism and dialogue. As he wrote, of course, he would have discovered that the qualities he associated with each genre could adhere in any. Still, even as he brought what he learned in one genre to the writing of others, he maintained a sense of their discrete forms and cultural meanings. Though *Cane* has always appeared defiant of convention, and though much critical ink has flowed in christening its new form (it has been called a "fictional thesaurus," an experimental novel, a "melange," a "potpourri," a "frappé," a "sequence of narrative forms," "an elaborate jazz composition," "a blur of genres," a "hybrid short story cycle," a "pastiche," and a "montage"), our emphasis on the mixture of forms in *Cane* has drawn attention away from the volume's own interest in formal distinctions.[21] In fact, the argument of *Cane* resides in the contrast of genres rather than in their combination, and what that contrast reveals is the precedence of poetry, despite Toomer's inclination to equate prose with substance.

To make such a claim for poetry is to insist on clear generic distinctions and thus to disagree with many recent readers who argue that Toomer developed a hybrid form in *Cane* for articulating a mixed racial identity. Yet *Cane* was "the blackest text of all" (Gates 200, 213) for another generation of readers, and that it is currently read as racially indeterminate is thoroughly consistent with Toomer's own simultaneous affirmation of an authentic Negro identity and insistence on a multiracial American reality. In *Jean Toomer and the Terrors of American History*, Charles Scruggs and Lee VanDemarr observe that we have been inattentive to Toomer's early political writings, which establish his deep engagement with African American politics and identity.[22] Though Toomer's post-*Cane* letters and essays develop the idea of a multiethnic "American race," a concept to which he remained committed for the rest of his life, his writings before and during the *Cane* period (and even after) suggest that he understood "Negro" as a fairly stable racial category, whether or not he considered himself a member of it. In "The Negro Emergent," for instance, an undated typescript that he may have written as late as 1924, Toomer attributes racial identity to biology as well as to social situation: "Biologically, the Negro sprang from what he sprang from: a Negro, or a Negro and white stock. These bloods are in him. No attitude can change this fact, else it would have the power to deprive him of his physical existence" (*Reader* 87). Given his complex understanding and experience of mixed-race identity, it is notable here that he unhesitatingly terms a person of "Negro and white stock" simply "Negro." Granted, the purpose of the essay is to argue that though African Americans are emerging from the slave past and the stereotypes it has engendered, still they are emerging *into* a sense of self that coheres around fairly familiar notions of race:

> The Negro has found his roots. He is in fruitful contact with his ancestry. He partakes of an uninterrupted stream of energy. He is moved by the vital determinants of racial heritage. And something of their spirit now lives within him. He is about to harvest whatever the past has stored, good and evil. He is about to be released from an unconscious and negative concern with it. (*Reader* 90)

That is, African Americans are not emerging from conventional racial categorization but only from its overtly negative influences. Thus, he is able to endorse "that lyricism which is so *purely* Negro" (90) or claim that African Americans are "detaching the *essential* Negro from the social crust" (92, my emphases), phrasing that confirms his belief in an essential African American identity, an identity that is fundamental to *Cane*. Indeed, in a letter to Sherwood Anderson (1922), Toomer imagines himself consolidating this identity for African Americans through his writing:

> The mass of Negroes, like peasants, like the mass of Russians or Jews or Irish or what not, are too instinctive to be anything but themselves. Here and there one finds a high type Negro who shares this virtue with his more primitive brothers. As you can imagine, the resistance against my stuff is marked, excessive. But I feel that in time, in its social phase, my art will aid in giving the Negro to himself. (*Reader* 85)

Again, the rhetoric of categorical thinking reverberates in "instinctive," "high type Negro," "primitive," and even in apparently neutral words like "themselves" and "himself"—pronouns that assume a homogenous class of people. He plans a magazine "that would consciously hoist, and perhaps at first a trifle over emphasize the negroid ideal" (85). And although he distances himself from "people within the race"—"People within the race cannot see it" (85)—his exception only proves the rule.

Readers like George Hutchinson, who argue that *Cane* "attempts to initiate a new American tradition, to provoke a new 'racial' consciousness that would displace the dualistic racial consciousness of 'white' and 'black' ("Racial Discourse" 231), have transformed our sense of *Cane* and greatly increased our understanding of that complicated text. However, it is equally important to acknowledge *Cane*'s competing articulation of an essential black identity that confronts dualistic racial consciousness by extolling a specifically "negroid ideal."[23] When the prostitutes Stella and Cora prepare to leave Halsey's shop the morning after the party in "Kabnis," for example, their essential identity emerges:

> The girls, before the mirror, are doing up their hair. It is bushy hair that has gone through some straightening process. Character, however, has not all been ironed out. As they kneel there, heavy-eyed and dusky, and throwing grotesque shadows on the wall, they are two princesses in Africa going through the early-morning ablutions of their pagan prayers. (113)

Indeed, at many points in *Cane*, racial "character" cannot be ironed out—"Race memories of king and caravan" (15), "nigger life breathing its loafer air, jazz songs and love, thrusting unconscious rhythms" (41), Dorris's instinctive dancing that evokes "canebrake loves and mangrove feastings" (55), Muriel's "animalism" (62), and the "portly Negress"'s "strong roots sink[ing] down and spread[ing] under the river and disappear[ing] in blood-lines that waver south" (65).[24] Moreover, these moments of unambiguous racial identification typically constitute rare glimpses of hope in the book. They are not, then, aberrant or atavistic instances of racial essentialism in a work committed to redefining race but rather expressions of an African American ideal that is absolutely central to *Cane*.

Toomer wrote *Cane* during a brief period of his life, a life characterized by intellectual searching and philosophical change. For *Cane* to have deployed essentialist formulations does not preclude its simultaneous interest in more fluid and complicated notions of identity.[25] Yet even as he moved away from *Cane*'s interest in African American identity, essentialist terms would remain a part of his thinking. In a letter to Waldo Frank, for instance, Toomer appears to defend himself against exhibiting a narrow racial interest in his work: "The only time that I think 'Negro' is when I want a peculiar emotion which is associated with this name" (*Reader* 95). Still, he equates specific qualities with "Negro," and this is not mitigated by insisting that "Negro" is only a word.[26] Likewise, in a letter to *The Liberator* editors (1922) answering their questions about his background, Toomer creates an ethnic equation in which seven equals two: "Racially, I seem to have (who knows for sure) seven blood mixtures: French, Dutch, Welsh, Negro, German, Jewish, and Indian. [. . .] I have lived equally amid the two race groups. Now white, now colored" (*Reader* 15). Toomer is juggling two discourses here, one that observes ethnic differences without assigning hierarchical value, and one that reduces ethnic and racial difference to a binary opposition whose hierarchical relation we know too well: white and colored. He says he has "striven for a spiritual fusion analogous to the fact of racial intermingling. Without denying a single element in me, with no desire to subdue, one to the other, I have sought to let them function as complements" (15–16). Yet he also avows a special responsiveness to his African American heritage: "Within the last two or three years, however, my growing need for artistic expression has pulled me deeper and deeper into the

Negro group. And as my powers of receptivity increased, I found myself loving it in a way that I could never love the other" (16). These passages are perhaps at this point too familiar to Toomer's readers, yet their reminder that the restrictive terms of American racial discourse frustrated and served him at the same time is crucial to understanding *Cane*.[27]

Thus, notwithstanding excellent recent scholarship on *Cane* that explores its efforts to break out of the fiercely inadequate binarisms of American racial discourse, I argue that *Cane*'s generic multiplicity amounts not to formal hybridity but to formal essentialism.[28] The juxtaposition of poetry and prose in the volume does not finally blur generic distinctions as a means of undermining racial distinctions but rather reinforces the differences between lyric and nonlyric forms—which for Toomer inevitably encourages distinctions between the pure racial past and the desecrated present of African Americans. Toomer was not alone among African American poets in regarding poetic forms as essential—especially racialized forms. In a far-reaching study of Sterling Brown's modernist aesthetics, Mark A. Sanders joins Kimberly Benston in identifying a static notion of artistic form in many Harlem Renaissance writers (Brown is the exception):

> Kimberly Benston sees in a number of Harlem Renaissance writers, particularly Langston Hughes, a tendency to view the past (and its cultural forms) as a "repository of finished structures to be mined in the poet's representation of an intensified but static pictorial moment" [34], reflecting an assumption of fixity in cultural idioms, particularly the blues. That "finished structures" or idiomatic forms exist in opposition to historical dynamics, rather than as products of them, again reiterates an unexamined investment in essences rather than process. (7)

The New Negro poets responded to the notion of a fixed cultural repository in distinctive ways. Hughes sought to tap into the authenticity of racialized forms like the blues; James Weldon Johnson, Claude McKay, and Countee Cullen rejected Negro dialect precisely because they regarded it as a finished structure that could not voice modern black concerns; and Brown, as Sanders skillfully demonstrates, "rework[ed] the language and tropes he ha[d] inherited in order to explore the inventive ways in which African Americans articulate their own presence and modernity" (9). Like, Hughes, Johnson, McKay, and Cullen, Toomer conceived of African American cultural forms as unchanging. He would simultaneously attempt to invoke those forms in order to preserve (or conjure) the cultural past and create modernist forms in order to address the cultural present. In both modes he understands the "everlasting song" ("Song of the Son," *Cane* 14) of his ancestors as everlasting precisely because it is an essence rather than a process. Our contemporary antipathy for essentialist notions of race allows us to see important aspects of *Cane*'s dilemma, especially the urge to reconcile racial antagonisms in the figure of a mixed-blood savior, the "[g]old-glowing child" (117) who ascends at the end of the book, the "new American emergent." But if we obscure *Cane*'s profound investment in an African American ideal, we miss something equally important about the book. As we shall see, the juxtaposition of poetry and prose casts this ideal in stark relief.

If Toomer was not engaged in a radical breakup of form to express a radical notion of identity, questions of literary form and racial representation did certainly arise for him simultaneously. In the months before *Cane,* he was struggling to sort out contradictory assumptions about literary form and ethnic identity that bore directly on his own art. He had been reading "many books on the matter of race and the race problem in America" (*Wayward* 120) and felt that he could do better than other authors since he had "seen both the white and the colored worlds, and both from the inside" (120). He wrote "several fragments of essays" to work out his position and then "formulated it with more fullness and exactness" in a poem called "The First American." It is significant that poetry provided the medium of "fullness and exactness" for his thoughts about race, and "The First American" turned out to be the germ of a major poem about American identity, "The Blue Meridian," which he would continue to work on for many years. Much of his reading in this period was poetry; he mentions Shelley, Whitman, Coleridge, Blake, Baudelaire, and "most all of the American poets" in one of his autobiographical fragments (*Wayward* 107–20) as important to his developing literary sense.[29] But the strongest influences came just before he left for Sparta, the trip that would inspire *Cane*:

> And now again I was reading only literary works. This was the period when I was strongly influenced, first, by the Americans who

were dealing with local materials in a poetic way. Robert Frost's New England poems strongly appealed to me. Sherwood Anderson's Winesburg, Ohio opened my eyes to entirely new possibilities. I thought it was one of the finest books I'd ever read. And, second, the poems and program of the Imagists. Their insistence on fresh vision and on the perfect clean economical line was just what I had been looking for. I began feeling that I had in my hands the tools of my own creation. (*Wayward* 120)

Toomer's debt to Anderson is well known. *Winesburg, Ohio,* like *Cane,* is a collection of short works concerning the lives of disparate "folk" whose geographical location draws them into a kind of community, even if each member is unaware of his or her part in the larger group. Indeed, the paradoxically shared isolation of the characters in these two collections is a crucial component of each text's meaning and is formalized in the structure of the books. Moreover, Toomer's correspondence with Anderson about the writing of *Cane* lends even greater authority to Anderson's influence. Yet the comparison between *Cane* and the prose collection *Winesburg* has emphasized the short story to the exclusion of other formal issues, most especially the function of the poems in *Cane.* We must also explore Toomer's poetic influences if we are to understand the force of lyric in the book.[30]

The New England poems that gave Toomer a model for handling "local materials in a poetic way" are probably Frost's blank-verse dialogues and narrative poems in *North of Boston* (1914), Frost's second volume of verse but the first to be published in America (1915).[31] Poems like "Mending Wall," "The Death of the Hired Man," "The Mountain," "A Hundred Collars," "Home Burial," "The Black Cottage," "Blueberries," "A Servant to Servants," "The Code," "The Generations of Men," "The Housekeeper," "The Fear," and "The Self-Seeker" are character studies in verse, and *Cane*'s portraits that reveal character in a single incident have much in common with these poems. For Frost, colloquial dialogue—people speaking to each other in their own idiom—crucially shapes narrative. What people can or cannot say to each other determines their actions, and the tragedy of "The Death of the Hired Man" or "Home Burial" or "The Housekeeper" turns on the problem of communication.[32] Frost's blank verse captures the verbal rhythms and idioms of poor New England farming folk. Frost, of course, is famous for his theory of the "sound of sense," the notion that meaning adheres not merely in words but in the cadences and inflections of speech.[33] Toomer's explorations of how local speech embodies a place, how communication is frequently miscommunication, and how people often speak to themselves rather than to each other owe a great deal to the poems in *North of Boston.*

The Imagists offered Toomer something quite different. If Frost alerted Toomer to the sound of sense, the Imagists provoked his visual imagination. The "fresh vision" of a line measured to its own image and to the graphic effect on the page rather than to traditional meter concentrated his poetic energies into brief flashes of sight or insight, a form that suited his tendency to epigrammatic expression. Free verse also offered a poetry unconstrained by literary tradition and therefore, presumably, well adapted to the making of modern literature.

Imagist free verse was also, of course, a crucial step in the high modernist rejection of conventional lyric forms, forms Robert Frost nevertheless continued to find vital. Toomer's position between these competing notions of modernist poetry is crucial to his deployment of both traditional and free-verse poetic forms in *Cane* (and after). Though the modernist suspicion of lyric poetry quickly became hegemonic, what Kellie Bond calls "the argument of [old and new] forms" continued to rage—and to produce important poetry—during the period. Thus, while Pound was "break[ing] the pentameter" and Stein and Williams were deriding the sonnet in particular, many other poets, notably African Americans and women, were adapting traditional forms to modernist uses.[34] "Far from being preeminently genteel," Cary Nelson insists, "poetry in traditional forms was a frequent vehicle for sharply focused social commentary" (23). And though Toomer was one of the most adept modern practitioners of conventional lyric forms, he finally doubted the efficacy of those forms for the cultural work he was doing. In Toomer's poetry, then, the argument of forms was won first by free verse and later by even more drastically antilyrical forms as Toomer increasingly associated modernity with cacophony, ugliness, and deformity.

And yet, *Cane's* most renowned poems are not in free verse but in traditional rhymes and meters: the ballads "Song of the Son" and "Georgia Dusk" and the sonnet "November Cotton Flower" are most frequently anthologized and receive the greatest share of critical attention. Moreover, I will argue that poems in traditional Anglo-European forms are the most successful poems in *Cane* and that ballads and sonnets, not free-verse poems, actually afforded Toomer the "tools for [his] own creation." This should not surprise us. Claude McKay's sonnet "If We Must Die" gained national notoriety, especially among African Americans, when it appeared in the July 1919 *Liberator* in a two-page spread of sonnets responding to the racial violence of the Red Summer (Cooper 12). Indeed, the sonnet would shortly become a potent form of social protest among African American poets. And though Langston Hughes would declare artistic independence for the Harlem Renaissance writers in 1925 by implying they marched to a different drummer, an African drummer, "[t]he tom-tom cries and the tom-tom laughs," iambic pentameter was the beat most of the poets followed ("The Negro Artist and the Racial Mountain" 181). In the same year, Countee Cullen spoke directly to the issue of Anglo-European poetic form and African American writers in his foreword to *Caroling Dusk*: "As heretical as it may sound, there is the probability that Negro poets, dependent as they are on the English language, may have more to gain from the rich background of English and American poetry than from any nebulous atavistic yearnings toward an African inheritance" (xi). Cullen's opposition between an imagined "ebony muse" and the more evident Anglo-European one presents a widely held assumption about black writers and traditional lyric forms. James Weldon Johnson's preface to his 1922 *The Book of American Negro Poetry* elaborates this assumption, implying a continuum between African American musical culture (which for him *is* inspired by the ebony muse) and African American poetry. The spirituals, the cakewalk, and ragtime are three of the "only things artistic that have yet sprung from American soil" (10), and these black musical forms (along with the blues) clearly constitute the African American writer's poetic credentials. People, black and white, tended to associate African Americans with lyricism (Johnson refers to "their natural musical instinct and talent" and "the Negro's extraordinary sense of rhythm" 12) and took for granted that traditional Anglo-European lyric poetry gave full vent to this African musicality.[35]

Nowhere is this more evident, or would it have been more influential, than in W. E. B. DuBois's renowned *The Souls of Black Folk* (1903), where African American and Anglo-European forms reside easily together on a continuum of lyric that includes both oral and written poetry. Anticipating Johnson's claim about African American cultural contributions, DuBois argued not only that the Sorrow Songs communicated "the soul of the black slave" but that "Negro folk-song—the rhythmic cry of the slave—stands today not simply as the sole American music, but as the most beautiful expression of human experience born this side of the seas" (536–37). DuBois's argument went beyond the thematics of the Sorrow Songs, claiming that the music itself articulated the sorrow and longing of the slaves, their connection to Africa, and their transformation in America: "The songs are indeed the sifting of centuries; the music is far more ancient than the words, and in it we can trace here and there signs of development" (538). Making good on the idea that the melody was as expressive as the lyrics, he introduced each chapter with "a bar of the Sorrow Songs,—some echo of haunting melody from the only American music which welled up from black souls in the dark past" (359–60), and none of these bars of music contained lyrics. Thus, pure musical notation signified a meaning that exceeded language, rendering the past accessible, despite barriers of age, land, and language, to the present.[36]

Given DuBois's correlation between African Americans and song, it is all the more remarkable that each musical inscription in *Souls* is preceded by a literary epigraph—an excerpt of conventional poetry drawn from a mostly Anglo-European repertoire: Arthur Symonds, James Russell Lowell, Byron, Schiller, Whittier, Omar Khayyám (Fitzgerald), The Song of Solomon, William Vaughn Moody, Mrs. Browning, Fiona Macleod, Swinburne, Tennyson, and again Mrs. Browning. Only in the final chapter on "The Sorrow Songs" does DuBois employ the words of a "Negro Song" for the literary epigraph. This relationship among different poetries in *The Souls of Black Folk* assumes a correspondence between song and poetry and, further, between African American and Anglo-American poetry, assumptions that also inform *Cane* and much other African American poetry of the early twentieth century. It is no surprise that DuBois accords song a special role in African American culture: folk songs are expressive of the spirit of black people, and song, he argues, links past and present, Africa and America, because the past adheres in melody. But the contiguity of folk song and literary poetry in *Souls* implies an affinity between Negro folk songs and Tennyson's or Mrs. Browning's poetry. That is, *The Souls of Black Folk* reflects a cultural life that includes African songs, African American folk songs, and traditional literary poems in one rich notion of lyric. Jean Toomer shared these ideas—indeed, he may have gleaned them from reading *Souls*—and *Cane* embodies the assumption that traditional lyric poetry can figure forth African and African American lyricism.

This point is a crucial one for contemporary readers, who too often cannot come to terms with *Cane's* poetry because they are prepared to acknowledge only sanctioned African American forms in this "blackest text of all." In *Playing the Changes: From Afro-Modernism to the Jazz Impulse,* Craig Hansen Werner quips about this tendency to read all African American literature as "purely" African American: "When in doubt, the unofficial critical truism concerning Black writing goes, say it comes from the blues" (149). Invariably, call-and-response, spirituals, blues, and jazz are assumed to be the basic structures of *Cane,* assumptions that exaggerate the significance of these forms at best and misrepresent them at worst. In an influential essay on *Cane,* for example, Barbara E. Bowen argues that a call-and-response structure underlies all the other forms of the book and reveals Toomer's search for a communal voice.[37] This leads her to read lyrical moments in *Cane* as "pure" African American utterances, as when she transcribes Barlo's prose preachment into what she calls "a perfect blues stanza" (12):

> They led him t th coast,
> They led him t th sea,
> They led him across th ocean,
> An they didnt set him free. (Bowen 13; *C* 23)

Likewise, Bowen terms the refrain in "Blood-Burning Moon" a "blues stanza" (16):

> Red nigger moon. Sinner!
> Blood-burning moon. Sinner!
> Come out that fact'ry door. (Bowen 16; *C* 31, 33, 37)[38]

First, the notion of a "perfect" blues stanza is troublesome since the blues have always been composed in a variety of forms. However, if a single stanza has come to represent the blues, in music and in poetry, it is the familiar tercet: three long lines, the first two of which are identical or almost identical, the third of which is different, all rhyming A Aa, as in this stanza from "Backwater Blues":[39]

When it rained five days and the skies turned dark as night
When it rained five days and the skies turned dark as night
Then trouble taken place, in the lowlands at night.
(Sachheim 50)

Clearly, Barlo's ABAB quatrains can be more accurately described as ballad stanzas, and this is appropriate because the folk ballad was an oral
form that preserved and conveyed African American history and culture,
as Barlo's song is doing—even if it also functioned similarly in Anglo-
European culture. Toomer considered sonnets, ballads, and other traditional lyric forms conducive to, even emblematic of, African American
expression, a correlation crucial to the poetry of *Cane*.[40]

Likewise, his contemporaries would have made just this equation between conventional poetry and African American expression. For instance, John McClure, the editor of *Double Dealer* who accepted Toomer's poem "Harvest Song" in December 1922, argues precisely this in a
letter to Sherwood Anderson written after *Cane* appeared. He tells Anderson that Toomer should concentrate his efforts on poetry: "I do not
think that Toomer can't write short stories. I merely think that his finest
work so far is lyrical and that if he ever does supreme work it must be in
a lyrical manner" (*C* 161). This is owing to his African heritage, a birth-
right, McClure assumes, of lyric: "If [Toomer] follows that African urge,
and rhapsodizes, he will be a commanding and solitary figure. For his
own sake, I feel that he ought to do that which he does best" (161). Next
evincing a suspicion of poetry that is not inconsistent with his contention that poetry is an African American genre, McClure is quick to defend himself against "a fondness for poetry":

> "Poetry" as a state of mind does not exist, in my philosophy. Poetry
> is merely verse, rhythm in speech which reaches the condition of
> music. The human spirit expresses itself in many ways and verse is
> only one. Toomer's character seemed to me to be lyrical—he is so
> intensely an individual that it is useless for him to attempt any-
> thing other than to express himself. (162)

While McClure attributes Toomer's lyricism to his African heritage, he
also casts it as a feature of Toomer's unique personality—which is to say
he subsumes Toomer's individuality into a generic racial identity. That

assumed "African urge," the instinct for song, characterizes all people of African descent, a stereotype Toomer himself often advanced.

However, this conjoined idealization and condescension regarding Toomer's lyricism could also take another form—in fact, just the opposite form—when notions of the ebony muse came into conflict with expectations about modern writing. The modernist suspicion of traditional poetic form as antiquated was widespread (one thinks of Ford and Pound insisting that "verse must be at least as well written as prose if it is to be poetry" [Ford, *Thus to Revisit* 201]), and Toomer, moreover, apprenticed himself to prose writers like Frank and Anderson, who could idealize the figure of the poet without taking much interest in his form.[41] Thus, for example, the narrator of "Hands," the first story in *Winesburg, Ohio,* claims to need the help of a poet: "The story of Wing Biddlebaum's hands is worth a book in itself. Sympathetically set forth it would tap many strange, beautiful qualities in obscure men. It is a job for a poet" (10); "And yet that is but crudely stated. It needs the poet there" (12). But *Winesburg's* repeated gestures to the poet do not issue in poetry, ironically, because "the poet" represents sympathy, beauty, obscurity, and refinement—the very qualities modern writers abjured. Similarly, Waldo Frank can refer to the archeologist Edgar Lee Hewett as a poet: "Dr. Hewett belongs, despite his age, to the uprising generation whom we shall first examine in the following Chapter. He should have been included among the Chicago poets. For, essentially, he is a poet" (*Our America* 116).[42]

Frank's influence on Toomer in this regard is particularly important since he was the reader Toomer trusted most in 1922. And though he shares McClure's belief that African Americans are peculiarly lyrical, he also echoes McClure's suspicion that one wouldn't want to be too "fond" of poetry. For instance, Frank bluntly judged the poem "Prayer" a failure because Toomer was "shackled and thwarted in the pure forms" of poetry. Earlier, in a detailed response to a sheaf of Toomer's work, much of which shortly went into *Cane,* Frank had indicated that Toomer's writing was weakest when he wrote poems: "although you are a poet, I dont think you'll find your final satisfaction in the mere direct lyric."[43] Toomer's lyricism succeeded best, Frank thought, when articulated to prose forms, succeeded so well, in fact, that he was compelled to call the prose sketches "poems": "Some of the poems are quite perfect. Seventh Street, Becky, Avey, (Daniel less so), Carma are lovely transcripts

of a world old in America but new in American expression" (*C* 159). After reading the completed manuscript of *Cane*, Frank reiterated these
judgments: "At best your 'lyrics' are your weakest. [. . .] You are a poet-
prose. [. . .] The circles & spheres of drama & story alone can house
your [. . .] song and pure lyricism" (*C* 153). And in his introduction to
the first edition of *Cane*, Frank codified his sense that Toomer was "finally a poet in prose" (*C* 140).

Toomer, too, attempted to isolate lyricism from poems as if suspicious of poetry, describing to Lola Ridge his "own contribution" to letters as a blending of "the rhythm of the peasant[r]y with the rhythm
of machines. A syncopation, a slow jazz, a sharp intense motion, subtil-
ized, fused to a terse lyricism" (*Reader* 17). Again, in a letter to Kenneth
Macgowan, editor of *Theatre Arts* magazine, he maintained that the
"best of my stuff is basically dramatic" but nevertheless the "language
tends more towards poetry than towards what is flat and commonplace"
(*Reader* 22, 23). "In my reflective moments," he wrote to Gorham Munson, "I desire the profound image saturated in its own lyricism" (*Reader*
21). Plainly, lyricism could saturate any sort of writing, and language
could tend toward poetry without producing a "mere direct lyric."

Ironically, Frank detects "pure lyricism" only in forms that are not
pure lyric, actual poetic form paradoxically reducing Toomer's work to
mere poetry. Here he betrays a depreciation of poetry in general, not just
of Toomer's poetry, as if poetry cannot address "a world old in America"
in a new American idiom. For Frank, that world was comprised of native
people, Jews, and other ethnic minorities, the working classes, farmers,
laborers, especially the young among these groups. Thus, Frank asserts
in his foreword to the 1923 edition of *Cane*, Toomer is giving voice to
"the Georgia Negro" and the residents of "the brown belt of Washington" (*C* 139)—two groups akin to the many marginalized Americans
whom Frank had celebrated in *Our America* (1919), perhaps the most
powerful influence on *Cane*.[44] Prose, inflected with lyric but not infected
by it, would constitute Toomer's best expression because it captured the
ancient lyrical essence of African American culture without betraying
too much fondness for the historical or aesthetic past. This contradiction
between an idealized notion of *lyricism*, which must be preserved, and
a cynical attitude toward *lyric*, which must be eschewed, encapsulates
Frank's paradoxical response to American history in *Our America*, where
a certain notion of the past is glorified (especially the ethnic past) while

another notion of the past is held up for scorn (the middle-class, "Puritan" heritage).[45]

But Toomer retained the poems in *Cane*, and not because he resolved the imagined contradictions between African American expressivity and modernist expression but precisely because he recognized the value of putting such contradictions into play. In "The Psychology and Craft of Writing," Toomer claims that the modern writer "has a wish to produce by experimentation a new form. Certainly he will aim to make an individual use of old forms" (qtd. in Jones, *Prison-House* 33), an assertion that nearly conflates the old and the new. One kind of new form, the passage implies, is old forms put to new uses. And after all, *Cane*'s fondness for poetry *is* partly a fondness for the past, even as it is also a more critical engagement with tradition. Moreover, the past is not uniformly something to resist because it is not, in fact, uniform. A crucial scene from a play Toomer wrote during the *Cane* composition period, "Natalie Mann," dramatizes this complex relationship to tradition, and to the written tradition in particular. Mertis Newbolt, a middle-class black woman who is feeling the constraints of her world, flips restlessly through her Bible in search of a text that reflects her conflicting desires for emotional fulfillment and middle-class respectability. She first reads from the Song of Solomon, then from Leviticus, then from the Sermon on the Mount. The lines from the Song of Solomon are sensual and lyrical: "Let him kiss me with the kisses of his mouth: for thy love *is* better than wine" (*Wayward* 271). As though to stave off her growing desire, she "[rises] to her feet" and "nervously turns the pages back to Leviticus," where the text drops into a prosaic, legalistic language that repudiates sensuality:

If a woman have conceived a seed, and born a man child, then she shall be unclean seven days; according to the days of the separation for her infirmity shall she be unclean.

And in the eighth day the flesh of his foreskin shall be circumcised.

And she shall then continue in the blood of her purifying three and thirty days [. . .]. (272)

But, unwilling to submit to such an unsympathetic order, she turns the pages once again, "[w]ith an abrupt change of mood," to Christ's Sermon on the Mount. There she encounters encouragement in her suffering and a promise of eternal reward. Her Bible is a complex and variegated volume, offering alike scriptures for her most radical and most conformist moods. Its very contradictions are what render the Bible meaningful to her.

Mertis Newbolt flipping the pages of her Bible shares something important with Toomer organizing his material for Cane. Part 1 of Cane bears many resemblances to the Song of Solomon; both treat love and sensuality, both are lyrical and full of promise. Likewise, part 2 and Leviticus share a suspicion of the world, a dread of nature and sexuality, and an attitude of atonement. Part 3, like the New Testament, seeks a Christ figure who will redeem this fallen world, but in Cane racism and racial violence reduce Kabnis to a false prophet who is consumed by fear. Though Mertis reads Christ's blessings, "Blessed *are* the poor in spirit: for theirs is the kingdom of heaven," Kabnis hears only curses that prophets invite, "Blessed *are* they which are persecuted for righteousness' sake," "Blessed are ye, when *men* shall revile you, and persecute you" (272). If the prophet is a poet in Cane, it is inevitable that Kabnis will fail in his role of spiritual savior. He clearly gives up all pretensions to such a calling in the last pages of the book, hanging his priest's robe suggestively on a nail, taking up a bucket of dead coals, and going doggedly to work in the wheelwright's shop—a crucified rather than risen prophet. And though Cane, like Mertis, attempts to turn its own page to a better story with the concluding sunrise that hints at the glory and promise of Revelation, the lyricism of the ending cannot transform Kabnis's tragedy. The loss of poetry is critical to the loss of hope, and Cane has no more pages to turn because it has no more poems to turn to.

But to understand why Cane is finally bereft of poems, why Kabnis at last is a "[b]ad poet" (111), we must turn back to the beginning of the book where poetry is full of promise. Centered on the title page below the word "Cane" is a brief lyric epigraph:

> *Oracular.*
> *Redolent of fermenting syrup,*
> *Purple of the dusk,*
> *Deep-rooted cane.*

The epigraph follows the title of the book, glossing the book's central symbol: *Cane* is "oracular," a term that suggests authoritative (even dictatorial) wisdom or expression; but *Cane* is also something quite different: it is "redolent" rather than decisive, evocative of "fermenting syrup," Toomer's trope for lyrical (as opposed to oracular) expression. Elaborating this lyrical component through the lyric form itself, line 3 offers another figure for cane. It is redolent as the "purple of dusk," a time of day, a quality of light that confounds conventional distinctions, as when the variegated flowers in the Crimson Gardens appear to be all one color in the shadows of dusk: "[T]he Gardens are purple like a bed of roses would be at dusk. [. . .] I came back to tell you, brother, that white faces are petals of roses. That dark faces are petals of dusk. That I am going out to gather petals" ("Bona and Paul" 80). That is, the epigraph reveals *Cane's* dual mission to be oracular like a prophet but also to be evocative like a poet. Similarly, the book promises to be both spiritual and earthy, for cane is at once lofty (associated through its fragrance with sky and air) and "deep-rooted" in the earth. Here we have the same conflict Toomer expressed in his generic diagrams for the volume. Is *Cane* finally oracular, earthy, deep-rooted—a book of prose; or is it lyrical, spiritual, evocative—a book of verse? Can the oracle be a poet? Can the poet allow his words to waft suggestively, lyrically, like the scent of fermenting syrup and yet still remain rooted in the ground of history? The epigraph suggests that these assumed contradictions can be held in productive tension through the form of lyric itself. How Kabnis comes to repudiate this lyric promise, how the book comes to its end dispossessed of poetry, is *Cane's* most basic concern.

2

An Everlasting Song

Cane, Part 1

IN "Earth-Being," an autobiography written in the late 1920s, Toomer recorded his impressions of Sparta, Georgia, where he had gone for three months in 1922 to serve as acting principal of an industrial and agricultural school for African Americans. His portrayal of the black South in "Earth-Being" has become a touchstone for understanding *Cane*:

> There was a valley, the valley of "Cane," with smoke-wreaths during the day and mist at night. A family of back-country Negroes had only recently moved into a shack not far away. They sang. And this was the first time I'd ever heard the folk-songs and spirituals. They were very rich and sad and joyous and beautiful. But I learned that the Negroes of the town objected to them. They called them "shouting." They had victrolas and player-pianos. So, I realized with deep regret, that the spirituals, meeting ridicule, would be certain to die out. With Negroes also the trend was towards the small town and then towards the city—and industry and commerce and machines. The folk-spirit was walking in to die on the modern desert. That spirit was so beautiful. Its death was so tragic. Just this seemed to sum life for me. And this was the feeling I put into *Cane*. *Cane* was a swan-song. It was a song of an end. (*Wayward* 123)

As Toomer looked back on the experience that inspired *Cane*, he identified the structuring conflict of the volume: the demise of the African American folk spirit and the trend toward modernization. The black past and black present momentarily confront each other in Toomer's memoir but only long enough for Toomer to recognize that the past was "certain to die out" as African Americans moved away from the land and into the modern towns and cities. Significantly, the aspect of African American life that instantiates this process is song. The "back-country Negroes," who only "recently moved into a shack" near Toomer, still retain the capacity to sing traditional songs. Their songs are his initiation into black folk culture, a contradictory experience of beauty, joy, and sorrow (the paradoxical feelings for which African American folk songs are renowned). The primacy of song in Toomer's recollection is absolutely crucial to understanding *Cane*. The encounter with the African American past was, for him, an encounter with black song. His sense that modern blacks were unable to hear how "rich and sad and joyous and beautiful" these songs are explains his prediction that "the folk-spirit was walking in to die on the modern desert" and his need to elegize that culture in his own book.

"Song of the Son," the poem widely recognized as *Cane*'s raison d'être, articulates Toomer's fears about the decline of African American culture and his commitment to capturing and memorializing the Negro folk spirit in his book before it became extinct:

> Pour O pour that parting soul in song,
> O pour it in the sawdust glow of night,
> Into the velvet pine-smoke air to-night,
> And let the valley carry it along.
> And let the valley carry it along.
>
> O land and soil, red soil and sweet-gum tree,
> So scant of grass, so profligate of pines,
> Now just before an epoch's sun declines
> Thy son, in time, I have returned to thee,
> Thy son, I have in time returned to thee. [...][1]

This apostrophe to the past asks the Southern land to reverberate with the echoes of ancestral song, so that the poet-son can listen, record, and preserve both the culture of the slaves and his connection to them. The poem itself formalizes the echo with repetitious sound effects (alliteration becoming even more emphatic later, "for though the sun is setting on / A song-lit race of slaves, it has not set"), repeated words and phrases, and refrain lines. Indeed, the euphony of the poem suggests it is the lyrical heart of the book; no other moment in *Cane* so powerfully expresses the book's elegiac and commemorative mission. And the emphasis on song is paramount here as it is in Toomer's autobiographical account of his Southern sojourn. In "Song of the Son" the speaker attempts to take up that "parting" song despite the deep contradictions that attend such a task.

Scruggs and VanDemarr provide a powerful account of these conceptual contradictions in the poem—and, ultimately, in *Cane*:

> Toomer defines the singer in "The Song of the Son" [sic] as the black descendent who has come back to celebrate a vanishing way of life. He is the poet-detective "returned . . . in time" to discover a peasant world before it disappears, before it fades into the common day of modernity; he is a "singing tree" whose "leaves"—the "songs" that make up *Cane*—will counter time's mutability with the permanence of art. The words "in time" convey a double meaning: the singer has returned to the South in the nick of time, but although he aspires to the universality of art, he is trapped as a mortal man in history, "in time." Indeed, the "plum" in "Song of the Son" plucked by the poet has an inescapable connection to the apple plucked from the Tree of Knowledge in the Garden of Eden. Once it is eaten, the "son," like Adam and Eve, has entered history and can only know good and evil, in Milton's words, "as two twins cleaving together." Taken by itself, "Song of the Son" only hints at this theme, but in the context of the book, the "son" soon learns that terror and beauty in the South are intertwined; the "singing tree" and the lynching tree are the same tree. (164)

And yet the formal harmonies of the poem are so perfectly executed that its conceptual dissonances are easily missed. The very repetitions that create the lyrical echo also produce insistent disturbances that will not be lulled by song here or elsewhere in the book. For instance, the obvious interplay of "son" and "sun" seems to indicate that the poet-son, the descendant of the "song-lit race of slaves," will function as an afterglow or final illumination of his ancestors. Moreover, it suggests that this relationship to his past is natural and timely, the result of a natural, generational progression. Yet the poem asks too much from the son/sun formulation and the notion of time that "naturally" extends from the figure of

sunset: as Scruggs and VanDemarr note, it wants to argue that time itself
has brought the son back to his roots ("in time, I have returned to thee")
and that he has returned just in time ("I have in time returned to thee").
This insistence on time that is paradoxically both cyclical, bringing the
son back like a blossom "returning" to the tree in spring, and linear,
bringing him back just in time to hear the final echoes of his past, produces subtle figurative confusions in the third stanza, where he says
again that he has returned

> In time, for though the sun is setting on
> A song-lit race of slaves, it has not set;
> Though late, O soil, it is not too late yet
> To catch thy plaintive soul, leaving, soon gone,
> Leaving, to catch thy plaintive soul soon gone.

"[S]ong-lit" suggests at once that those slaves lives were "lightened"
(both brightened and eased) by song, their own folk songs and spirituals,
and that the poet-son will illuminate their nearly extinguished lives and
culture with his contemporary song. The image of the setting sun uneasily represents this combination of loss and recovery, of historical
time, which brings an epoch to its end, and cyclical time, which renews
it. Thus, the repeated "leaving" refers both to the souls of the slaves, who
are "leaving, soon gone," and to their son, who is leaving his own present
moment in order to attend to their song: "Leaving, to catch thy plaintive
soul soon gone." The son who returns to the past is indeed a "setting
sun" not only because he addresses himself to a culture in decline but
because he acknowledges his own inevitable decline in claiming a continuous connection to the past. He, too, is "in time." The archaic pronouns invoke a close relationship to the past, which will be harder to
express in a contemporary idiom. In fact, the temporal paradox at the
heart of the son/sun figure is perhaps what inclines the speaker away
from the sunset metaphor in the final two stanzas. Here, in a closing
apostrophe to the "Negro slaves," a plum tree figures forth the relationship of the modern African American to his ancestors:

> O Negro slaves, dark purple ripened plums,
> Squeezed, and bursting in the pine-wood air,
> Passing, before they stripped the old tree bare
> One plum was saved for me, one seed becomes

An everlasting song, a singing tree,
Caroling softly souls of slavery,
What they were, and what they are to me,
Caroling softly souls of slavery.

In the metaphor of natural change, of course, the fruits of one generation blossom in the next. However, the ripened plums here are "[s]queezed, and bursting," and the singing tree is nearly stripped bare. These descriptions recall not a family tree, flowering with successive generations, but, as Scruggs and VanDemarr say, the lynching tree, where those slaves and many of their descendants were literally crushed.[2] Moreover, the image of the bursting plum is not merely generative but sexual, raising the specter of explicitly sexual violence carried out against black men during lynchings: castration. The idea of plucking the last plum suggests lynching, castration, and the destruction rather than the preservation of "black seed." We know, of course, what the son means to say, but the volatile coincidence between his metaphors for inheriting the ancestral culture and the iconographic metaphors for lynching cannot be ignored. Nevertheless, the poem does seem to ignore this aspect of its own imagery and concludes with the lovely, lisping echo of a beautiful past and the promise that the son will listen to and preserve the "souls of slavery" in his own songs.[3] Yet such a hopeful resolution will be difficult to carry out in the rest of the book. Indeed, almost every other page of Cane will demonstrate that elegizing a golden age of African American culture will be an impossible task, first, because no such ideal past exists and, second, because the relation of the modern black man to his slave past must inevitably be sorrowful and ambivalent.

One more detail of "Song of the Son" hints at the way the whole book will simultaneously reveal and repress its ambivalence about the past. The word "passing" in the penultimate stanza uneasily connects the son to his ancestors. As the Negro slaves are passing away, their descendant almost passes them by, yet the two cross paths in the syntactic doubling of a word that is also a loaded term in its own right: "passing," of course, refers to identifying oneself as something one isn't. Thus, the "slaves [...] [who are] [p]assing" away meet up with the son who in "[p]assing [them discovers that] [...] / One plum was saved for [him]." He discovers his relation to them, but this connection is recorded in a word that also registers the denial of such a relationship. A troubled association between the decline of one generation (its passing away) and the denial of ancestors by their descendants (passing for white) may figure in the fact that this son almost misses hearing the echo of the slaves (almost passes them by). Indeed, the elegiac impulse of the poem, and of the book, is partly motivated by the son's need to sever his connection to a brutal past and partly by his desire to establish that very connection. The sheer beauty of "Song of the Son" seems proof of the son's capacity to carry on the "everlasting song" precisely because it mutes the conceptual dissonance of such a project—most significantly, what separated him from them in the first place and to what extent he can take up their song now.

The intricacies of such passing are treated in another poem that did not appear in *Cane*. "And Pass" (*Collected Poems* 5) was written during the same period as *Cane*, but Toomer neither included it there nor apparently planned to publish it in his projected (and copyrighted) volume of verse, "The Blue Meridian and Other Poems."[4] Here again, sunset marks a time of contradictory passings:

When sun leaves dusk
On far horizons,
And night envelops
Empty seas
And fading dream-ships;
When the stars have eyes,
And their light blends
With darkness—
    I stand alone,
    Salute and pass
    Proud shadows.

In *Cane* dusk on the horizon will describe the color of a light-skinned black woman ("Karintha"), and night will be a time when different colors look the same ("Bona and Paul"). Here the ideal of overcoming racial difference by "blending" white and black appears as the blending of light and dark. Yet this is the moment, ironically, just as the horizon and the night sky emblematize such merging of differences, when the speaker feels alone. He does not join the "proud shadows"—which can be read as the dark shades of his ancestors—but salutes them in a contradictory gesture of recognition and farewell. That a poem replete with Toomer's particular images of racial indeterminacy foregrounds passing in its title and conclusion suggests how complicated the relationship to history was for him. Indeed, Toomer himself lived out the profound contradictions between his pride in his African ancestry and his ability to pass for white. He consistently sought freedom from either racial identity, calling himself a member of the "American race," a new race emerging in the peculiarly multiracial United States, promising a return to the old race, the human race (Kerman and Eldridge 341–42). However, such a position naturally forced him to expend a greater effort in denying his black-ness than his whiteness. For instance, he suggested that his grandfather Pinchback was white and may have passed as black to gain political ad-vantage during Reconstruction (Kerman and Eldridge 18), and he denied his black heritage when a school inquired about his daughter's racial makeup before admitting her (Kerman and Eldridge 293). He was easily able to pass as white, and quite often did, yet he received his only artistic recognition for being Negro. Like Toomer, the speaker of "And Pass" clearly admires the proud shadows of his dark ancestors yet also clearly takes pride in remaining aloof and passing them by.

It is important to note that in the free-verse poem "And Pass" the speaker bids the shades farewell, while in the traditional "Song of the Son" he greets them. "And Pass" is a calm and meditative poem but one in which the free verse does not contribute to an aural argument about continuity between past and present through its own lyricism. In "Song of the Son," on the other hand, the persuasive euphony aids in idealizing the past and in creating a sense of harmony between past and present. Indeed, these are the special tasks assigned to lyric poetry in *Cane*, especially to lyric poetry in conventional forms: selective memory, idealization, continuity, and optimism are registered in the pleasing re-liability of rhyme, meter, and traditional stanza forms. This is one reason why the son's poem is a song.

"Song of the Son," like Toomer's autobiographical piece, proposes that the echo of the African American past persists in song and that the son most likely to hear that echo and best equipped to take up that song is the lyric poet. One might have expected, in a book saturated with refer-ences to folk seculars and spirituals, that the son would be an actual rather than a metaphorical singer, a blues- or jazzman rather than a poet;

however, the distinctly African American forms in *Cane*, folk songs and spirituals in particular, almost always appear as fragmented snippets and frequently as corrupted lyrics that mock the traditional songs and register their loss. For instance, the blurring of morning and evening, dawn and dusk, birth and death, that patterns the book is reproduced in one of the echoes of a spiritual in "Kabnis":

> My Lord, what a mourning,
> My Lord, what a mourning,
> My Lord, what a mourning,
> When the stars begin to fall. (93)

The substitution of "mourning" for "morning"[5] and the apocalyptic image of stars falling where we would expect a sun to be rising indicate a modernist suspicion of nature and song that characterizes parts 2 and 3 of *Cane*.[6] Even in part 1, the section of the book dedicated to the folk spirit, the folk songs only appear in corrupted form.[7] Still, part 1 holds out hope that a new song, lyric poetry, can bridge the gulf between "[w]hat they were, and what they are to me," between the African American past and its present. Why literary poetry rather than song? Perhaps Toomer hopes that the page will preserve the past in ways he thinks an oral tradition cannot. Lyric poetry in *Cane* takes many forms: sonnets, ballads, free verse, and even a work song. That is, literary poetry does not constitute a complete break from oral poetry; instead, Toomer seems to regard these two traditions as two ends of a spectrum of forms,[8] representing not complete opposites but different historical moments and different artistic resources. Nevertheless, if left to hang in the air of an oral tradition, the folk spirit will be "soon gone." "The folk-spirit was walking in to die on the modern desert." The folk songs and spirituals were "certain to die out," being replaced by "victrolas and player-pianos" (*Wayward* 123). The songs of the son would have to survive modernity. One could argue that the victrolas and player pianos are merely the modern equivalent of banjos and guitars, that is, that the folk songs and spirituals were developing into blues and jazz rather than being extinguished by these newer musical forms. However, Toomer's phrasing, "certain to die out" and "being replaced by," suggests that he simultaneously viewed modernity, its technology, and its musical forms as paradoxically derived from yet antithetical to past forms. This is one of the many contradictions in *Cane*. Ironically, then, he hoped to preserve the oral folk tradition by incorporating it into a new literary form, a form he conceived of as both related to and distinct from the folk tradition. Literary poetry offered the conventions of an established tradition, the physical durability of writing, and the immediacy and flexibility of free verse. The son would have to be a modern poet, and like other moderns, his effort to restore order to the world by making poetry new would involve a deep nostalgia for the past and a vexed engagement with its forms and conventions.

In "Natalie Mann," a play Toomer completed in 1922 while writing many of the sketches for *Cane*, he orchestrates past and present forms in precisely the way he must have hoped to do in *Cane*. Indeed, the moment when past and present merge in "Natalie Mann" is the point in the play when Nathan Merilh, an aspiring black artist based on Toomer himself, reads one of his recently written manuscripts to a group of white, New York bohemians.[9] The piece he chooses to read is almost word for word the story "Karintha" that would shortly become the first prose portrait in *Cane*. Here in "Natalie Mann," however, Toomer the dramatist is able to envision a performance of that story that would release the words on the page into an aural environment of folk song. The stage directions describe a presentation of "Karintha" that would have joined the past and the present, folk songs and modern literature, oral and written forms, in a coherent and powerful way:

(Merilh fumbles around with some papers. The rest comfortably re-settle themselves. Nathan selects a MS, shows it to Natalie who picks up the [guitar and mandolin], giving the mandolin to Brown. These latter begin to play and hum an adaptation of a Negro spiritual. Merilh reads. As he progresses, one by one the others in the room join Natalie and Brown in humming. When Nathan finishes, the curtain begins to descend. The humming continues till it is down.) (*Wayward* 310)

To encounter "Karintha" this way—the words of the story set off against the strumming and humming of a spiritual, a curtain lowering in concert with the final lines, "Her skin is like dusk on the eastern horizon / [. . .] When the sun goes down. / Goes down . . . "—would be to witness the formal ideal Toomer hoped to realize in *Cane*. However, the play was never produced or published in Toomer's lifetime. Instead, the book *Cane* would have to accomplish this formal mission, and modern literature would have to find a way to keep the son's promise to his past with only the resources of the page.

The most explicit demonstration of the power of traditional lyric poetry to transfigure a degraded modern world is the sonnet "November Cotton Flower" in part 1, which I will discuss momentarily. First, though, that poem takes its title from a phrase in "Karintha," the opening prose portrait in *Cane*: "Even the preacher, who caught her at mischief, told himself that she was as innocently lovely as a November cotton flower" (3).[10] Instead of learning to live more fully from observing Karintha, however, the men around her wait impatiently for her to become a woman, so they can possess her sexually. Their desire to "ripen a growing thing too soon, could mean no good to her" (3), and she will be drained of her vitality by them. Thus, she changes from an innocent, vivacious twelve-year-old to a sexually experienced, contemptuous woman in the course of two paragraphs. The narrator's euphemistic treatment of sex, pregnancy, and childbirth seems initially to be motivated by irony: he responds to Karintha's degeneration with sardonic platitudes. For instance, he describes sex as natural and divinely ordained: "One could but imitate one's parents, for to follow them was the way of god" (4). Yet this is an excuse for childhood sexual experiments that lead to Karintha's ruin: "That started the whole thing" (4). However, his attempts at irony are repeatedly subsumed into something more like euphemism: he tries to maintain an ironic distance from the most troublesome aspects of Karintha's life, but the more tragic the details, the less able he is to confront them, with irony or without.[11] Karintha seems to have become a prostitute ("They all want to bring her money" [4]), though he never explicitly says this, and she commits infanticide, though this most horrific fact is almost lost in the distracting, preoccupied prose:

A child fell out of her womb onto a bed of pine-needles in the forest. Pine-needles are smooth and sweet. They are elastic to the feet of rabbits . . . A sawmill was nearby. Its pyramidal sawdust pile smouldered. It is a year before one completely burns. Meanwhile, the smoke curls up and hangs in odd wraiths about trees, curls up, and spreads itself out over the valley . . . Weeks after Karintha re-

turned home the smoke was so heavy you tasted it in the water.
Some one made a song:

> Smoke is on the hills. Rise up.
> Smoke is on the hills, O rise
> And take my soul to Jesus. (4)

It is easy to miss the death of Karintha's baby since the narrative interest
darts from the infant on the pine needles to the qualities of the needles
and then to how the pine needles would feel to rabbits. The implication
could be that Karintha's baby has been birthed like an animal—thus,
that Karintha herself has been degraded to that level—but the narrator
shifts his focus to rabbits too completely, too literally, for a point about
Karintha's degradation to have any force. Indeed, some readers do not
realize that the baby is left to die under the smoldering sawdust pile, even
though its "pyramidal" shape suggests a pregnant woman's womb and
the year-long burning parallels the period of gestation.[12] The "wraiths"
of smoke from the smoldering pile, finally, ought to indicate the presence
of the ghost of Karintha's baby, but the narrator persists in avoiding the
implications of his own imagery. The ellipses register his faltering and
refusal. As the imagery becomes intolerably pointed—"the smoke was
so heavy you tasted it in the water"—the narrator evades the realities of
the prose by slipping into poetry: a song that "some one" made up, presumably in response to these unacknowledged events, at once curtails
the sense building in the prose that Karintha's tragedy permeates everything and elevates her tragedy to a spiritual plane where "some one" can
lyricize it rather than gag on it. Ironically, the song could be read as addressing the death of the baby more explicitly than the narrator has been
able to do: "O rise / And take my soul to Jesus." However, the narrator is
put in mind of Karintha's soul rather than the baby's: "the soul of her
was a growing thing ripened too soon" (4). His interest is not in the
physical death of a baby but in Karintha's metaphorical death. Yet, the
best evidence we have for the destruction of Karintha's "soul," her innocence and vitality, is that she destroys her own child. The girl who taught
others how to live grows up to be a woman who kills. The other song,
presumably the narrator's, that frames the story and occurs once in ab-
breviated form midway through it, renders the apotheosis of Karintha
in her decline:

Her skin is like dusk on the eastern horizon,
O cant you see it, O cant you see it,
Her skin is like dusk on the eastern horizon
. . . When the sun goes down.

Goes down . . . (4)

Indeed, the beauty he wants to celebrate is the embodiment of decline. Her tawny skin is like the sky at nightfall; in a mixture of opposites that Toomer frequently employs, the colors of sunset on the eastern horizon, not the western, best describe Karintha's beauty. This detail suggests figuratively that sunrise, renewal, is not possible because sunset "colors" everything (a formulation that will recur throughout the book) and dusk is always falling. The verbal and visual repetition of nightfall at the end of the story, "When the sun goes down. // Goes down," reinforces the sense that death and decline are inevitable—and, moreover, beautiful. Karintha *is* the setting sun, a goddess of decline, indeed, a "natural" event in a world defined by loss. The framing song aestheticizes and mythologizes Karintha's fate much as "Song of the Son" glorifies the "souls of slavery."[13] The ways that song is functioning in "Karintha" reveal one of the purposes of lyric throughout the book. Song frequently averts attention from the "realistic" and often tragic details of African American life, instead creating a lyrical realm in which gruesome realities give way to idealistic impressions.[14] No wonder, then, that Karintha's tragedy can be utterly transformed into a positive (super)natural event in the sonnet "November Cotton Flower" (6).

In fact, the poem does not, strictly speaking, concern Karintha's tragedy but the general, one might even say mythical, implications of her particular story. The phrase "November cotton flower" here again regards the sudden, untimely introduction of beauty in an ugly world:

Boll-weevil's coming, and the winter's cold,
Made cotton-stalks look rusty, seasons old,
And cotton, scarce as any southern snow,
Was vanishing; the branch, so pinched and slow,
Failed in its function as the autumn rake;
Drouth fighting soil had caused the soil to take

All water from the streams; dead birds were found
In wells a hundred feet below the ground—
Such was the season when the flower bloomed.
Old folks were startled, and it soon assumed
Significance. Superstition saw
Something it had never seen before:
Brown eyes that loved without a trace of fear,
Beauty so sudden for that time of year.

Whereas in "Karintha" the advent of innocence and beauty in a ruined
world cannot transform that world, "November Cotton Flower" leaves
the impression that these same traits are redemptive. The withering failure of nature in the first eight lines of the poem provides an uncongenial
setting, to say the least, for beauty, innocence, and hope. Rodents are taking over a landscape already destroyed by drought and cold; the plants
have failed, and birds have died in their futile search for water. Yet, the
whole wasted scene can be preempted with the flick of a dash that ends
the octave's pessimism and signals the coming of the flower and the
hubristic optimism of the sestet: "Such was the season when the flower
bloomed." The blooming of the flower out of season, a perilous image
of the fragility of beauty and innocence in "Karintha," is treated here as
an omen of good fortune, not bad. The superstitious optimism that the
speaker attributes to the "old folks" is reiterated in the structure of the
poem, itself an "old form." The closing couplet at once personifies and
mythologizes the cotton flower and significantly gives no hint that its
beauty and innocence will be destroyed by the world of the octave:
"Brown eyes that loved without a trace of fear, / Beauty so sudden for
that time of year." Indeed, the penultimate line introduces an equation
the poem has strategically reserved for the end—the untimely blossom
is like an innocent lover—exposing it to the surrounding wasteland only
long enough to idealize it by contrast. The whole poem drives toward
this idealization of its subject, as the rhetorical structure of the sonnet
supersedes the problem of its octave with the vision of its sestet. The
poem concludes with the notion that the sudden beauty of the November cotton flower *answers* the ugliness of the world (it quite literally has
the last word in the poem), while "Karintha" chronicles the destruction
of the cotton flower's innocence and beauty in that same environment.
    If, in a certain sense, both "Karintha" and "November Cotton Flower"

are about innocence and beauty in a fallen world, then the prose treatment handles that subject with pessimism and the poetic treatment with optimism. Though *Cane*'s generic distinctions are finally more complicated than this, these two pieces do roughly represent the tasks the book assigns to different genres. Prose is the discourse of realism, modernity, and tragedy; poetry of idealism, the past, and hope. As we've already seen in "Karintha," of course, the book does not always keep its generic modes apart. Eruptions of lyric in the prose sections suggest the book's pained intolerance of its own desire for realistic representation. Lyric functions at these times like whistling in the dark; its role is to repudiate the tragic facts of African American life in the modern world through a lyricism that is often more macabre than consoling.

The poetry/prose distinction, however, is not the only generic contrast in *Cane*. Poetry itself takes many forms. I have said that Toomer sometimes imagined a spectrum of verbal art, with lyric at one extreme and prose at the other.[15] He similarly conceived of poetry on a subspectrum: oral forms, folk songs and spirituals, are situated on the end associated with the past; and literary forms, especially free-verse and Imagist poems, are located on an opposite end associated with the present. Literary poetry in traditional forms—sonnets, ballads, or any stanzaic pattern employing rhyme and meter conventionally—offers a structure in which past and present, oral tradition and writing, can coexist. And, more than merely coexisting, the traditional literary form preserves the oral culture it embraces in ways that culture's own (oral) forms cannot. Thus, older folk songs and spirituals typically occur in the prose because they are more susceptible to change and corruption than written forms, incomplete and eerie echoes of a lost past erupting into the "prosaic" present.[16] Other poems treat "folk" material—farmers, sawmill workers, rural lovers—in traditional *literary* forms. Finally, free-verse, imagistic poems conceive of poetry in distinctly modernist terms as a form that offers a vivid, immediate, and unmediated picture of the present, a picture that can only, in its formal "honesty," expose the vicious truths of modern life. Toomer's generic spectrum, then, begins in the past with oral folk song and concludes in the present with written prose; between these two extremes various forms of literary poetry trace the distance between a glorious past and a doomed present in the "breakdown" of conventional versification into free verse. This is not to say that free verse or prose is devalued in Toomer's scheme; each genre has its merits and functions. Still, in associating poetry with a golden age and prose with modernity, Toomer inevitably implies different valuations of different genres.

We have already begun at the middle of this spectrum, and, not co-incidentally, right at the middle of part 1 of *Cane*, with "Song of the Son," a literary poem in traditional form that attempts to call the ideal-ized ancestral past into being by its very structures. "Reapers" (5), the first such traditional poem in the book, deploys an arsenal of poetic sound effects for its disturbing subject matter. The first quatrain uses the alliteration of *s*'s to invoke the manual labor of the black workers, the sharpening and then swishing of their blades through the grass:

> Black reapers with the sound of steel on stones
> Are sharpening scythes. I see them place the hones
> In their hip-pockets as a thing that's done,
> And start their silent swinging, one by one.

Here, in the stanza devoted to the past, black workers, probably share-croppers, do the necessary, even natural work of bringing in the har-vest. The ominous figurative sense of language like "Black reapers" and "scythes," suggesting the darkness of death and the Grim Reaper, is pres-ent but held in check by the insistence on the literal and ordinary mean-ing of the scene: these are dark-skinned men who must harvest the crops.[17] The ominous overtones of the imagery are tucked away, at least momentarily, like the hones: put away into homely hip pockets as a simple, ordinary "thing that's done." The second quatrain, however, moves with-out warning to the present period when horses pulling mechanized har-vesting equipment have replaced the human workers and where every word now gives itself to foreboding connotations:

> Black horses drive a mower through the weeds,
> And there, a field rat, startled, squealing bleeds.
> His belly close to ground. I see the blade,
> Blood-stained, continue cutting weeds and shade.

B's and hard *c*'s replace the sibilance of the first quatrain, and the im-agery of reaping is now clearly grim. Black horses have replaced black men working in the field; indeed, the field rat, squealing, bleeding, ignored by the very force that destroys it, seems a metaphorical replacement for the missing workers, who have also been "cut down" by mechanical progress. Here, the formal resources of traditional literary poetry do not simply invoke an idealized prior time but do so to capture its loss. The quiet, pleasingly cadenced lines, the couplets of perfect rhyme, the hushed insistence of the alliteration: all of this bespeaks an artistic harmony that cannot be discovered outside of "archaic" poetry. The poem about the reapers is quite beautiful and harmonious even as the reapers' actual lives are destroyed by modernity like the field rat crushed by the mower blade. The unity, harmony, and coherence of the conventional poetic form render the modern scene even more brutal by contrast.

Still, those very qualities of conventional versification can be employed more innocently to conjure an idealized past. "Georgia Dusk" (15) set conspicuously next to "Song of the Son"—and contributing to the nostalgic center of part 1[18]—recurs to the vision of African Americans working the soil, singing, and, in doing so, enacting a spiritual connection to their African past. It is no surprise by this time in *Cane* that dusk is the period of ritual and memory. Even more aspiring than "Song of the Son," "Georgia Dusk" witnesses the transformation of field and mill workers into "[h]igh-priests" and "juju-m[e]n" as sunset falls and "[r]ace memories" rise in song. After a long day at labor, the workers return home under a sky extravagantly described as too lazy to prevent sunset: "too indolent to hold / A lengthened tournament for flashing gold, / [the sky] Passively darkens for night's barbecue," imagery suggesting that some formerly more heroic context has given way to barbecues and orgies. Nevertheless, caught up in the glory of the sunset, the "genius of the South" surprises himself "in making folk-songs from soul sounds":

> Meanwhile, the men, with vestiges of pomp,
>   Race memories of king and caravan,
>   High-priests, an ostrich, and a juju-man,
> Go singing through the footpaths of the swamp.
>
> Their voices rise . . the pine trees are guitars,
>   Strumming, pine-needles fall like sheets of rain . .
>   Their voices rise . . the chorus of the cane
> Is caroling a vesper to the stars . .

O singers, resinous and soft your songs
   Above the sacred whisper of the pines,
   Give virgin lips to cornfield concubines,
Bring dreams of Christ to dusky cane-lipped throngs.

As "soul sounds" are shaped into "folk-songs," the scene of African American rural workers going home is organized into conventional five-beat lines and rhymed quatrains. The order and euphony of the form lend cohering power to the scene, and the poem itself, like "Song of the Son," constitutes an instance of the saving grace of song. Indeed, the song rises out of the cacophony of modern life—"The sawmill blows its whistle, buzz-saws stop"—to recreate the world only grasped in echoes in "Song of the Son." These are not poet-sons but ordinary black men, whose extraordinary souls emerge at night during their brief respite from labor and under the influence of the celestial sphere; and they do not take up a song whose echo is quickly fading but rather their own prosy soul sounds become song in this mystical environment. All of nature contributes to the "chorus of the cane" as tree boughs strum, pine needles fall like background music, and the wind whispers in the trees. In such a setting, profane words and sounds become sacred, and concubines are virgins once again. Thus, the song in the cane fields is at last a "vesper to the stars," a prayer that brings "dreams of Christ" to the transformed workers.

It is not completely clear what forms the dreams of Christ take, however. Certainly, the poem has been escalating from song to prayer, and it may be that such inspired singing inevitably inspires a religious experience. Yet, there is also the sense that the song makes the men think of themselves as Christlike, mistreated and misunderstood sons of a deity who will ultimately exonerate and glorify them. Typical of Cane's poems, the last line reaches an emotional crescendo that is puzzling. The lazy, wanton Georgia scene is transformed through sunset and song into a vision of universal harmony and spiritual ecstasy. As the reference to Christ suggests, it is redemptive. But how such a vision informs part 1 is more difficult to assess. We turn the page to "Fern," another prose portrait of a fallen, devitalized woman, whose life cannot be touched by the lyricism and vision of "Georgia Dusk." The contrast between the poem and the prose piece, however, is not hard to evaluate. "Georgia Dusk" achieves in poetry something that the prose sections cannot even imagine: a harmonious continuum of past and present, Africa and African America, the profane and the sacred. Dusk once again is a moment when opposites blend, and that is a moment when anything is possible.

One last poem in this mode, "Evening Song" (21), similarly idealizes rural Southern life, this time in a romantic rather than spiritual setting. Here, the speaker and his lover, Cloine, nestle together as the full moon rises. The poem holds at bay the more negative connotations of these images, especially the figure of the full moon, which will illuminate the lynching in "Blood-Burning Moon," and of the sleeping woman. In "Carma," "Fern," "Esther," and "Avey," Toomer depicts sleeping women as either deceitful or devitalized, a danger or a dangerous disappointment to men. In "Evening Song," however, Cloine falls asleep peacefully on the chest of her lover; she is like the moon, "[r]adiant, resplendently she gleams," a natural part of sundown. The poem is composed of three quatrains, rhyming ABBA CDDC ABBA, with exact rhymes throughout and the repetition of the initial rhyme sounds in the final stanza bringing the poem to a satisfying aural conclusion. However, the meter is erratic, with first lines of four, six, and seven beats and great variation in the number of unstressed syllables. Likewise, lines 2 of each quatrain vary from three to five beats, and the fourth lines from three to four. Only the third line of each stanza—"Cloine tires," "Cloine sleeps," and "Cloine dreams"—achieves the metrical regularity typical of the closed-form poems in *Cane*:

Cloine, curled like sleepy waters where the moon-waves start,
Radiant, resplendently she gleams,
Cloine dreams,
Lips pressed against my heart.

The result is a poem in which the slight disturbance of metrical irregularity is eased by perfect rhymes, consistent rhyme scheme, envelope stanzas, and, most of all, by the quiet containment in the two-beat "Cloine" lines. Here Toomer casts folk material in a form that simultaneously suggests the past, in its rhyming quatrains, and the future in alternating long and short lines typical of his free-verse poems. In the context of part 1, "Evening Song" captures an idyllic moment between lovers that cannot be found anywhere else in *Cane*. Its formal regularities contribute to the idyll even while its slight irregularities seem to acknowledge that such a scene cannot be preserved. Thus, the two-beat lines in which Cloine drowses and sleeps contract to a dream world of rural love, while the restless longer lines reach uneasily away from that vision to the surrounding texts and their contradictory vision.

Like "Evening Song," "Cotton Song" (11) straddles the past and present by treating folk material from a contemporary perspective, and, again like "Evening Song," it bears the traces of this tension in its form.[19] Composed in work-song style, the poem is ostensibly about lifting bales of cotton: "Come, brother, come. Lets lift it; / Come, now, hewit! roll away!" Yet the ambiguous "it" in the first line is also the song itself. In one register, the song calls upon fellow workers to lift the bale together, so the cotton can be "roll[ed] away," presumably on a cargo ship. However, another register calls the workers to lift their song, a song that enables them to work in unison and, ironically, permits them to express something more than the need to work together. The difficulty of moving the heavy cotton bale is likened to the difficulty of walking with shackled feet and then to the limitations of the body (as opposed to the freedom of the soul). The call to work is a call to song—"Lets lift [our song, so we can lift the cotton bales]"—yet song appears to rouse a rebellious spirit:

> Cotton bales are the fleecy way
> Weary sinner's bare feet trod,
> Softly, softly to the throne of God,
> "We aint agwine t wait until th Judgment Day!
>
> Nassur; nassur,
> Hump.
> Eoho, eoho, roll away!
> We aint agwine t wait until th Judgment Day!"

If heavy bales of cotton are hard to move but can be set in motion through concerted effort, then they are like souls that are shackled by the body but will be liberated by God on Judgment Day. "Shackled," of course, also raises the issue of bodies literally bound in slavery. In a familiar formulation from African American spirituals and folk seculars, the soul of the slave will transcend earthly captivity in death and resurrection. As Bernard Bell has observed, the phrase "roll away" suggests the stone rolling away from Christ's tomb on the morning of the Resurrection as well as the cotton bales that must be moved (*Afro-American Novel* 323). We would expect the song to argue that hard work and suffering on earth will lead to everlasting peace in heaven. Indeed, Udo O. H. Jung links the "fleecy" cotton in stanza 3 to the "fleecy way," a derivation of the Milky Way, the path to heaven in folklore (331). Yet the refrain of these stanzas is "We *aint* agwine t wait until th Judgment Day!" The communal song seems to incite workers to sing on their own behalf; by the end of the song, it is not the cotton bale that's rolling, and it is not the analogous boulder at Christ's tomb; instead, the workers themselves assert their intention to "roll away":

> God's body's got a soul,
> Bodies got to roll the soul,
> Cant blame God if we dont roll,
> Come, brother, roll, roll!

The suggestion seems to be that the communal hoisting of the cotton bale inspires the workers to escape the shackles of their labor. They are not going to wait for spiritual transcendence. In fact, in the last stanza, the soul functions like a boulder to weigh the body down (as a religious doctrine of submission to suffering constrains believers) rather than the expected reverse. It's the body's job to "roll the soul." God cannot be blamed for their bondage and, by extension, cannot be counted on for release. The cotton workers must employ their physical strength for their own escape; lifting the song together seems to be a crucial part in their liberation.

"Cotton Song" and "Evening Song" are poems in traditional forms that push toward something untraditional. "Cotton Song" invokes the call-and-response work song structure to urge the brothers to "roll away" not just from their labor and captivity but from a religious view that would ask them to wait for liberation in the afterlife. "Evening Song" depicts an idyllic world but casts it in a form that qualifies rural love as a *mere* idyll. Both of these poems demonstrate *Cane*'s practice of invoking conventional poetic forms in order to register the difference between a version of the past and the present. The stevedores in "Cotton Song" and Cloine in "Evening Song" don't quite fit into the formal moments of their poems, the stevedores because they are too modern, Cloine because she is too old-fashioned. The poems in part 2 will make much less subtle use of the fact that traditional forms can be deployed to sound a dissonance—sometimes hopeful but more frequently discouraged—between the past and the present.

The part 2 poems will also confirm the even greater dissonance between an idealized past and a profane present that free verse can expose. Throughout *Cane* free-verse poetry offers lyric forms that are devoid of the very qualities associated with traditional lyric poetry: melodic continuity with the past; conventional, idealizing figures; archaic sentiment; an oracular voice; and visionary confidence. In addition to the six conventional poems in part 1, then, four poems in free verse, "Face," "Nullo," "Conversion," and "Portrait in Georgia," register a more modern and thus more ominous vision. In these brief lyrics, three of which were published together in *Modern Review* as "Portraits in Georgia," Toomer shifts conspicuously away from "song" to explore visual rather than aural poetic resources, as the word "portraits" suggests. As we know, Toomer's adoption of the Imagists' "fresh vision" marked an important step in his progress as a writer (*Wayward* 120). Yet, even as he claimed to have discovered his essential tools in Imagism, he also recoiled from what he argued was its overemphasis on visual imagery and the resulting devaluation of sound and emotion, qualities of poetry he obviously associated with each other. In a 1921 unpublished review of Richard Aldington's "The Art of Poetry," Toomer takes Imagism to task for its infatuation with sight:

> We of the Western world, whose thoughts have been shaped and moulded by the poets from Plato (Goethe, Ibsen, etc.) to Whitman suddenly roll on our back with our face toward China and the Chinese. Charmed by their pictorial, suggestive loveliness we no longer hear the mighty voices of the past. Or rather, we hear them, but as a tired man hears a symphony; there is an auditory titillation, but no soul expansion—the spirit is too weary to respond.
>
> I have used "we." I think it would be nearer the truth to say "they." By "they" meaning [Aldington] and similar ones whose eyes are so charmed and fascinated by the gem, by its outward appearance, by its external form, that the spirit behind the gem is not perceived. Which is perfectly all right. I simply say that I do not

believe such an attitude characteristic either of the Western poets or of their readers. Overnight our voice and hearing have not
shrunk into an eye. ("Selected Essays" 4)

Notice the association of auditory qualities—voice and hearing—with
spirit and emotion. The "mighty voices of the past" carried spirit and
emotion in "rousing message[s]" that moved readers beyond titillation.
Aldington's preferred poetry is intellectual, while Toomer's is emotional
(5). Indeed, the depiction of contemporary readers, supine, facing East,
mesmerized by a trinket of a poem, indicates spiritual exhaustion and
debasement. Toomer clearly wants to reject the notion that his fellow
readers are reduced to this, that they are "shrunk into an eye," but his
own vivid image of decadent Imagists belies his faint rebuttal.

It is precisely this contradictory attitude toward Imagist poetry that
informs the free-verse poetry in *Cane*. What Toomer seems to want from
these poems is not the evocation of a glorious, lyrical past offered in
a poem like "Song of the Son" or "Georgia Dusk" but rather a stark, realistic look at the conditions of African American life in the modern
world. Whereas in "Song of the Son" he recovers a utopian past, and in
"Georgia Dusk" or "Reapers" he links the contemporary, degraded moment to a meaningful past through song, in the Georgia portraits he exposes the surface realities of black life in America, refusing to listen to
the mythical echoes that reverberate in the traditional lyric poems and
therefore refusing to transform what he sees into something grander.

Thus, the three Georgia portraits are visions of racism, violence, and
death. The title "Face" (10), for instance, flaunts the challenge of *Cane*'s
Imagist poetry to "face" the realities revealed in these portraits:

Hair—
silver-gray,
like streams of stars,
Brows—
recurved canoes
quivered by the ripples blown by pain,
Her eyes—
mist of tears
condensing on the flesh below

And her channeled muscles
are cluster grapes of sorrow
purple in the evening sun
nearly ripe for worms.

"Face" alludes ironically to the blazon tradition, in which a poem offers
an inventory of the physical traits of a woman.[20] The gesture of celebrating female beauty is short lived, however, as the potential loveliness of
silver hair "like streams of stars" gives way to eyes that are full of tears
and pain.[21] The visual imagery moves quickly and relentlessly from silvery streaks of hair to a vision of the woman almost dead from suffering.
Her face muscles are contorted by pain into "cluster grapes of sorrow /
purple in the evening sun," an image that anticipates and qualifies the
"purple ripened plum" in "Song of the Son." In fact, "Face" turns out to
function less like a blazon and more like a fugitive slave poster, or even
a slave auction bill, listing the physical attributes of the anonymous black
woman and suggesting that such commodification of human qualities
is an inhumane practice that leads inevitably to death. The poem "Portrait in Georgia" (29) operates exactly the same way, though here the
context of a specifically African American oppression is explicit:

Hair—braided chestnut,
        coiled like a lyncher's rope,
Eyes—fagots,
Lips—old scars, or the first red blisters,
Breath—the last sweet scent of cane,
And her slim body, white as the ash
        of black flesh after flame.

Again the poem offers a list of physical features, and again it titillates us
with an appealing figure in the opening line: braided chestnut-colored
hair might be the beginning of a beautiful description. However, the
picture is spoiled almost immediately as the coiled hair is likened to a
lyncher's rope. Suddenly, the dangers attending beauty and desire in an
African American context are horribly explicit. The poem represents
beauty, desire, and destruction as impossible to separate. To be a beautiful black woman in Cane is to be vulnerable to the violence and corruption of desire. Like Karintha, who "matures" from an innocent child

to a fallen woman in the course of a sentence, the women depicted in "Face" and "Portrait in Georgia" are destroyed, whether by hardship or violence, as quickly as the speaker can look from their hair to their eyes. Indeed, he cannot seem to visualize a beautiful woman without seeing her demise, as if visual representation, by definition, exposes the ugliness that feeds on beauty in Toomer's South. The sense that the poem is structured like an auction announcement or "wanted" poster again overwhelms the structure of the blazon. The beauty of African American women leads ineluctably to death, as it will for Tom Burwell in "Blood-Burning Moon," the story of a lynching that directly follows "Portrait in Georgia." Here, the black or mulatto woman herself is cast as the lynched victim—her distinctive beauty burns until its blackness is transformed by death to whiteness: "And her slim body, white as the ash / of black flesh after flame."[22] If we set these two poems beside "Song of the Son" or "Georgia Dusk," we cannot ignore the aesthetic equation in operation, an association between formal, lyrical poetry and the idealization of African American culture on the one hand and between imagistic, free-verse poetry and the harsh realities of African American life on the other.

"Conversion" (28) is the last of the poems published in *Modern Review* as the Georgia portraits. Like the other two, it depicts the destruction of blackness as it comes into contact with whiteness. African spirituality is corrupted and lost, the "African Guardian of Souls" replaced by a "white-faced sardonic god." The cultural transformation in "Conversion" moves in the opposite direction from that presented in "Georgia Dusk," where the black laborers, animated by nighttime partying, are transformed into African high priests and juju-men. Here, conversion marks the loss of African traditions, and the bacchanalian drinking and feasting render the deity drunk and debased:

African Guardian of Souls,
Drunk with rum,
Feasting on a strange cassava,
Yielding to new words and a weak palabra
Of a white-faced sardonic god—
Grins, cries
Amen,
Shouts hosanna.

Rum and cassava place this conversion in the West Indies, where slaves were transferred in their journey from Africa to North America. This is significant since it locates the conversion from authentic African beliefs to ineffective western religion before the slaves reached the American South—a fact that calls into question *Cane*'s idealization of the Southern slave experience. The new words and weak palaver are the alien, inauthentic tenets of Christianity, which the African Guardian of Souls shouts out only because he is drunk.[23] Once again the lack of lyricism lends the poem a corrupt, fragmentary quality; the form of the poem registers a conversion from the rhythmic African chants whose echoes linger in the traditional poems to this unmelodious shouting and crying. These new words are noticeably not as aesthetically compelling as the words of "November Cotton Flower," "Song of the Son," "Georgia Dusk," or even "Reapers." The loss of spirituality that characterizes Toomer's account of the move from Africa to America parallels the loss of lyricism in the move from past to present. The wisdom and beauty of African prayer are lost as Africans convert to Christianity, but *Cane* seems to want to believe that these things are reclaimed again in the South in the slaves' songs. Part 1 paradoxically captures the echo of those songs and simultaneously records their degeneration into the "new words" and "weak palabra" of modern poetry. The Georgia portraits are poems whose poetic resources have shrunk into an eye, and they are especially disturbing because *looking* at African American life, as opposed to *listening* to it, will always reveal an ugly truth. Indeed, what part 1 refers to as "new words" part 3 will bluntly term "ugly words" as the suspicion that poetry can no longer address and appease contemporary suffering grows to an admission of fact.

Still, though poetry can no longer aspire to be the everlasting song, it retains a certain force even when it occurs only in random fragments. All of the poems in this first section succeed in the terms they set for themselves, whether those terms are idealistic or realistic, glancing backward to an imagined better time or scrutinizing the present moment. In addition to the poems proper, part 1 contains many snippets of lyric that intrude into the prose, disquieting eruptions of a voice that lacks conventional lyric authority but is nevertheless disruptive precisely because it is so strange.

Of the six prose pieces in part 1 of *Cane*, four are punctuated with poetry. "Karintha," as we have already seen, "Carma," and "Blood-Burning

Moon" all employ a songlike stanza that responds to and comments upon the story proper in the manner of the chorus in a Greek tragedy. In "Becky" lyrical eruptions are less formalized and therefore more disruptive. The comparison to Greek tragedy is apt in both cases, however, since the Greek chorus articulated the wisdom of traditional religion and society, especially as that society became secularized. That is, the chorus expressed a traditional perspective, even an anachronistic one, and it is not surprising that it did so in a conventional, even archaic, form:

> [T]he ch[orus] remained the conservative soul of the play, the articulate spokesman for traditional religion and society, clinging stubbornly to the forms and wisdom and even the style of the worshipping group from which it arose. This conservatism is visible not only in the elaborately figured archaic lyrics, with their "poetic" syntax and heavy load of Doricisms in sharp contrast to more colloquial dialogue, but in the traditionalism of its moral beliefs, its conventional theodicy, and its commitment to proverbial social wisdom.[24]

The Greek chorus embodies a conservatism of form and perspective that we also find in *Cane*'s aesthetic and thematic nostalgia. Recall the lyric voice in "Karintha" intruding on the narrative precisely when the contemporary prose mode finds itself unable to manage the tragic details of Karintha's life. The distracted prose and the faltering ellipses give way to a song that recasts Karintha's tragedy as Christian myth. A similar opposition between the tragic present moment of the prose and the mythical context of the intrusive poetry structures "Carma" and "Blood-Burning Moon," though much less successfully as the transforming power of lyric decreases over the course of part 1.

"Carma" is the story of another spirited Southern black woman whose social environment restricts her. Like Karintha and Fern in part 1 or Avey, Dorris, and Muriel in part 2, Carma embodies a mythical African female power that the male narrator glimpses but cannot possess. We first encounter Carma driving a mule wagon home at sunset. The opening paragraph of the story handles this scene in a realistic, colloquial style: "Carma, in overalls, and strong as any man, stands behind the old brown mule, driving the wagon home" (12). However, Georgia dusk inspires the narrator here, as almost everywhere else in the book, to recreate this or-

dinary scene as myth. The second paragraph, sequestered within parentheses, offers another vision:

> (The sun is hammered to a band of gold. Pine-needles, like mazda,
> are brilliantly aglow. [. . .] A black boy . . . you are the most sleepi-
> est man I ever seed, Sleeping Beauty . . . cradled on a gray mule,
> guided by the hollow sound of cowbells, heads for them through a
> rusty cotton field. [. . .] A girl in the yard of a whitewashed shack
> not much larger than the stack of worn ties piled before it sings.
> Her voice is loud. Echoes, like rain, sweep the valley. Dusk takes the
> polish from the rails. Lights twinkle in scattered houses. From far
> away, a sad strong song. [. . .] She does not sing; her body is a song.
> She is in the forest dancing. Torches flare . . juju men, greegree,
> witch-doctors . . torches go out . . . The Dixie Pike has grown from
> a goat path in Africa. (12)

In this parenthetical account of nightfall in Carma's world, sunset ignites
a different sensibility, one that can hear the lives of the African American
folk and can sound out the differences between their voices and the narrative voice, first in the overheard snippet of dialect conversation ("you
are the most sleepiest man I ever seed, Sleeping Beauty") and then in the
song, which is at once literal ("Her voice is loud") and figurative ("She
does not sing; her body is a song"). As song creates a link between the
contemporary black man and his ancestors in "Song of the Son" or draws
out a repressed African identity in "Georgia Dusk," the song here creates
a continuum between the present moment on the Dixie Pike and the
ancient "goat path in Africa." When we leave the parenthetical realm,
however, we return to a profane world where "Carma's tale is the crudest
melodrama" (13), where she is unfaithful to her husband and thus responsible for his anger, violence, and his resulting incarceration on a
chain gang.

The crude melodrama of Carma's life is framed by a stanza of poetry
about song:

> Wind is in the cane. Come along.
> Cane leaves swaying, rusty with talk,
> Scratching choruses above the guinea's squawk,
> Wind is in the cane. Come along. (12, 13)

The poem situates the song between the cacophonous gossip of the local men, who generate "boasts and rumors" about their sexual exploits with Carma (theirs is the "rusty," "[s]cratching" "squawk"), and the sacred strains of the African scene (which, notably, is not described). Though the voice of the wind in the cane is harsh and strained like the townspeople's talk, it nevertheless communicates an invitation to "come along"—an ambiguous command at once to attend to Carma's tale and to move beyond her tragic story to its mythic potential.[25] It is, of course, only in poetry that the harsh talk of ordinary life can be transformed into the "chorus of the cane." However, the three instances of formal poetry in "Carma" remain isolated from the action of the story. The parenthetical mythical transformation is likewise structurally sealed off from the story it wishes to recast. Carma's story remains a crude melodrama, unchanged by the lyrical invitation to "come along" to another version and another mode. In "Karintha" the prose voice ultimately submits to the song that deifies Karintha; here, however, the natural song sounds sadly like the profane chatter of the gossips. The poetry frames the story but does not subsume the tragedies of the prose into the mythical realm of lyric.

This generic disappointment is played out in another way. The visual image of the setting sun in "Carma"—"The sun is hammered to a band of gold. Pine-needles, like mazda, are brilliantly aglow" (12)—receives a second treatment in a free-verse poem a few pages later:

A spray of pine-needles,
Dipped in western horizon gold,
Fell onto a path.
Dry moulds of cow-hoofs.
In the forest.
Rabbits knew not of their falling,
Nor did the forest catch aflame. ("Nullo" 20)

The title, "Nullo," one of Toomer's many coinages, from the Latin *nullus*, suggests something invalid, insignificant, amounting to nothing. That the dramatic spectacle of sunset, a (super)natural event that elsewhere in *Cane* transforms the mundane world into the sacred as a flame transforms darkness into light, goes unnoticed indicates how much has been lost in part 1 by this point, just over halfway through the section. Back at the beginning, when the pine needles were "smooth and sweet" and "elastic to the feet of rabbits," the sunset had the power to confer meaning and glory on the fallen world. In "Nullo," however, only the Imagist eye of the speaker notices the beauty of the sunlit pine needles. Within the world of the poem, the gilded needles fall to the ground unseen; not even the rabbits recognize the event, and, even more discouraging for the speaker, the illuminated pine needles do not ignite a poetic vision: "Nor did the forest catch aflame." Similarly, the mythic potential of the sunset in "Carma" is limited to a parenthetical aside, and the speaker is recalled from his imaginative reveries when night falls and "Foxie, the bitch, slicks back her ears and barks at the rising moon" (12).

We might argue that in "Nullo" the Imagist vision of sunset amounts to nothing because it can be seen but not heard: it is a poetic moment shrunk into an eye. Without the specifically *lyrical* aspects of lyric poetry —melodiousness, rhythm, rhyme—the image fails to make spiritual and emotional contact with the mythic realm. Likewise, the "far away [. . .] sad strong song" of "Carma" is dispelled as mere fantasy when the dog's bark snaps us back to a world where even the natural song of the wind is unpleasant, its message now no different from the chattering of the gossips. This reduction of song to talk may account for the fact that the poem in "Carma" can't keep its imagistic mind on cane, that is, on the book's central symbol for the age-old harmony between African Americans and the land. Halfway through "Carma" the poem appears with one word changed: "Wind is in the *corn*" not the cane (13, emphasis added). Though the story proper occurs in and near a cane field, there is also mention of a cotton field (12) and here a corn field. These variations create a subtle tension between the realistic setting, where various crops are grown, and the mythic arena, where the cane field is the symbolic space of African American myth and tradition.[26] Thus, "[t]ime and space have no meaning in a canefield. No more than the interminable stalks" (13). If the same song rustling in the cane field rustles in the corn and cotton fields, then no wonder the chorus of the cane is now merely a scratching sound, hardly distinguishable from the squawking of birds—or worse, the "weak palabra" of the prose. The cane field has become as ordinary and profane as a corn or cotton field.

In "Blood-Burning Moon," the final piece of part 1, poetry is not merely ineffective but corrupt—given *Cane*'s urge to associate lyric with beauty and authority. Like the full moon that casts an evil eye over the story and is clearly an omen of evil, the lyric voice intrudes with a taunting reminder of the inevitability of violence and a demonstration of the perversion of song. Notable here is that song does not echo some golden age that we can no longer see but *could* hear if we would only listen. The background sounds of "Blood-Burning Moon" are all harsh noises: dogs yelping and howling, chickens cackling, roosters crowing (30–31), and, most terrible, the yelling of the lynch mob (36). Even the women singing do so not to create beautiful sounds but "to stop their ears" against the cacophony of their environment. Indeed, this is what Louisa does at the end of the story when she sings in a futile attempt to retreat from the violence of the lynching and recreate a sense of community that is now irrevocably lost: "She'd sing, and perhaps they'd come out and join her. Perhaps Tom Burwell would come. At any rate, the full moon in the great door was an omen which she must sing to" (36). Tom Burwell, her black lover, has been lynched for killing Bob Stone, her white lover, and their deaths destroy any possibility that Louisa will be part of either community. She sings, then, not because song will be transforming but because she has lost her mind in losing everything else. Sitting alone after the lynching, the evil moon shedding its red light upon her, singing *to* that moon, Louisa is an emblem of "lunacy"[27]; and in this moment, the final moment of part 1, the lyric voice is similarly defeated as song becomes the expression of evil and madness and the embodiment of corruption.

The poem that constitutes this song is a brief triplet that occurs at the end of each of the three sections of the story—and therefore simultaneously concludes "Blood-Burning Moon" and part 1 of *Cane*:

Red nigger moon. Sinner!
Blood-burning moon. Sinner!
Come out that fact'ry door. (31, 33, 37)

The direct address to common people, colloquial diction, and dialect spelling suggest that this is a folk song. Indeed, on first reading it recalls several spirituals that hail sinners away from work to church and that employ the blood-red moon as a figure of God's judgment. For instance, "The Day of Judgment" uses the red moon as a sign of the Last Judgment: "And de moon will turn to blood / In dat day"; "Stars in the Elements" similarly recognizes ominous celestial events as signs of the apocalypse: "O the stars in the elements are falling, / And the moon drips away into blood, / And the ransomed of the Lord are returning home to God. / O blessed be the name of the Lord!"[28] In "Blood-Burning Moon," however, the folk are called away from work to witness the lynching, and the red moon is not an emblem of God's judgment but of a godless world governed by racism, hatred, and violence. As we've seen before in part 1, the figurative tradition of the poem—in which the red moon signifies the upheaval of the apocalypse and Last Judgment, with its promise for Christians, especially long-suffering black Christians, of resurrection and everlasting life—is betrayed by a literalization of the image. In "Karintha" the actual dead baby is ignored in favor of the metaphorical death of Karintha's innocence as poetry works to idealize the narrative events; here, however, the metaphorical meaning of the "blood-burning" moon is diminished to a terribly literal sign of the lynching in which Tom's blood does actually burn: "Now Tom could be seen within the flames. Only his head, erect, lean, like a blackened stone. Stench of burning flesh soaked the air. Tom's eyes popped" (36).[29] In such a context, the song voices a perverse irony, mocking the faint echo of faraway spirituals that promised a heavenly reward for earthly suffering and insisting instead on the inescapable finality of violence.

A similarly defeated and corrupted archaic text occurs in "Becky," another prose story about a fallen woman, this time a "white woman who had two Negro sons" (7, 9). Here, however, the snippets of poetry that intrude upon the narrative bear almost no formal trace of lyric, though we recognize them as deriving from spirituals: "O pines, whisper to Jesus" (8) and "O fly away to Jesus" (7). These hapless appeals to an absent savior reiterate the prose's frequent references to the loss of spiritual guidance and the emptiness of conventional religious discourse. Indeed, the frame text of "Becky," which is written in prose but functions much like the poetic frames of "Karintha," "Carma," and "Blood-Burning Moon," calls our attention to the impotence of biblical text in particular—the text, of course, from which the spirituals took their lyrics: "Becky was the white woman who had two Negro sons. She's dead; they've gone away. The pines whisper to Jesus. The Bible flaps its leaves with an aimless rustle on her mound" (7, 9). This frame, which attempts to summarize and draw a moral from Becky's story, fails to do so partly because it fails to resolve the formal tensions between the lyrical ejaculations, which appeal to Jesus for help, and the prose admission that no such appeal can be answered. The phrasing, "flaps its leaves," comes ridiculously close to conjuring up a preacher "flapping his lips" in pointless prayer. In fact, this is exactly what happens at the end of the story when Becky's house has collapsed and the townspeople want to conclude that she lies dead beneath the rubble. Instead of trying to dig her out—either to save her if she's still alive or give her a Christian burial if she's dead—Barlo, "mumbling something, thr[ows] his Bible on the pile" (9). The frightened men then bolt back to town, where they recount the story to others at a safe distance from Becky's house. Significantly, the speaker refers to their gossip as the "true word of it" (9), a bitterly ironic phrase that suggests gossip has replaced gospel and reveals one source of Becky's mistreatment: these people do not *read* the Bible, a book which would teach them something of Christian charity; instead, they gossip maliciously while the pages of the Good Book are turned over by the uncomprehending wind.

The tension between a lingering desire for spiritual authority and the complete debasement of religion in "Becky" accounts for the weirdly schizophrenic prose texture. As the narrator's starkly realistic description of the scene begins to acknowledge a supernatural element, lyrical outbursts express an anxiety that cannot be contained by the prose:

> It was Sunday. Our congregation had been visiting at Pulverton, and were coming home. There was no wind. The autumn sun, the bell from Ebenezer Church, listless and heavy. Even the pines were stale, sticky, like the smell of food that makes you sick. Before we turned the bend of the road that would show us the Becky cabin, the horses stopped stock-still, pushed back their ears, and nervously whinnied. We urged, then whipped them on. Quarter of a mile away, thin smoke curled up from the leaning chimney [of Becky's cabin] . . . O pines, whisper to Jesus . . . Goose-flesh came on my skin though there still was neither chill nor wind. Eyes left their sockets for the cabin. Ears burned and throbbed. Uncanny eclipse! fear closed my mind. We were just about to pass . . . Pines shout to Jesus! . . the ground trembled as a ghost train rumbled by. The chimney fell into the cabin. (8)

One of the disruptive aspects of the outbursts is the uncertainty about their source. Are they the speaker's cries? Elsewhere he employs similar phrasing in prose description: "The pines whisper to Jesus" (7, 9) and "The pines whispered to Jesus" (7). And immediately preceding the scene quoted above, he seems to speak the line himself in order to brace up to the unmanageable possibilities of his subject: "Becky if dead might be a hant [ghost], and if alive—it took some nerve even to mention it . . . O pines, whisper to Jesus . . . " (8). While the narrator has good reason to feel threatened by Becky's story, most especially because he is implicated in her isolation and suffering but also because her tale exceeds the certainties of realism—the lyrical intrusions also bespeak an anxiety manifested in the prose itself, the prose as a genre with certain capacities and tasks. Becky's story taxes the limits of prose in Toomer's scheme because it includes things that are inaccessible to the modern world with its religious skepticism and objective reporting. A contradictory story like Becky's, of ostracism and compassion, self-righteousness and guilt, realism and supernaturalism, is one that cannot be fully rendered in an "objective" mode. Some vestige of Christian charity haunts Becky's neighbors just as some vestige of Christian lyric haunts the prose.

Lyric also haunts the prose in two other short stories in part 1, "Fern" and "Esther." With "Becky" these three stories are distinctive for not containing stanzas of poetry or snippets of folk songs outright, yet lyric continues to nag the prose with the concerns it has embodied elsewhere in part 1: connection to the past, expression of spiritual authority, transformation of the mundane into the mythic. Many readers have noted Cane's numerous titular females, especially in part 1: Karintha, Becky, Carma, Fern, and Esther; like the Georgia portraits, these short stories are vignettes of Southern women and, again like the portrait poems, of women whose vitality has been depleted by life in the modern South. At times Cane seems to want from its women characters the same things it wants from poetry; thus, the book tends to idealize and even deify them, on the one hand, while inevitably depicting their degradation on the other. Karintha is both a goddess and a fallen woman; Carma has unusual strength but her story is a crude melodrama; Fern inspires men with her beauty but disappoints them with her remoteness. The tensions between prose and lyric in these stories frequently reflect tensions between the idealization of the woman and the realization of her failure to embody it. Thus, poetry effectively textures "Karintha" and "Carma," reproducing the split between the narrator's desire and his subjects' reality at the level of genre. "Becky," "Fern," and "Esther" register this tension more subtly. These three stories are bereft of poetry—that is, no stanzas of poetry or fragments of song appear in the prose—yet the myths and ideals associated with lyric persist to measure how far the women have fallen from the narrator's ideal.

Fern is one more light-skinned Southern black woman in whom the narrator desires to invest his vision of the African American South. Like all the other men who see and desire her, he wants something from her she cannot give, intimate, passionate contact with a woman who embodies a continuity with the past that the narrator himself cannot achieve on his own. Here, that past endures in the form of the Southern landscape, which flows into her eyes in a mystical blending of her beauty, the Southern landscape, and God: "[I] Saw her on the porch, head tilted a little forward where the nail was, eyes vaguely focused on the sunset. Saw her face flow into them, the countryside and something that I call God, flowing into them" (19). Though he asserts that "[w]hen one is on the soil of one's ancestors, most anything can come to one" (19), nothing does come to him even despite his near-vision while holding her in the cane field:

> Her eyes, unusually weird and open, held me. Held God. He flowed in as I've seen the countryside flow in. Seen men. I must have done something—what, I don't know, in the confusion of my emotion. She sprang up. Rushed some distance from me. Fell to her knees and began swaying, swaying. Her body was tortured with something it could not let out. Like boiling sap it flooded arms and fingers till she shook them as if they burned her. It found her throat, and spattered inarticulately in plaintive, convulsive sounds, mingled with calls to Christ Jesus. And then she sang, brokenly. (19)

Throughout the story, he has described Fern as looking like a Jewish cantor singing; that is, he has compared how Fern appears to how a cantor sounds: "Her nose was aquiline, Semitic. If you have heard a Jewish cantor sing, if he has touched you and made your own sorrow seem trivial when compared with his, you will know my feeling when I follow the curves of her profile, like mobile rivers, to the common delta" (16). The common delta is the related suffering of African Americans and Jews. The ripples of pain and channels of sorrow in "Face," the curves of Fern's face, and the song of the cantor all converge at one point of articulation—song: like the mouth of a river, rich with alluvial deposits, the songs of the Jewish cantor, of the slaves, and now the songs of the son are cultural and emotional repositories. Strangely, however, the narrator imagines all of this flowing *into* Fern's eyes; little wonder, then, that his gestures of intimacy ignite all of this suffering within her, so that she seems to boil over with pain, like sugar cane boiling up or Tom Burwell's body boiling and bursting during the lynching. Significantly, her pain wells up into a song, but the song is broken and sounds like a "child's voice, uncertain, or an old man's" (19). As she sings, dusk falls until the narrator can no longer see Fern: "Dusk hid her; I could hear only her song" (19). The obsessive emphasis on eyes and sight in "Fern" gives way to pure sound, a development in part 1 that has previously produced the transformation of the mundane into the mythic world, of ugly reality into glorious ideal. Sadly, though, Fern's song does not recuperate the ancestral world but only anticipates the broken lyrics of part 2 and the "ugly words" and "bad poetry" of part 3. Instead of being transfigured, Fern faints from the anguish of her song, and the narrator leaves the South without getting from or giving to her what he wants. As he departs, he sees her from the train, her "eyes vaguely focused on the sunset" (19). Fern's song has reverted to one more dusky portrait, and *Cane's* poetry has once again shrunken into an eye.

If part 1 of *Cane* has been searching for an ideal Southern African American woman in its female portraits and an ideal artistic form for embodying the cultural richness she represents in its poetry, then "Esther" is the end of a process of steady deterioration and disappointment recorded in the prose of "Karintha," "Carma," and "Fern" (Becky is a white woman) and in the poetry of "Face" and "Portrait in Georgia." Esther is a "dictie" (27), with a "chalk-white" face (22) and thinning hair (25). In girlhood, while Karintha "was a wild flash that told the other folks just what it was to live (3), Esther looks "flat" and "dead" (22). Indeed, Esther has more in common with the introspective, romantic, frustrated male narrators than with her female counterparts. She is a witness to African American culture rather than a participant, and she harbors perverse and pathetic fantasies of connection with that culture. She falls in love with King Barlo, a "clean-muscled, magnificent, black-skinned Negro" and sometimes preacher (22), and dreams of having his child. Her dream combines immaculate conception, sexual repression, violence, and disaster in a formula that suggests the complete corruption of generation and cultural perpetuation: "Her mind is a pink meshbag filled with baby toes" (26). Her mind, like her face, is more white than black, and the imagined child she would have with Barlo is nothing more than a jumble of amputated fragments. Predictably, then, no poetry frames or punctuates Esther's story, no lyric voice attempts to reclaim Esther as an icon of African ancestry. As in "Becky" the only bit of lyric we hear is embedded in the prose, a faint echo of a song that once preserved African American history. King Barlo delivers this echo of the past in a prophetic trance:

And while [the black man] was agazin at th heavens, heart filled up with th Lord, some little white-ant biddies came an tied his feet to chains. *They led him t th coast, they led him t th sea, they led him across th ocean an they didnt set him free. The old coast didnt miss him, an th new coast wasnt free, he left the old-coast brothers, t give birth t you an me. O Lord, great God Almighty, t give birth t you an me.* (23, emphasis added)

Here, embedded in the prose of a short story about a black woman who has lost all but her twisted yearning for African ancestry, in a character who is as much faker as fakir, is lodged the history behind "Song of the Son." African Americans descend from Africans who were kidnapped from their homeland and transported to a hostile world but who preserved their culture and history in song and assured their own future by surviving the ordeal and giving birth to their children. The history embedded in Barlo's utterance is not merely thematic but formal, for the story of the slave trade falls into lines that scan and rhyme as ballad stanzas. Ballads like the one alluded to in Barlo's speech were crucial to the preservation of the African American past. Barlo's cadenced speech moves the black folks to song ("Fragments of melodies are being hummed" [23]) and even touches the whites. The last words of Barlo's speech parallel the appeal of *Cane*: "Open your ears—" (23). But it is already too late in the book for such an appeal to transform Esther—or anyone. At the end of the story, after Esther has approached Barlo in a gambling den and been rejected, as the gamblers and prostitutes are laughing at her, "Esther doesn't hear" (27). Instead, she *sees* how degraded and evil Barlo is: "She sees a smile, ugly and repulsive to her, working upward through thick licker fumes. Barlo seems hideous. The thought comes suddenly, that conception with a drunken man must be a mighty sin" (27). Finally, this vision of King Barlo speaks louder than his oracular speech years earlier; Esther "draws away, frozen" and walks "stiffly" back to her empty life "[l]ike a somnambulist" (27). Esther is one of the walking dead, a race of people we'll encounter in part 2 when Southern blacks move north to the urban industrial centers, lose their idyllic connection to the Southern soil and their past, and become modern automatons, fragmented, lost, and degraded denizens of the modern wasteland. The echo of lyric in Barlo's outburst has been moving, disturbing, but not transforming.

If part 1 is *Cane's* Song of Solomon, Song of *Songs,* then Toomer is sounding out the resources of an intensely lyrical and idealizing discourse. The Song of Solomon is love poetry, a unique biblical instance of erotic and lyric exuberance, that figuratively associates the body of the beloved with the geography of the homeland.[30] Its concerns are remarkably similar to the issues in part 1 of *Cane*: erotic desire, lyric beauty, lover and land as oases from a harsher world, the transforming power of linguistic play. Though the song of the son may take its inspiration from the Song of Solomon, however, the lyric impulse in part 1 only intermittently achieves its desired—and promised—end: to be an "everlasting song" (14). The trajectory from the apparently celebratory lyric that opens "Karintha" (and the book) to the ominous refrain that closes "Blood-Burning Moon" (and part 1) marks a gradual descent from the promise of song to the corruption of that valued form. Though the seeds of its demise, of the demise of the ideals of the past, the South, the folk, women, and lyric, are present from the first page of *Cane*, part 1 falteringly reveals the former power and authority of lyric even as it traces its dissolution. Like Mertis Newbolt in "Natalie Mann," we must inevitably turn the page from the Song of Solomon to Leviticus. But before moving to part 2 and the destruction of lyric, it is crucial to recognize that poetry is the heart of part 1. In the cadences of song and the formal structures of the past are lodged ancestral voices, ancient wisdom, and emotions and experiences that have been extinguished in the modern world. Part 1 relentlessly demonstrates that the son cannot fully take up the song of his ancestors, cannot therefore recuperate what he imagines to be their idyllic, pastoral world. But he can register its loss by recording the faint echo of a better time, and he can exert his own contemporary poetic powers to articulate his own epoch. Though part 1 does not offer a pastoral, Southern, folksy haven from the realities of the United States in 1923, it does poignantly capture the tensions between the ideal and the real, the past and the present, the mythic and the mundane, and it does so because of the particular powers of poetry, especially the transforming potential of figuration and lyricism. To dismiss the lyric strain as peripheral or ornamental, as even Toomer himself did at times, is to ignore the one resource in the book that makes all the rest of it possible.

3
Discordant Snatches of Song

Cane, Part 2

IF PART 1 OF *Cane* regards the son who is committed to his Southern past, part 2 regards his brothers who have gone north, a geographical move associated with the loss of memory, culture, and spiritual bearings. The "brothers" of part 2 are bewildered, fragmented automatons, struggling to survive in an urban wasteland that cannot sustain them. "Rhobert," the first prose portrait of the section, describes a man who is at once the antithesis of the poet-son in part 1 and a type of the men in part 2. His name is an emblem of his condition: "Rhobert" is an anagram for "brother," the meaningful term of kinship now just a jumble of letters suggesting the loss of familial and cultural connections and the attendant loss of meaning. Ironically, while the anagram obstructs positive connotations, it creates a sinister pun, for Rhobert, as many have observed, is a robot, deprived of his humanity by the conditions of life in the North: "Rhobert wears a house, like a monstrous diver's helmet on his head. [. . .] Rods of the house like antennæ of a dead thing, stuffed, prop up in the air" (42).[1] Part robot, part insect, part living, part dead, Rhobert lives in an alien environment that forces him to adapt in precisely the ways that will destroy him. The house he wears is like a diver's helmet in that it is a bulky mechanical contraption, helpful only under water. But the water is "being drawn off" in this wasteland, and the helmet weighs him down, causing him to sink in the mud and slime. If he takes the helmet off, he'll die because he cannot survive in the atmosphere of this alien environment; but if he leaves it on, he'll be crushed under its weight and smother in the mud. Damned if he does and damned if he doesn't, "[h]e is way down" (42), a refrain phrase that registers his predicament not just figuratively but literally.

Yet the monstrous helmet is only the most extreme symptom of Rhobert's malaise; he also has rickets, a skeletal weakness and deformity resulting from a failure to assimilate calcium and phosphorus, normally caused by insufficient sunlight. A subtler metaphor for the deficiencies of the Northern and urban environment than the helmet, rickets destroys a person's very foundations. Thus, Rhobert is "banty-bowed and shakey" (42) not just because he struggles under the weight of the helmet but "because as a child he had rickets" (42). Like all the brothers in part 2, Rhobert is a child of the North, one of the number of African Americans born or raised away from the South, and therefore apart from the natural and cultural sustenance associated with the South. These men can conjure up the South only in dreams and fantasies—and, significantly, many of those pastoral dreams take the form of lyric poems. If the tragedy of part 1 was that the idealized Southern landscape insistently revealed a history of estrangement and violence, the tragedy of part 2 is that the whole Southern past—not only the land, but also women, songs, and spirituality—is so remote as to be unreal.

The strange image of wearing a house like a helmet is an emblem of this racial and cultural amnesia. The blacks up North are hindered by attitudes and perspectives that are no less debilitating than Rhobert's helmet for being less absurdly visible. Throughout this section, rows of city houses are personified as domesticated African Americans, rigid, middle class, conformist, and "locked up," while the actual residents are systematically dehumanized. In "Calling Jesus," for instance, a woman denies her soul, figured forth as a stray dog, by closing "the big outside storm door" and leaving her soul "in the vestibule" (58). In "Box Seat" the narrator describes lighted houses as "shy girls whose eyes shine reticently upon the dusk body of the street" (59). Characters inside houses are trapped in convention, as Rhobert is trapped inside his house-helmet: "Muriel's chair is close and stiff about her. The house, the rows of houses locked about her chair" ("Box Seat" 63). Like many other characters in this section of Cane, Rhobert has taken on alien values and obligations, epitomized by the house, values that render him dependent on a materialist world that will only destroy him. Part of its destructive power is the fact that it separates him from nature; indeed, the natural environment in "Rhobert," whether water or air, is dangerously unnatural to him. The air is filled with "shredded life-pulp" (42) and must be piped in through the helmet, and the water is "murky, wiggling" (42), muddy, and draining away. Even more insidious than the destruction of nature, however, is Rhobert's internalization of wasteland values: "Like most men who wear monstrous helmets, the pressure it exerts is enough to convince him of its practical infinity" (42). The claustrophobic, artificial space inside his helmet seems to be the whole world to him, and this reduced perspective is the most disturbing feature of life in the North. The men in part 2, whether narrators in stories, speakers in poems, or characters in the fiction, all want to break out of the North and its rigid, suffocating system of values. Again and again, these impotent prophets attempt to lead others, especially women, back to a better time and place—the ancestral past that only exists in fantasy. The Northern son in part 2 will not find his way back, then, and it will remain the task of Kabnis in part 3 to return to the South and renew his connection to the slaves. Yet the effort to reestablish "[w]hat they were, and what they are to me" ("Song of the Son") will be hindered for the Rhoberts in part 2 and for Kabnis in part 3 by the fact that poetry no longer functions as a continuum between the past and the present.

Nellie McKay has observed that "[i]n general, a language in concert with the sounds and vibrations of the city replaces lyricism and nature" in part 2 (126). Herbert Rice rightly acknowledges that part 2's antilyricism is not just aesthetically dissonant but "bitterly sarcastic" (444).[2] This is true of all lyric forms in the second section of *Cane*. Every poem and snippet of song in part 2 registers the decline of lyric. The tension between the idealizing vision of traditional poetry and the imagistic objectivity of free-verse poetry is absent in this section. Instead, the poetry unequivocally articulates cynicism, confusion, and loss. The narrator of "Rhobert" calls for an elegiac song, a verbal monument to mark Rhobert's descent into the slime meant to parallel the "monument of hewn oak, carved in nigger-heads" (43) that he proposes to erect on the site where Rhobert sinks. But his elegy can only exacerbate our sense of loss. In *Poetry of Mourning: Modern Elegy from Hardy to Heaney*, Jahan Ramazani demonstrates that modern elegies often disallow the traditionally recuperative effects of the genre. He describes modern elegists as "melancholic mourners" who, "[u]nlike their literary forebears or the 'normal mourner' of psychoanalysis, [. . .] attack the dead and them-

selves, their own work and tradition; and they refuse such orthodox con-
solations as the rebirth of the dead in nature, in God, or in poetry itself"
(4). It is especially significant here that "[m]odern poets direct their melancholic ambivalence not only at themselves and the dead, nor only at
elegiac and social convention, but also at their own elegies" (6). "Every
elegy," he continues, "is an elegy for elegy—a poem that mourns the diminished efficacy and legitimacy of poetic mourning" (8). The speaker's
broken song marks not just the death of Rhobert but of elegy itself.

Both verbal and sculptural monuments, then, indicate an ironic relationship to the past: carved African heads suggest the vogue among early
century whites in "exotic" African art, the consequent commodification
of the "primitive" black past, and the violent fragmentation of African
Americans in the North; likewise, the song, a corrupted spiritual, registers both the desire for a spiritually coherent past and the destruction of
that ideal in the present. The narrator's call to erect a statue on the very
spot where Rhobert perishes is sarcastic at best since the statue, like
the man, will sink into the mud. "Deep River," cannot be "uplifting" in
this context; instead, the "deep river" of the spiritual—the river Jordan,
which believers cross over to heaven—is literalized into just one more
sinkhole in the Northern waste:

> Brother, Rhobert is sinking.
> Lets open our throats, brother,
> Lets sing Deep River when he goes down. (43)

The most obvious failure of the song, of course, is that this is not a stanza
from "Deep River." Like the sardonic anagram "brother/Rhobert" that
denies Rhobert's humanity and disrupts the positive connotations of
"brother," the poem that follows the call for song is only a painful perversion of the spiritual. Thus the actual spiritual's emphasis on crossing
over the river Jordan ("My home is *over* Jordan," "Lord, I want to *cross
over* into camp ground") and on the resurrection of the soul to heaven
("I'll go into heaven, and take my seat," "Oh, when I get to heav'n, I'll
walk about") is replaced in the poem with the language of downward
defeat ("Deep River" 765, emphasis added).

In such a context, the repeated command to "open our throats" and
sing makes song itself seem dangerous, even deadly. In part 1 song is consistently associated with uplift: "Come, brother, come. Lets *lift* it" (11),

"Scratching choruses *above* the guinea's squawk" (12, 13), "And let the valley *carry* [song] along" (14), "Their voices *rise*" (15). Here, however, in an atmosphere of water, mud, and only limited air, inhaling air in order to sing could be fatal. Thus, the emphasis on Rhobert's straining and gulping for breath and the uncharacteristic synecdoche of throats for song (*Cane* typically refers to lips when it wants to suggest idealized song): "One thing about him goes straight to the heart. He has an Adam's-apple which strains sometimes as if he were painfully gulping great globules of air . . air floating shredded life-pulp" (42). The loaded language—"globules" of air, "gulping," usually associated with liquids,[3] and the notion that the air is filled with dead bodies—suggests that it is not in fact air but mud that Rhobert strains to inhale. Such imagery makes clear that opening our throats would be risky, and the call for song makes the end of "Rhobert" as suffocating for those who would sing Rhobert's elegy as Rhobert's end is for him.

Rhobert is the antithesis of the "Song of the Son" speaker, the antithesis of everything *Cane* wants for African Americans, and his vignette introduces the problems of part 2. Blacks have moved north in search of employment, cultural opportunities, and freedom from Southern racism. In doing so, however, they have broken their connection to the land, a bond that *Cane* perceives as essential to African American spiritual and cultural wholeness. Up North, these people have lost their bearings in a concrete, sunless maze, where mechanized work, or, worse, unemployment, and rows of identical houses dehumanize them. Governed now by bourgeois values, they repress their "natural" instincts—sexuality, spirituality, and musicality. These basic impulses, always associated with authentic African and slave identity in *Cane,* erupt violently in the frustrated, impotent male narrators and characters, who typically attempt to force the female characters to acknowledge their lost heritage. Rhobert embodies the fragile, dehumanized, doomed existence that the other men in part 2 desperately seek to avoid. The bitter sarcasm in the vignette registers the section's profound ambivalence toward the Northern brothers as it expresses both compassion and contempt for blacks who have left the South.

The role of song in "Rhobert" is also emblematic of lyric in part 2. Lyric gasps for breath in the Northern, industrial context, an environment lacking all that part 1 associated with poetry: nature, tradition, spirituality, ancestry. The reduced quantity of poetry is one indication of its demise. Part 1 contains ten poems and six prose pieces. Part 2, in contrast, has only five poems but seven stories, and the poems are shorter and the stories longer than those in part 1. The number of pages devoted to each genre gives an even better indication of the dramatic shift in quantity: 10 pages of poetry and 24 pages of prose in part 1; 5 pages of poetry and 35 pages of prose in part 2. More significant than quantity, however, is how lyric functions in this section devoted to the North. By design, part 2 poems don't work in the terms they clearly set for themselves. Hymns are revised to register doubt and cynicism rather than faith; all metaphors are disturbing and awkward, and figures from nature are especially perverse, as though the speakers in these poems have never seen the natural world; a love poem renders intimate contact dangerous; a work song reveals the exploitation of laborers; and verse that aspires to reach beyond the wasteland in prayer deflates into self-centered babble. Significantly, all five poems in this section are written in free verse, and four of them attempt to develop a single image; and, here again, as in part 1, free verse and Imagism work to expose realities that traditional lyric poetry tends to obscure or even idealize. The lingering desire of poetry to associate itself with ancient, natural truths struggles for expression in poems relentlessly committed to representing the loss of all that part 1 posited as good and saving. Lyricism, nature, love, and other ideals strain unsuccessfully for voice in this corrupting environment. When the lyric voice opens its throat in part 2, song goes down.

Thus, "Beehive" (50) and "Storm Ending" (51), the first two poems of part 2, must strain to represent life in the urban, industrial North because they employ an outmoded, even unintelligible, natural idiom. The speaker of "Beehive," like so many other men in part 2, watches the bustle of the city but cannot participate in it. Unemployed, drunk, he feels useless and longs for an escape that liquor cannot offer:

Within this black hive to-night
There swarm a million bees;
Bees passing in and out the moon,
Bees escaping out the moon,
Bees returning through the moon,
Silver bees intently buzzing,
Silver honey dripping from the swarm of bees

Earth is a waxen cell of the world comb,
And I, a drone,
Lying on my back,
Lipping honey,
Getting drunk with silver honey,
Wish that I might fly out past the moon
And curl forever in some far-off farmyard flower.

The imagery of the "black hive" connotes a large city, perhaps even more specifically a black ghetto, where millions swarm, escape, and return, "intently buzzing." The poem makes a fairly obvious analogy between a beehive, buzzing with its busy bees, and the city, astir with human activity. Yet the speaker is a drone—that is, a male bee that does not work, whose role is purely sexual—living on the labors of others. No more than a parasite, he lounges around lapping up the honey that others work to provide.[4] He is in company with the numerous unemployed, heavy-drinking men in part 2.

If "Beehive" appeared in part 1, it would likely communicate the parallel between drones in a hive and unemployed African American men in Northern cities adeptly.[5] Here, however, the imagery of the hive takes on strange aspects, the most prominent of which is the notion of the hive as a figure for the whole universe, not just the city. The black hive where a million bees swarm "to-night" is night itself; that is, the *hive* is black, not simply its inhabitants. If the night's blackness is the interior of the hive, and the moon marks the entrance to the hive (suggesting an illuminated sphere outside the hive), then the stars must be the bees since they are the only things in the scene that appear to be both silver and flying around the moon. On this cosmic scale, earth is only "a waxen cell of the world comb," the place where the drone is trapped. He longs to escape, not just the hive and his own situation, but earth itself: "[I] Wish that I might fly out past the moon / And curl forever in some far-off farmyard flower." Beyond the moon, of course, is empty space, not farm yards and flowers. But he can't know this since, like Rhobert in his helmet, he never leaves his "cell." Consequently, he invokes nature first as a metaphor for his world but then as a figure for an ideal world that he can only imperfectly imagine. Two things occur in this process: the city and the natural world are shown to have little in common, and, more to the point, the natural world is understood to be utterly out of the speaker's ken. He wants to curl up forever in some idealized place, a place that certainly doesn't exist in outer space. Ironically, the imaginative picture he has of that utopian place derives from an agrarian past he has never actually experienced. The speakers and characters in part 1, by contrast, have experienced it—cane fields, pine trees, red soil, sunsets—they simply aren't able to idealize it persuasively since so many atrocities occur in those natural settings. To the Rhoberts of part 2, that past is just a faulty, fragmentary illusion.[6]

Another important way that "Beehive" troubles this illusion is in its vexed rhetoric of escape: "passing," "escaping," "returning," and "buzzing" are the verbs describing the activity of the workers, who, unlike the speaker, have mobility and purpose. Still, the language hints that their flight achieves an escape that is merely "passing," a word we know to be a loaded term and that here indicates an extremely qualified release—a release likely to end in return. These bees go "*in* and *out* the moon" in a restless motion of escape and return. (Presumably, those who would consider getting out of the hive an "escape" would not choose to come back to it.) If "passing" can be read as pretending to be white, then escaping the hive involves denying one's past. As we've seen, in *Cane* such passing inevitably leads to return: even when you pass for white, you remain black, and your origins will inevitably call you back; thus, escape will always entail return. In part 2, however, the idea that one cannot escape his "true" identity is complicated by the fact that the ancestral past has been lost. Characters can pass for white if they are light-skinned ("Bona and Paul"), or they can aspire to white social norms even if they can't pass ("Box Seat"), but they will be haunted by an original identity too fragmented and illusory to be sustaining. In this context, the speaker's dream of escape is understandably contradictory: immobile, he longs for motion that will bring him to another stasis. His idea of liberation is to curl up forever in a flower, a situation eerily like the one he's in. His only escape, then, is his dream of escape, a dream, moreover, that thematizes dreaming. The sense of defeat could not be greater. The idealized rural past is obviously only a dream; for African Americans raised in the North, there is literally nowhere to return to because their connections to the South, the past, their ancestral culture have been severed. Taken together, the action verbs in "Beehive" ultimately imply that the lively bustle of the city—passing, escaping, returning—signifies a frenzied effort to leave that place rather than, as first seemed, a celebration of urban activity and opportunity. That "a million bees" "swarm," that they are "intently buzzing," come to suggest not the productive labor of African Americans up North but their desperation and dehumanization. Little wonder, then, that the speaker is immobile, "Lying on [his] back, / Lipping honey," sedating himself with liquor and fantasies of escape to an even more static and enclosed world.

"Storm Ending" (51), on the facing page of "Beehive," similarly employs distortion of nature imagery to suggest the unnaturalness of life in part 2; and, again, at stake is not simply the inappropriateness of the urban setting but the complete loss of connection with the agrarian past. Like the other free-verse poems in *Cane*, this one opens with a promise of natural beauty, "Thunder blossoms gorgeously above our heads," only to deny the very expectations its first line raises:

> Great, hollow, bell-like flowers,
> Rumbling in the wind,
> Stretching clappers to strike our ears . .
> Full-lipped flowers
> Bitten by the sun
> Bleeding rain
> Dripping rain like golden honey—
> And the sweet earth flying from the thunder.

The end of the storm is heralded when the sun comes out from behind the clouds, the rainwater reflects the sun's golden light, and the thunder dies away. Though one can extract these conventional details of a storm passing from the images in the poem, such a reading requires omission and selection that amount to misreading. In fact, the poem's depiction of the end of the storm is quite gruesome and contradictory, the loveliness of rainwater catching the sunlight denied by the comparison to blood dripping from bitten lips. The synesthesia of the first line—the sound of the thunder is like the blossoming of flowers—captures the aural and visual drama of a thunderstorm, and more, the relationship between visual and aural events in a storm.[7] Thunderclouds amass in the sky, bolts of lightning flash out from them, the roar of thunder follows: visual phenomena produce sound.

The potential of such synesthetic imagery to figure forth nature's complexity in richly associative forms is denied in this hostile environment where everything that should be beautiful is horrific. Thus, "Storm Ending" cannot finally control the discrepancies between the visual and aural qualities of bells, the underlying figure for the storm. The thunder is first compared to "bell-like *flowers*" to establish the analogy between a bell and a thundercloud, but even more at this point, to offer an analogy for the rising and falling sound of thunder. To say that "thunder blossoms gorgeously above our heads" is to equate the noise of the thunder, its first faint rumble, full ferocious boom, and final falling off, with the life cycle of a flower from small bud to full bloom to fallen petals. But the other thing the poem wants from this analogy is the "*bell*-like" quality of the storm: like bells, clouds appear huge and hollow yet produce great sound; bolts of lightning stretching from the clouds look like bell clappers, and, again like clappers, create sound when they "strike." Significant in all this is that the bell figure is sufficient: it bodies forth both the aural and visual aspects of the thunderstorm. Why, then, does the poem insist on the simile "bell-like flowers," that is, on the notion that the thunder is like flowers? It does so because flowers, unlike bells, are natural, alive, and vulnerable to the elements—here, to the sun that destroys the clouds as it can destroy flowers. Just when the thunderclouds are in "full bloom," the sun comes out and "bites" them as it would scorch delicate blossoms. The parched, shriveled edges of flowers are analogous to the edges of clouds lit by sunlight, an unexpected comparison that views the sun coming out from behind storm clouds as wounding. "Storm *Ending*" is not a poem celebrating the passing of a terrible storm but rather an elegy to the destruction of a "gorgeous" natural phenomenon.

Two things are wrong with this picture. First, another natural phenomenon, sunshine, is cast in the role of destroyer. The poem depicts a natural world at war, the beautiful thunderclouds crushed by the sun just as flowers are crushed by sunlight and heat. Conventionally, of course, the sun is a positive force that provides relief and calm after a violent storm or that enables flowers to bloom. However, this is not a nature poem—as the second figurative problem, the personification of the "full-lipped flowers," indicates—but a poem about vulnerability, power, wounding, and the desire for escape: that is, this is a poem about people. Indeed, it is the desire for escape that motivates the speaker to idealize nature in the first line of the poem and the impossibility of escape that turns the poem off its course. The suggestively full-lipped flowers are "[b]itten by the sun"; the thunderclouds are "[b]leeding rain." It is *personification,* not nature, that produces the violent, destructive hierarchy of power in the poem, a hierarchy in which everything beautiful and "sweet" is rendered victim to everything else. This is the only way to explain the final line in which the whole earth is trying to escape . . . not from the sun, oddly, but from the thunder: "And the sweet earth flying from the thunder." The once-gorgeous thunder, victim of the sun, is now victimizing the earth.

And though they try, the closing lines cannot elude the violence of the preceding images. Saying that "Bleeding rain" is "like golden honey" does not reclaim the gruesome image of rain as blood; instead, it undermines the positive associations of golden honey. Perhaps this is why the poem shifts perspectives at the end. The last line views the passing storm clouds from an unusual angle: it proposes that the earth, not the clouds, is moving away, that the wounded earth is in flight from the terrible thunderclouds (which are, in turn, in flight from the biting sun). And yet, the word "sweet" decisively links the earth and the storm (honey is sweet), revealing that escape is impossible. The earth is surrounded by the atmosphere that produces storms; there is nowhere to fly. How does the poem propose to introduce sweetness into such a scene? In two ways: first, by attempting to idealize nature in the face of overwhelming evidence to the contrary, and, second, the thing that makes such ungrounded idealizations possible, by having no real familiarity with nature.

Indeed, one way to gauge the speakers' inexperience with nature in "Beehive" and "Storm Ending" is that the idealized "land," so reminiscent of part 1, is not *land* at all but *planet.* "Earth is a waxen cell of the world comb" and "sweet earth flying from thunder" are images that view the earth from the perspective of outer space. No longer a place to be rooted, a natural environment, a garden where diurnal and seasonal cycles faithfully promise renewal, a haven—earth is a tiny, vulnerable speck in a huge, inhospitable universe. This remote, unsympathetic perspective occurs throughout part 2.[8] If this is the view of nature, it is easy to understand why the speakers' depictions of the natural world are so "far off." Sadly, they've never actually been there and thus cannot make persuasive poetry out of it.

And yet both poems reveal a bittersweet connection to that unknown natural world. "Beehive" seeks to create an analogy between city life and nature *and,* failing that, to posit nature as an escape from city life. Likewise, "Storm Ending" attempts to understand violence and power by conceiving of them in natural terms, *and,* failing that, to naturalize suffering if it cannot be escaped. These contradictory but deeply related impulses come together repeatedly in the volume, as well as in these two poems, in the figure of the lips.

Lips are consistently associated with song in *Cane.* "Georgia Dusk" introduces the figure when the "cane-lipped scented mouth[s]" of the African American workers produce "folk-songs from soul sounds" (15). And song, in that idealized and idealizing context, restores "virgin lips" to cornfield concubines and "dreams of Christ to dusky cane-lipped throngs" (15). "Cane-lipped" denotes the mouths of people who have actually tasted sugar cane and consequently suggests the *natural* sweetness of their songs; it also conveys the notion that such lips are full of sweetness, as cane is. Indeed, the songs are "resinous and soft" like cane syrup, and even the profaned lips of prostitutes are sanctified when anointed with this sacred substance.

Moreover, the full lips that *Cane* idealizes are distinctly racialized lips, one of Toomer's images for people whose African ancestry is still felt, and thus still visible in their physical features. John, whose connection to his African ancestry is weak, has lips that are "too skinny" (55). (Another physical feature repeatedly associated with ethnic inauthenticity is chalky white or lemon-colored skin [22, 83].) In contrast, African Americans who retain their connection to the African past are typically full lipped; for instance, the dancers in "Theater" are "full-lipped, distant beauties" (52) and Dorris's lips in particular are "curiously full" (53)— curious because her face is "lemon-colored" (53). If Dorris's physical features are warring characteristics in a contest between authentic and inauthentic identities, then her lips are decisive evidence that she is capable of authenticity, as the story demonstrates. "Box Seat" makes an explicit connection between full lips and song: there, such lips are "flesh-notes of a forgotten song" (59) and "flesh-notes of a futile, plaintive longing" (62), the unusual image "flesh-notes" suggesting that the stereotypically thick lips of contemporary African Americans are all that is left of ancestral song. These positive associations of voluptuous lips are felt in "Evening Song," where Cloine's lips are "pressed to [the speaker's] heart" (21), and "Her Lips Are Copper Wire" (57), where the beloved's lips conduct erotic energy. Thus, when lips are wounded—for instance, in "Portrait in Georgia," lips are "old scars, or the first red blisters" (29), or in "Box Seat," the lips of the dwarf are "battered" (68) and bloody—song, too, is in crisis. Bloodied, blistered, or scarred lips represent something beautiful, sensual, and essentially African American under assault. Wounded lips cannot carry forth the ancestral song as could the cane-scented lips of part 1.

Perhaps this explains why the full-lipped beauties in part 2 are dancers, not singers, women who can still communicate a sacred past with their bodies but who cannot do so in song—the book's privileged vehicle for truth. Indeed, a dwarf wrestler in "Box Seat" is one of only two singers in part 2 (nearly every story and poem in part 1 thematizes song), but his voice is "high-pitched" and "sentimental" (68), and his lips are bloody from the wrestling match. Song itself is literally dwarfed and battered in part 2: four of the five poems are brief and figuratively deformed, their images not merely awkward and illogical but explicitly grotesque. If this is hard to recognize in part 2 poems, it is not because the individual poems are ambiguous but rather because we have been conditioned by part 1 to expect something grand from poetry. Indeed, part 2 toys cruelly with our expectations for lyric beauty and affirmation. Looking at a poem in part 2 is like looking at one of that section's full-lipped beauties: they promise the ideal but fail to deliver it. This is nowhere more apparent than in "Her Lips Are Copper Wire" (57), the most misread poem in Cane, where a lyric love poem about a full-lipped beloved cannot contain the contradictions between its ideals and its reality:

whisper of yellow globes
gleaming on lamp-posts that sway
like bootleg licker drinkers in the fog

and let your breath be moist against me
like bright beads on yellow globes

telephone the power-house
that the main wires are insulate

(her words play softly up and down
dewy corridors of billboards)

then with your tongue remove the tape
and press your lips to mine
till they are incandescent.

Bowen calls "Her Lips Are Copper Wire" "*Cane's* most stunning single piece" (14), Jones singles out the poem as one of the "only illuminated moments of vision" in *Cane* (*Prison-House* 56), and Whalan terms it "the only moment of mutually rewarding sexual communion and communication" in the volume. Only Fahy recognizes how disturbing the poem is: "the imagery reveals the narrator's inability to control and connect with women. The final stanza contains one of the most disturbing images of a silenced woman in the entire work [...]" (58). Scruggs and VanDemarr invoke Toomer's claim that he was "a natural poet of man's artifices" (174) in relation to this poem: "Copper sheets were as marvelous to me as the petals of flowers; the smell of electricity was as thrilling as the smell of earth after a spring shower" (*Wayward* 43).[9] That is, electrical imagery is not innately unpoetical, and the poem is consistently read as if it makes good on its analogy between sexual energy and electricity.[10] In such readings, copper aptly describes the color of a light-skinned African American woman, lips bestow the positive associations of song and ethnicity to sensuality, and electricity provides an appropriate metaphor for sexual energy and attraction.[11]

Moreover, the poem conveys not only the speaker's confidence with these propositions but also his unusually intimate tone. The syntax of the first line, "whisper of yellow globes," is incomplete, suggesting not fragmentation in this case but the lack of need for a more complete utterance. That is, the poem itself seems to open on a partial, intimate whisper, partial precisely because it is intimate, as though the speaker has no need of rigid grammatical or interpersonal relations that would distinguish between subject and object. Further, a series of imperative apostrophes, "let your breath be moist against me," "telephone the powerhouse," "remove the tape / and press your lips to mine," suggests conventionally gendered speech in which the male speaker seduces his female lover to increasingly intimate acts.[12] Strangely, though, only the poem's tone communicates these things, and yet its tone is so powerful and persuasive that it seduces *us* not to notice how disturbing its imagery actually is.

The equation between electricity and sexual energy is not surprising;

Whitman's "I Sing the Body Electric" had celebrated a divine spark operating in the human and natural realms in 1855, and artistic interest in the new electrical technology is everywhere evident early in the twentieth century.[13] In fact, it is the tension between these two types of electricity, the dynamic natural force and the imposing industrial force, that animates Toomer's poem. And, yet, this too is familiar: romance is attractive, but sometimes you get burned. If the electrical danger were simply metaphorical here, "Her Lips Are Copper Wire" would be more conventional (and less interesting). However, the electrical imagery in the poem ventures too close to its literal sources until the *figure* of electricity as sexuality itself explodes. The distinctive modernism of this poem adheres once again in a terrible disjunction between past formulations and present realities.

Like "Beehive" and "Storm Ending," "Her Lips Are Copper Wire," despite its title's reference to modern technology, addresses itself to a past tradition of nature poetry that isn't viable in part 2. The poem opens clearly enough in the urban environment, where lamps posts line the streets. Nevertheless, at first this seems like a promising beginning for romance; the light is just a "whisper," the "lamp-posts [. . .] sway" in the mist, and, though we don't actually encounter any people in the first stanza, we can imagine the swaying lovers, their whispers. Helping us in these associations is the conventional context of a bacchanalian love scene that "Her Lips" invokes. Nighttime, nature, intoxication, intimacy lead "naturally" to undressing and sexual consummation ("remove the tape / and press your lips to mine / till they are incandescent"). And yet this is precisely the poem's problem: that the "moist," "dewy" bacchanalian scene provides a dangerous setting for the modern electrical imagery.

In the context of other part 2 pieces, like "Seventh Street," "Avey," "Beehive," "Box Seat," and even "Bona and Paul," "Her Lips" is very likely spoken by one more idle, drunken dreamer, perhaps himself a "bootleg licker drinker in the fog," outside, alone, tottering from drink and thus perceiving the lamp posts as swaying. In fact, though the poem has an extremely intimate feel, it's one more instance in which the modern industrial environment is personified, a move in part 2 that has consistently contributed to the dehumanization of the urban inhabitants. Here, the street lights are figured as people, their yellow lamps like gleaming faces, their posts like swaying bodies; even the "whisper" of the lovers probably alludes to the humming sound of early electrical lights. This association between technological apparatus and human bodies generates a figurative conflict between moisture and electricity, nature and culture, and ultimately between the ideal and the real.

When the speaker urges his lover to "let your breath be moist against me / like bright beads on yellow globes," he pictures the mist and fog condensing on the globe of a street light as intimate, human contact. Moreover, he proposes a figurative marriage of nature and technology that will be crucial to the poem. At first, this union seems natural enough: the soft yellow glow and misty atmosphere appear well suited to romance. But with his next command—"telephone the power-house / that the main wires are insulate"—the electrical imagery suddenly drops its pretensions to being natural and exposes itself as thoroughly industrial. In fact, it's hard to imagine that this particular utterance is addressed to the lover, even though other similar rhetorical structures ("let your breath," "remove the tape," and "press your lips") would incline us to hear all imperatives as issuing from the speaker to his beloved. Whatever this abrupt and intrusive command would mean ("communicate to the source of sexual energy that the apparatus is ready to go"?), the language of telephones, power-houses, wires, and insulation will not be conducive to love. The aggressiveness of the command and the awkwardness of the imagery in stanza three disturb the intimacy of the preceding stanzas. Stanza four contributes to the sense that the speaker is now addressing someone apart from the two lovers: "(her words play softly up and down / dewy corridors of billboards)"; the parentheses suggest that this is an aside, and the shift in pronouns from the second person to the third indicates an external point of view.

Too, those "dewy corridors of billboards" do not merely romanticize the urban setting but also suggest the female body. The parentheses lend graphic support to this. The potential eroticism and intimacy of "dewy corridors," however, is figuratively at odds with the public and commercial connotations of "billboards," and the contradictions in the poem between human connection and modern modes of communication become exposed here. The very restlessness of the figures indicates the poem's awareness of these tensions. The electrical imagery had already shifted from a light bulb to a telephone in stanza three. Still electrical but now an explicitly verbal figure (and also now a less distinctly visual one), the image of telephone wires might indicate the erotic energy "communicated" between lovers in whispers. Like electrical impulses that carry words from one party to another along telephone lines, the lover's talk "play[s] softly up and down" the receptive nerves of the speaker. But a corridor of billboards seems less a metaphor for telephone wires or for a lover's receptivity than a description of a city street, perhaps that same street where the poem began, the crass words of advertising billboards softened by the mist and fog. Whether stanza four is trying to picture an urban scene transformed by night and mist into a congenial setting for love, an analogy between telephone communication and sexual connection, the physicality of the lover's body, or simply the erotic current that flows from lover to lover, the image of "dewy corridors of billboards" troubles the electrical imagery, interrupting the figurative and thematic "flow" of energy, and returns the speaker to the cold, damp outside world just when he achieves intimacy with his lover.

The figure of the lips recurs in the final stanza, and along with it, the image of the electric light; these images are ushered back into the poem with the word "then," as if their return were the result of some logical figurative process. Yet if lamp posts, telephone lines, billboards, and light bulbs can be associated with human attraction and intimacy, then the electrified city—its tall lamp posts capped with glowing bulbs, its buzzing network of electrical and telephone wires—all this can be a figure for the modern body, the industrial city as lover not simply as the locale of love. That is, not merely is electrical energy associated with sexual energy in "Her Lips," but the whole industrial terrain is a metaphor for human relations. Since the premise of Cane is that African Americans are "natural" people who belong close to the land, such an analogy between urban landscape and human intimacy is lethal. And when the speaker asks the lover to remove the insulation tape *with her own tongue* (a striking image of imminent danger), so that, "undressed," they can kiss, the technological imagery does indeed falter. In a disturbing pun and image that reveal the impossibility of romanticizing the city, the *tongue* of the lover exposes the lips like "tungsten" filaments in a light bulb, and light is produced when the two uninsulated wires touch—and the lips become "incandescent." The *idea* is appealing. Erotic energy is like an electrical current; words, gestures, and some intangible spark flow back and forth between lovers. Sex, too, is like electricity: lovers are naked and unprotected, and their sexual union produces physical and emotional radiance. However, because the poem locates its love scene in a traditional romantic environment—to the extent that it can do so in a northern, industrial setting—its electrical figure is dangerously situated in wetness, an aspect of the "natural" scene that problematizes the use of electricity.[14] What would happen in this conjunction of moisture and electricity is not, in fact, incandescence but electrocution. And though the final stanza asks us to see the lovers as a glowing light bulb, the whole poem creates a thoroughly uncongenial setting for its conclusion. More-over, the vision of the two lovers as filaments in a light bulb recalls Rhobert with a globed contraption for a head, and we see them as merely mechanized bits in an inhuman world. Indeed, the allusion imbedded at the level of syntax in "Her Lips"—the imperative "let" clause in the poem ironically echoing God's "Let there be light"—casts the construc-tion of urban robots in contrast to the creation of the natural world, and most especially places the poem's modern lovers in contrast to Adam and Eve in the Garden of Eden. The lovers' world in part 2 of *Cane* is an anti-paradise, where light emanates from a vast industrial structure, not from God, and where light destroys rather than creates.

Finally, how exactly lips are like copper wire is an important question readers haven't asked the poem. Copper is a rich, reddish-gold color, obviously, and is consistent with *Cane*'s descriptive imagery for light-skinned African Americans. We expect, then, that copper-colored lips belong to someone like the full-lipped beauties in "Theater." Yet her lips are not like copper but like copper *wire,* a word suggesting thin, cold, mechanical devices located in an industrial world—and even hinting at torture and electrocution.[15] The wire figure may be necessary for the analogy between electricity and sex, and it may even suit the familiar idea that romance is a species of torture, but it nevertheless introduces more deeply troubling associations into a love poem than such readings can accommodate. Her wire lips, like Rhobert's helmet and rods, signal a dehumanizing adaptation to the northern environment.[16] And yet the northern woman in "Her Lips" seems every bit as idealized as Karintha was in her southern setting. Indeed, the sexual desire in "Her Lips" dis-tracts attention from a much deeper desire: *Cane*'s longing to revive a romantic, pastoral realm where Rhobert can remove his helmet and be Brother Robert again, where African American women can revive an an-cient and natural sexuality, and where African American men can connect with that past by uniting with them. But if the ideal woman is all filaments and wires, she cannot perform her mythic function. Such is the sexual failure we witness repeatedly in part 2.

The failure of these human connections will be dramatized most fully in part 3, where Kabnis, a character who epitomizes the difficulties of *Cane*'s poet-prophets, is unable to establish a sexual connection with women. Even the prostitutes he hires mock him for spending all night talking (109). Indeed, the entire volume is populated with visionary, "poetical" men whose impotence is verbal as well as sexual. Again and again, in fact, their idealistic speech intrudes upon intimate scenes, spoiling the moment, and demonstrating that these men are "all talk"—a sign of defeat in a world where words have lost their potency but retain their mystique. Ironically, these speakers' impotence is matched by their verbosity as if they could make up for the failure of meaning by the sheer volume of words. The narrator of "Avey," for instance, tells Avey his dreams while they recline in the park: "I talked, beautifully I thought, about an art that would be born, an art that would open the way for women the likes of her. I asked her to hope, and build up an inner life against the coming of that day. I recited some of my own things to her. I sang, with a strange quiver in my voice, a promise-song" (48). He discovers momentarily that Avey, the weary prostitute, has fallen asleep; his grand schemes and self-important "promise-song" have no meaning for a woman in her situation. His only appeal to Avey is that she can sleep safely in his company for a few hours—not that she can sleep *with* him—precisely because he is just talk and poses no sexual threat. Dan Moore in "Box Seat" similarly can't interest Muriel in his grandiose optimism. His attempt to inspire hope in her fails: "'But Muriel, life is full of things like that [her recent tragedy]. One grows strong and beautiful in facing them. What else is life?'" (61). Muriel isn't moved by his rhetoric: "'Whats the use? Lets talk about something else. I hear there's a good show at the Lincoln this week'" (61). And in "Bona and Paul," Bona disappears when Paul runs off to announce his epiphany to the black doorman; it is significant that his insight concerns his relationship with *Bona,* the very person he absents himself from in order to deliver his oration. Paul's repeated declarations that "something beautiful is going to happen," that he is "going out [to] gather petals," that he is "going out [to] know [Bona]" (80) have an unmistakable similarity to the over-confident assertion of the speaker in "Her Lips" that it's time to "telephone the power-house." Almost to a person, the men in *Cane* cannot unite words and actions. This may explain the fact that "Her Lips Are Copper Wire" shifts metaphors from the light bulb to the telephone and billboards; that is, the speaker tends towards metaphors involving words, yet words, as the poem ultimately reveals in its own linguistic failures, cannot unite people in the part-two world. "Her Lips" thus reenacts in small the larger tensions between what Ezra Pound termed melopoeisis and phanopoeisis, between lyricism and Imagism, in *Cane*: the speaker's inclination is to turn the electrical metaphor towards song ("words *play* softly up and down"), but this will not work in a world in which words are profaned by modern communication technologies.[17] If the words of lovers must be submitted to electrical wires in order to be conveyed, if words appear on billboards as visual texts, then the primal connection between words and voice—the connection necessary for song—has been severed. Thus, the poem moves from figures for words to the purely visual metaphor of the light bulb. The command to "remove the tape" from the lips is not, then, as we might expect, a call to unrestricted expression but rather an admission that the lovers need to get past words—or at least that the poem needs to get past the imagery of words. But, as we have seen (in varying ways in part 1 and part 2), the move to the more visual Imagist mode is deadly. And it is so partly because *Cane* imagines the move from song to visual imagery as destructive of the one saving grace poetry could offer: a formal connection to the voice of the past.

The problem of voice is nowhere more exacerbated than in the fourth poem of part 2, "Prayer" (70). Having failed to enact a lyrical connection with nature, in "Beehive" and "Storm Ending," and with women, in "Her Lips Are Copper Wire," part two offers a poem that attempts to speak directly to God. "Prayer" unabashedly admits its longing to escape the helmeted modern self by communicating with a divinity outside the individual, but, predictably, divinity is something the speaker cannot quite put his finger on:

My body is opaque to the soul.
Driven of the spirit, long have I sought to temper it unto the spirit's
    longing,
But my mind, too, is opaque to the soul.

A closed lid is my soul's flesh-eye.
O Spirits of whom my soul is but a little finger,
Direct it to the lid of its flesh-eye.
I am weak with much giving.
I am weak with the desire to give more.
(How strong a thing is the little finger!)
So weak that I have confused the body with the soul,
And the body with its little finger.
(How frail is the little finger.)
My voice could not carry to you did you dwell in stars,
O Spirits of whom my soul is but the little finger . .

A poem called "Prayer" raises certain generic expectations in taking that genre as its title. A prayer is a sacred address meant to establish communication between the supplicant and the deity; Christian prayers typically close with the word "amen" ("so be it") to indicate conclusion as well as to acknowledge the supplicant's submission to a greater power. The most basic thing the prayer form indicates is that the speaker believes he can address something outside of himself.

Yet the problem of this "Prayer" is that the speaker cannot transcend his own bodily limits. The trinity he struggles with is not the Father, Son, and Holy Spirit, but the triad of his own fragmented self: body, soul, and mind. He senses that his problem is precisely this: his soul is somehow related to the Spirits he would petition, but both his body and mind are "opaque" to his soul. He feels driven by spiritual longings, but such feelings only make him aware that he cannot apprehend his own spirituality. Like so many characters in Cane, he is haunted by a vague sense of spirituality but only enough to trouble him. Body and mind fail to temper themselves to the spirit's longing, as the word play suggests: "long have I sought to temper it unto the spirit's longing."

Fragmented body parts, which have come to characterize the dislocation and dehumanization of part 2, prevent the self from reaching physical and spiritual unification. Indeed, the figure for spiritual blindness is one more grotesque assemblage of confused body parts: "A closed lid is my soul's flesh-eye." Simply casting spirituality in bodily terms suggests the impossibility of transcending physical limitations. But the speaker's problems are even more serious than this. The soul's "eye" is closed because it is a "flesh-eye" rather than an organ of purely spiritual vision—like full lips, which are only the vestigial "flesh-notes" of song, not song itself, the flesh-eye represents the reduction of spirituality to a physical appendage. This establishes an inescapable link between the body and the spirit in the most negative sense: the spirit will always be mired in the body. Thus, the speaker imagines needing a little finger—that is, another bodily appendage—to open the spirit's flesh-eye.[18] He vacillates between conceiving of this little finger as an extension of the spiritual realm he hopes to reach ("O Spirits of whom my soul is but a little finger") and suspecting that the little finger is nothing more than the pinkie finger on his hand, a particularly diminutive part of his physical body that could never open his spiritual vision ("I have confused the body with the soul, / And the body with its little finger"). This confusion engenders others: is the little finger "strong" or "weak"? That is, does he have more spirituality in his little finger than most people have in their whole beings (as the saying goes), or is he weak, blind, and confused because he has so little spirituality?

If we schematize the hierarchy of terms in "Prayer," the latter appears to be true. The poem seems to privilege its various "parts" in the following order: Spirits, soul, mind, body, little finger. The poem settles on the little finger as the final measure of the speaker, a phallic image suggesting a spiritual impotence that is part and parcel of the sexual and social impotence characteristic of the men in *Cane*. He recognizes toward the end of the poem that he is merely a little finger and that as such he is frail. The penultimate line issues the real prayer in "Prayer," the desire to possess a *voice* (not a bodily appendage) that could reach to the spiritual realm—"My voice could not carry to you did you dwell in stars"—but its syntax registers defeat. *Even if I had a voice,* he admits, it would not carry all the way to the Spirits; and then, even more disheartening, it would not carry all the way to the Spirits *even if they were in heaven.* "Did you dwell in stars" expresses the recognition that they don't; small wonder then that the final line returns to the grotesque and limiting body. The apostrophe to Spirits and the insistence that the speaker is a part of them, if only a severed part, cannot establish the connection between body, mind, and soul that the poem prays will be possible—and certainly cannot link the human and the divine. The partial ellipsis, always a signature of *Cane*'s verbal defeat, leaves the poem trailing off hopelessly.

Anticipating Carrie K's challenge to Kabnis regarding his lack of faith in part 3, the ellipsis raises a worrisome question, "is that your best Amen?" (117).

Like Rhobert, bent under the weight of modern life, or the dwarf in "Box Seat," a beaten stub of a man, the first four poems in part 2 are ill-made, stunted Imagist verses, shrunk into an eye and struggling to adapt to their urban materials. Still, despite the fact that these poems are figuratively situated in the contemporary northern environment, each longs in its own way to be the song of the son, to transform its setting and transport its speaker back to the pastoral, pre-modern realm that the son in part 1 believed he could reach. Yet the capacity of lyric to reverberate with ancient song has been lost along with the part 1 world; the ability of Imagism to figure forth contemporary reality is all that remains to poetry here, and that one resource exposes a world that cannot be made analogous to the bucolic ideal. Moreover, under pressure from a reality it can neither escape nor transform, imagery takes on a grotesque quality as the poetry gasps to fulfill its role as soothsayer of an unstable truth. Poetry struggles to negotiate its commitment to the past and its obligation to the present, a struggle it cannot win.

Thus, while part 1 expressed the tensions *between* the past and the present, the ideal and the real, in competing generic forms, part 2 registers a further stage of cultural loss in its contrasting forms. Here, no cotton flower is snatched from the withering prose environment to flourish again in lyric; no voices rise from the mundane to the sacred in song. Instead, poetry delimits the same world we encounter in the prose and, in fact, is itself delimited by that world. If part 1 raised certain expectations about lyric—that it articulated truth, provided a formal link to the past, transformed ugliness into beauty, and transcended the prosaic everyday world—part 2 poems uniformly disappoint those expectations. That is, generic difference, a source of hope in part 1, becomes one more symptom of defeat in part 2.

Another striking difference between the poetry in the first two parts of *Cane* is the loss of community in part 2. Five of the ten poems in part 1, notably those in conventional forms, regard fellow workers, neighbors, and ancestors, and even some of the free-verse Imagist poems situate individual concerns (beauty, love, nature, spirituality) in a larger historical context. For instance, "Conversion" explicitly historicizes the loss of African spirituality, and "Portrait in Georgia" links beauty to brutality in the racist South. Part 2 poems, in contrast, thematize isolation: The speaker in "Beehive" is alone in a crowd, "Storm Ending" concludes with an image of flight, "Her Lips" can be read as someone talking to himself, "Prayer" explores spiritual isolation, and "Harvest Song" articulates utter estrangement. Moreover, the relationship in part 1 between traditional community and traditional poetic form becomes reified in part 2 where the first four poems simultaneously demonstrate the extreme limitations of individuality and of modern verse, as if to be without traditional poetry is to be without community.

For these reasons, the poems in part 2 consistently fail to realize their generic expectations. Poetry does not provide escape or consolation in part 2; instead, it reads like "poetical" bits extracted from the prose but only typographically different from it. Many have praised *Cane* for its lyrical prose, especially in part 2, but this quality only evidences the draining away of lyric into prose. When poetic language lacks formal boundaries that ritualize and elevate it, lyricism operates as mere embellishment, or worse, as empty ostentation. Part 2 seems to acknowledge this profanation of poetry: only the dwarf in "Box Seat" and the impotent narrator in "Avey" recite poems or sing songs, and both performances are ridiculous; the narrator of "Rhobert" calls for a song as a way to mock Rhobert and celebrate his defeat; and Dan's prophetic rantings, again in "Box Seat," are formatted as verse, giving graphic form to his poetic pretensions. As in the first section, stanzas of poetry frame or conclude the stories, lyrical refrain lines call out from the prosaic abyss, and self-fashioned poet-prophets erupt in "lyrical" pronouncements, but every instance of poeticalness here serves only to confirm the impotence of language, especially poetic language. Lyric poetry is still painfully associated with ancestral voice, ancient truths, and authentic African American identity; however, the "ugly words" of "bad poetry," to anticipate Kabnis's terms, can do no more than verify the loss of these cultural ideals.

Given the decline of lyric, then, it is significant that only the first vignette of part 2, "Seventh Street" (41), will be framed by a stanza of song, a vestigial structure from part 1 that will not survive long in this section of the book. Functioning much like the framing stanzas of "Karintha" and "Carma," poetry elevates the situation in the prose to mythic status. Here the poem glorifies urban bootleggers whose fleet Cadillacs, in contrast to the public transit system, which ordinary people ride, emblematize their fast money and fast lives. The brisk, rhythmic quatrain introduces the second section of *Cane* with the buoyant confidence appropriate to such men:

> Money burns the pocket, pocket hurts,
> Bootleggers in silken shirts,
> Ballooned, zooming Cadillacs,
> Whizzing, whizzing down the street-car tracks.

This opening song of part 2 rejects the ending of part 1; here, well-dressed bootleggers make an extravagant show of money and mobility, while there, hard-working Tom Burwell was tied up and burned at the stake. Remarkably, one short stanza of jazzy song seems to dispel the sinister connotations of "burn" just a page after Tom's lynching; indeed, the entire vignette employs blood imagery and metaphors of violence not to recall life in the South but to affirm life in the North. The mood of "Seventh Street" is combative and aggressive: African Americans have moved into urban areas where Northern blacks have lost their vitality to bourgeois existence. The arrival of their Southern brothers disrupts the "white-washed," "soggy" routine of Washington's black and white citizens, promising to destroy that compromised world and erect a vital black society in its place:

> [Seventh Street is a] crude-boned, soft-skinned wedge of nigger life breathing its loafer air, jazz songs and love, thrusting unconscious rhythms, black reddish blood into the white and white-washed wood of Washington. Stale soggy wood of Washington. Wedges rust in soggy wood . . . Split it! In two! Again! Shred it! . . the sun. Wedges are brilliant in the sun; ribbons of wet wood dry and blow away. Black reddish blood. Pouring for crude-boned soft-skinned life, who set you flowing? (41)

Yet the description of black life as "crude-boned" and "soft-skinned" throws an uneasy emphasis on African American bodies, and the vulnerability of Tom Burwell's body, soft skin burning away to crude bones, haunts the celebratory tone of "Seventh Street."

Nevertheless, in this context the imagery is affirming *because of* its destructiveness. The prose argues that Southern blacks invigorate Northern African American society; consequently, the imagery employs the pastoral figure of an ax and wedge splitting away old, pale, deteriorated wood. The rustic vitality of the Southern brothers drives a wedge into the complacent urban existence of the Rhoberts and opens a place for the sun to shine in. This reading explains the odd intrusion of the ellipsis followed by the words "the sun" into the prose: the text attempts to reproduce typographically the introduction of "natural" energy into enervated social structures. The compromised life up North must be destroyed, or it will destroy the transplanted Southerners; because the wedges would "rust in soggy wood," that wood must be hacked away, so the sun can shine and the wedges remain bright. In the sun the "wedges are brilliant" and the old, worn wood shrivels up and blows away. This notion that rural blacks rejuvenate the cities explains the unequivocal imagery of demolition and renewal; however, the metaphorical violence required to clear away that bourgeois conformity cannot fully extricate itself from the physical violence of Southern racism in part 1 or even from the psychological ravages African Americans will experience in part 2.[19]

Thus the imagery of black bodies returns, reducing the indestructible iron wedges to blood, bones, and skin. "Blood" generates the repeated phrase "Who set you flowing?" a question that asks several disturbing things: who set so many rural blacks flowing into the cities, who unleashed their energy by making liquor available to them (another kind of flowing), and in what sense is black redemptive blood "flowing"? The claim that "[w]hite and whitewashed disappear in blood" suggests that the new vitality "colors" their pallid existence in positive ways, yet the negative connotations of disappearing in blood cannot be limited to that benign metaphor. The black blood, which might be a figure for African American vitality, is also described as "reddish," a modifier that makes it impossible to read the blood as purely figurative. Indeed, the image of "black-reddish blood" as a tonic stronger than liquor ("Blood sucker of the War would spin in a frenzy of dizziness if they drank your blood. Prohibition would put a stop to it" [41]) is also, of course, an image of that vitality consumed by the vampire North. Similarly, flood imagery—flowing, eddying, swirling, and even sucking—gives a disturbing connotation, again distressingly literal, to the idea of flowing blood. The undeniable sense that metaphorical violence has become literal, and that real violence is aimed at African Americans, is confirmed in a new metaphor that views the migratory "flood" from a suddenly remote perspective. "Who set you flowing" changes to who set you "[s]wirling like a blood-red smoke up where the buzzards fly in heaven?" and we seem to be looking down not on city bustle but on the aftermath of Tom's lynching ("blood-red smoke")—now horribly multiplied by millions. The aggression of the opening has led ineluctably to an urban holocaust.[20]

Recoiling from the contradictions and dangers put into motion by the prose, the text reverts to poetry as if to manage those unruly associations. The little stanza about the bootleggers diminishes the energy released in the preceding glorification of violence, reducing "burns" to a euphemism for spending money and the mythic "thrusting unconscious rhythms" of African American culture to the mechanical movements of cars. The extravagant, wild denizens of Seventh Street were meant to inaugurate part 2 with energy and élan, but black vitality is not in fact more at home in part 2 than it was in part 1. The Rhoberts up North will die a different kind of death from Tom, but they will be extinguished just the same. And the dueling generic modes of "Seventh Street" reveal that poetry can only momentarily dodge the reality of the prose. The stanza that opens and closes "Karintha" deifies her, elevating her individual tragedy to myth in song; in contrast, the stanza that frames "Seventh Street" rings hollow in relation to its violent prose. The childish diction—"pocket hurts," ballooned, zooming, whizzing—while celebratory, is inadequate to the task of rectifying the vision of the prose. A jazzy ditty lauding zoot-suited bootleggers cannot dispel the violence of the move to part 2.

To return briefly to that point when the sunlight breaks through the shredded, soggy wood, and where the ellipsis and phrase ". . the sun" break through the text, it is important to note the rhetorical strategy at work here. "Truth" intrudes into the prose texts repeatedly in this manner in part 2, as indeed it did on occasion in part 1. These eruptions of truth are associated with lyric authenticity, and not just formally, with ragged right margins and figurative language, but thematically. And yet their effect is confusing rather than epiphanic. The men in part 2, as I have said, are to a person impotent poet-prophets. Their prophetic outbursts do not have the rhythm and power of Barlo's pronouncement in "Esther"—nor do they have the meaning. Instead, their ruminations and rantings produce fragmentary, weird, irrational utterances that mark them as pariahs rather than prophets. If there is any truth to this outburst in "Seventh Street," or to Dan's or Paul's or any number of other similar rhetorical moments in part 2, it is lost in the disjointed, perplexing delivery. Lyric eruptions are now wholly associated with fragmented minds and will typically involve "ugly words" rather than poetry.

"Rhobert," the second vignette in part 2, is the only other prose piece in this section that employs poetry, and again the lyric form is not able to counter the discouraging vision of the prose. When the first prose paragraph ends "Life is water that is being drawn off," a couplet formatted as poetry takes up that sentiment as song: "Brother, life is water that is being drawn off. / Brother, life is water that is being drawn off" (42). Yet the line does not gain in lyricality or meaning simply by virtue of its being repeated and set off as poetry. If the text seeks to elevate Rhobert's tragedy to myth by recasting it as poetry, then the story reveals that such a move is no longer possible. By the end of the story, the narrator seems fully aware that the move to song can only be cynical. Calling to a community of brothers that no longer exists, he suggests a chorus of "Deep River" in honor of Rhobert's defeat. But just as this narrator and others in part 2 can no longer sing the spirituals—or compose viable poetry— the closing stanza can only mock Rhobert and parody a culture once rooted in song.

The dwindling of lyric in the poems proper and the association of lyric with failure and insanity in the prose are what give poetry its gasping, fated quality in part 2. If song is the link between modern African Americans and their ancestral past in Africa and the South, then the loss of poetry clearly signifies the end of that connection. Still, part 2 is not yet willing to dissociate African America from the musical constitution that *Cane* posits is essential to that culture. "Natural" rhythm continues to define the characters in this section of the book; however, that cultural pulse is no longer felt in poetry or song but in dance. Dance replaces song as the vehicle of African American expression in part 2—as theaters and dance halls replace the cane fields and pine forests. Yet *words* are lost in the shift from verbal enunciation to bodily gesture, and dance will prove an inadequate substitution for song. Moreover, in a world where bodies are vulnerable and fragmented, dance cannot unite past and present. Part 2 will continually offer dance as an alternative source of cultural meaning and expression only to expose its crassness and inadequacy. Thus, dance occurs in vulgar, artificial settings and is inevitably associated with theatricality in the most pejorative sense. "The past" exists only in performance in part 2 and consequently is always inauthentic. Part 1 posited an authentic African American identity that, though fading, could be recovered in song; part 2 reveals that such identity can now only be imperfectly performed—and, even at that, only performed in dance where the semantic force of poetry does not operate.

"Theater" and "Box Seat," two stories set in music halls in Washington D.C., establish the notion that African American identity has been reduced to a racial spectacle that does not transmit cultural authenticity. "Theater" takes place in the Howard Theater, where both performers and audiences were African American, and yet Dorris, the dancer, and John, the manager's brother (clearly another Rhobert, as the epithet "brother" will indicate throughout part 2) cannot connect through dance the way others in *Cane* have united in song.[21] John is very much like the speaker in "Prayer," a man divided by different desires, paralyzed because he cannot unite his mind and his body. As he sits down to watch the women rehearse their dance, he appears half in light and half in dark to emblematize, as Darwin Turner points out in a footnote to the text, the conflict between sensuality and intellect:

> Light streaks down upon him from a window high above. One half his face is orange in it. One half his face is in shadow. The soft glow of the house rushes to, and compacts about, the shaft of light. John's mind coincides with the shaft of light. Thoughts rush to, and compact about it. Life of the house and the slowly awakening stage swirls to the body of John, and thrills it. John's body is separate from the thoughts that pack his mind. (52)

The thoughts that pack John's mind are familiar in *Cane*: desire for sexual union with beautiful African American women, longing for cultural wholeness through artistic ritual, but also insecurity, arrogance, attraction, revulsion, ecstasy, anger, and a disabling romanticism that underscores all the contradictions plaguing him. Predictably, John's "lips are too skinny" (55), and he longs to witness a display of authentic African identity because he knows himself to be inauthentic. And yet he is ambivalent about African American culture. What is striking in part 2 is that his ambivalence resonates in the narrator's point of view as well, suggesting that *Cane* itself is conflicted about modern black American culture. As the rehearsal begins, jazz animates the dancers *and* John, but the narrator's comments remain reserved and critical:

> A pianist slips into the pit and improvises jazz. The walls awake. Arms of the girls, and their limbs, which . . jazz, jazz . . by lifting up their tight street skirts they set free, jab the air and clog the floor in rhythm to the music. (Lift your skirts, Baby, and talk t papa!) Crude, individualized, and yet . . monotonous . . . (52)

John echoes the narrator's skepticism, telling himself that the female energies released by jazz will momentarily be brought under the sway of a lifeless, "white-washed" culture: "Soon the director will herd you, my full-lipped distant beauties, and tame you, and blunt your sharp thrusts in loosely suggestive movements, appropriate to Broadway" (52). John's interior monologue posits an opposition between the natural, instinctual (indeed, animal) rhythms of the women and the contrived musical taste of a debased culture, and it may be hard to recognize that this opposition includes the aesthetics of a debased African American culture. Here, jazz is "[c]rude, individualized, and . . yet monotonous," as the narrator says; and John also notes that the improvised dances of the women, like the improvised music of jazz, are "[t]oo thick. Too easy. Too monotonous" (53). While we may want to claim that black jazz is diminished by the white culture that appropriates it (the Howard Theater vs. Broadway provides a convenient contrast), "Theater" actually argues that jazz itself is a diminution of the ancestral culture. Thus, improvisation, a quality highly valued in jazz, is devalued in *Cane* because it replaces ritual, its antithesis. John may prefer the sharp thrusts of the dancing women to the domesticated dances of Broadway, but the narrator objects to the very transience of such improvisational art forms: "Girls laugh and shout. Sing discordant snatches of other jazz songs. Whirl with loose passion into the arms of passing show-men" (53). His diction—discordant, snatches, loose, passing, and show-men—registers dissatisfaction with modern African American musical forms for being ephemeral, commercial, and false. Further, once again the word "passing" introduces the ongoing problem in *Cane* that authentic black culture is passing away as contemporary culture passes into an alien world. Yet, the ambivalence of the text is even deeper than a simple opposition between past and present.

The schizophrenic eruptions of the text, which are not limited to characters' interior monologues, reveal that contradictory assumptions, desires, and claims are straining the narratives in part 2. The hope in "Seventh Street" was that textual rupture would permit the intrusion of truth into falsity, of sunlight into the dim environment up North. However, since truth has been lost with part 1, only a fragmented, partial, distorted echo of truth can break through. More precisely, part 2 cannot posit a decisive opposition between truth and falsehood, past and present, poetry and prose, authenticity and inauthenticity because it has only a partial recollection of the first terms in each of those oppositions. Consequently, the prose buckles with contradictions at both the thematic and structural levels. When the pianist "slips" into the pit and "improvises" jazz, a careless, unsystematic activity, the "walls awake," suggesting dead things coming back to life; however, the personification of buildings in part 2 inevitably implies the dehumanization of people. The girls, too, are animated by the music, but their movements "jab the air" and "clog the floor," verbs and images reminiscent of Rhobert and suggesting congestion, awkwardness, and even violence associated with the North. Still worse, the focus on body *parts* (arms, limbs) contributes to the fragmentation, chaos, and cacophony of the scene. Into this already contradictory description, further textual conflicts intrude: the words "jazz . . jazz" interrupt the narrator's prose, as does the parenthetical shout, "(Lift your skirts, Baby, and talk t papa!)." These textual eruptions introduce a frenzied energy but also destabilize the point of view. The vacillating perspectives and voices in "Theater" have been read as a jazzy, improvisational structure—or what critics too readily assume is a call-and-response form. In fact, however, the shifting perspectives capture the isolation of the various characters, not their commonality or reciprocity.

Moreover, "Lift your skirts, Baby, and talk t papa!" has an especially disturbing resonance in *Cane*. That exposed female parts can "talk" to men may be simply another version of the idea in "Carma" and here in "Theater" that the movements of black women's bodies are a kind of song: "Glorious songs are the muscles of her limbs" (55). However, the word "snatches," which follows quickly on the parenthetical call to "talk t Papa," registers a more vulgar meaning. In the profane realm of the dance hall, perhaps the only orifice that "sings" is in the dancer's "snatch," a vulgar term for the female pudendum.[22] The narrator directs the women to lift their skirts in order to express themselves, but it's not entirely clear whether he valorizes the expressivity of black women's gestures or debases song and speech by associating it with one more isolated body part—and a particular body part that is historically regarded with the same combination of fascination and repulsion that characterizes John's response to the dancers. The narrative voice in these outbursts is, obviously, pumping itself up as it cheers on the dancers; as elsewhere, however, such expressions of textual self-encouragement ("telephone the power-house," "Lift your skirts," "Split it! In two! Again! Shred it!" "Open your liver lips to the lean, white spring" [59]) ring disturbingly violent, awkward, and self-hating. At these moments, the narration reiterates the tensions and contradictions that torment the male characters.

All of this is to say that the vitality and spontaneity so many readers, like McKay, Griffin, and North, have appreciated in part 2 represent unruly, unpredictable energies about which this section of the book is at once optimistic and skeptical. Given that *Cane* has already cast its philosophical lot with the past in part 1, it is understandable that change of any sort is regarded with ambivalence here. Part 2 wants to celebrate the infusion of "black red blood" into the whitewashed African American urban world, but it also recognizes that black vitality is invigorating an alien realm—and changing in that context from something creative to something destructive. The text of part 2 repeatedly demonstrates that what appears to be revivifying energy and activity may actually be frenzied desperation. As the culture of the city music hall gains power, the culture of the slaves, and their African ancestors and Southern descendants, fades. Yet these changes have already been "set flowing" and cannot be stopped. Part 2 simultaneously propels itself forward, northward, toward the present and backward, southward, into the past, and this division wracks the text at every level.

Thus, in part 2, the idealized world, so frequently accessed through song in part 1, is sealed off in unreality and cannot be brought into contact with daily life. The split between John's sensuous nature and his rational mind, figured forth at the beginning of the story when his face is half illuminated and half shadowed, anticipates a larger structural division between his defeated, realistic thoughts and his fantasy world. As Dorris's meaningless jazzy dance becomes more "natural" and authentic, John shifts from being a spectator to a dreamer:

Dorris dances. She forgets her tricks. She dances.
Glorious songs are the muscles of her limbs.
And her singing is of canebrake loves and mangrove feastings.
[...]   Dorris dances . . .
John dreams:

> Dorris is dressed in a loose black gown splashed with lemon rib-
> bons. Her feet taper long and slim from trim ankles. She waits for him
> just inside the stage door. John, collar and tie colorful and flaring,
> walks towards the stage door. There are no trees in the alley. But his
> feet feel as though they step on autumn leaves whose rustle has been
> pressed out of them by the passing of a million satin slippers. The air
> is sweet with roasting chestnuts, sweet with bonfires of old leaves.
> John's melancholy is a deep thing that seals all senses but his eyes, and
> makes him whole.
>
> [...] They are in a room. John knows nothing of it. Only, that the
> flesh and blood of Dorris are its walls. Singing walls. Lights, soft, as if
> they shine through clear pink fingers. [...]
>
> John reaches for a manuscript of his, and reads. Dorris, who has no
> eyes, has eyes to understand him. He comes to a dancing scene. The
> scene is Dorris. She dances. Dorris dances. Glorious Dorris. Dorris
> whirls, whirls, dances . . .

Dorris dances. (55)

In the book, the text of John's dream is indented and set in slightly
smaller type; the phrase "Dorris dances" frames the dream in regu-
lar type at the extreme right margin. Like the parentheses in "Carma,"
which will simultaneously preserve and isolate the narrator's romantic
vision of sunset and song, this framing of John's dream marks it as dis-
continuous with the story's reality. Indeed, his dream is a weird mixture
of pastoral idyll, sexual innuendo, and elegiac imagery. John, dressed up
like the flamboyant bootleggers in "Seventh Street," meets Dorris in a
back alley where there are no trees. Nevertheless, he feels as if he's walking over autumn leaves, the decline of the year suggesting the passing of
the natural world, and the air is filled with the scents of an earlier time
and place. Dorris, too, exudes the past in her fragrance, which is elegia-
cally compared first to old flowers and then to the book's icon of the past,
a Southern cane field, as if "old" and "Southern" were synonymous. The
emphasis on scent in the dream is curious since the crucial sense organ

here is eyes: "John's melancholy is a deep thing that seals all senses but his eyes" and even Dorris, "who has no eyes, has eyes to understand him" (55). While vision is associated with realism elsewhere in *Cane,* John's dream depicts sight as the one human faculty that can "[make] him whole." Here eyes, not mouths, speak, and the lovers understand each other completely *because* they don't have to communicate in words. The romantic cliché that the lovers' bodies speak louder than words, that words are unnecessary between lovers whose perfect communication supersedes talking, rests uneasily in a book that idealizes words. Inevitably, then, *Cane* must introduce song into this silent fantasy since song is the genre of the ideal; it does so by transforming Dorris's body into the theater itself (a move anticipated in the opening of the story when the stage lights look as if they "shine through clear pink fingers" [52] and the walls, "sleeping singers until rehearsal begins" [52], awaken when the dancers begin to rehearse [53]) so that the impotent, paralyzed John can get inside of her simply by being in her presence. By the end of the dream, the setting has become a bizarre conglomeration of various (incongruent) things the men in part 2 desire: femininity, sex, black blood, pink skin, and, inexplicably, song—apprehended through sight, which is to say not a literal song but a series of analogies between visual phenomena and song.

Having dreamed himself into this soft, light, warm haven, John does what most of the other men in *Cane* do at moments of sexual intimacy: "[He] reaches for a manuscript of his, and reads." The doggerel bit "Glorious Dorris" gives some indication of the quality of his poetry. But worse, having retreated in fantasy to a wordless realm of pure understanding, John now spoils it with words. Inevitably, then, reading returns him to reality; he comes to a scene in his manuscript in which "Dorris dances," and the dream ends, having come full circle to the dance rehearsal; that framing phrase punctures the dream, as it were, by appearing within it. Real sound now intrudes violently as the "pianist crashes a bumper chord" and the "whole stage claps" (55). The story switches to Dorris's point of view, and when she looks at John for confirmation that her dancing has moved him, she discovers that he is lost in the shadows, his face "a dead thing" (56). Her eyes, full of tears, can see only the "whitewashed ceiling," not the glow of lights through pink fingers; and the theater now smells of "dry paste and paint, and soiled clothing," not chestnuts, bonfires of old leaves, flowers, or Southern cane fields (56). The two cultural resources *Cane* hopes will restore a lost past—dancing black bodies in part 2 and African American song in part 1—fail to effect transformation and unification in "Theater."[23]

Because there is nothing left in the world that can bridge the gulf between the past and the present, the ideal and the real, John advises himself to disengage from reality. "Keep her loveliness. Let her go" (53) is John's warning to himself and his motto for life in a degraded culture. The ideal can only be maintained by accepting that it's purely imaginary. If he were to join with Dorris, "she'd bore [him] after the first five minutes" (54). Even though Dorris herself is able to "[forget] her tricks," those crass, predictable movements of the rehearsal, and dance with glorious songs in her muscles, creating movements of "canebrake loves and mangrove feastings" (55), John cannot meet her in that imaginary canebrake. In his dream the setting is a city alley, only nostalgically tinged with the scent of canebrakes and mangroves. Despite his longings for something more idyllic, John's own mind is bordered by the profane world he dwells in, exactly like Rhobert in his helmet. Thus, the only way to preserve Dorris's ideal beauty and meaning is to refuse to realize them. And even such self-denial and repudiation of the world cannot protect him from reality; his own dream leads him right back to the contemporary nightmare, where dreams come to nothing and Dorris's beauty cannot be "kept," even in imaginary form.

"Theater" is thus ambivalent at best about modern African American musical culture. The story, like John, seems fascinated with black vitality and creativity, as expressed in jazz and dance, but suspicious of these artistic forms as well. It wants to idealize African American bodies, especially female bodies, as the locus of culture and meaning in the absence of the South and the past, but it recognizes that dance cannot adequately replace song. Acknowledging that the cane-lipped choruses of song are silenced in this environment, it hopes to recover an ancient musicality it associates with spirituality in contemporary musical culture. Failing that, the story can only follow John into a dream world that is significantly devoid of sound. But the effort to replace real song with metaphorical song fails, and John returns abruptly to a clangorous stage where an ideal African American identity can only be mimicked in awkward movements that describe its loss. Even when Dorris breaks out of the staged dance into something more authentic, her dance remains a spectacle because John cannot join with her in ritual.

This emphasis on theatricality appears repeatedly in part 2, suggesting that *Cane*'s ideals can be staged but not truly attained. "Theater," "Box Seat," and "Bona and Paul" are explicitly set in theatrical environments, but the notion that identity is a performance permeates the entire section. The bootleggers in "Seventh Street" make a display of wealth and power, "Rhobert"'s narrator calls for a chorus of song to accompany Rhobert's defeat, and the narrator of "Avey" *recites* his poems to Avey; of the stories in part 2, only "Calling Jesus" (58) does not invoke performance. Instead, following directly on "Her Lips Are Copper Wire," "Calling Jesus" alludes sardonically to the telephone, as though Jesus could be reached through modern technology. Indeed, the title refers doubly to the *call* of African American oral culture (the call-and-response form invoked unsuccessfully in "Theater" as well as field calls associated with agricultural work and shouts during religious services) and to making a telephone call. It participates in the personification of city buildings and the attendant dehumanization of city inhabitants that has become the icon of part 2. Here, the soul of the urban woman is figured as a pathetic dog who must spend each night cold and lonely in the vestibule of her apartment building. Only in dreams does the soul remember the songs and scents of Southern life, of a place where buildings don't need vestibules and storm doors to keep out the cold. The cold, of course, is more than the Northern climate; it represents the spiritual numbing of modern African Americans. The soul abandoned in the vestibule is one more instance of that separation of body and spirit we witness so often in part 2. Also typical of part 2, the text of "Calling Jesus" erupts with snippets of "song"—vestiges of the lost oral culture break through the modern narrative, carrying with them the ellipses that signify the wordless gulf between this world and that: "Some one . . . eoho Jesus . . . soft as a cotton boll brushed up against the milk-pod cheek of Christ" and "Some one . . . eoho Jesus . . . soft as the bare feet of Christ moving across bales of southern cotton" will, the eruptions promise, come in through the storm door and comfort the soul—indeed, will unite the body and soul: will "carry it to her where she sleeps: cradled in dream-fluted cane." "Eoho" is a field holler, a remnant of work songs like "Cotton Song" in part 1, a musical device for communicating from one field to another while working the land; the holler was also invoked during religious services as a call to God. Significantly, then, both the woman and her soul retreat imaginatively to the cane field, a mythic place where field hollers would enable people to communicate—with each other and with God. But "eoho Jesus" intrudes here only as a fragment of something lost. Jesus cannot be reached through the old hollers and songs any more than he can be called by telephone.

It is this failure of direct, authentic, oral communication that makes performance necessary in part 2. Given that people are dehumanized and alienated from their own souls, that the ancestral voice has been silenced by modern clamor, that the land is covered with asphalt and the sun blocked by concrete buildings, the ritual aspects of African American culture are denied meaning and reduced to mere spectacles. "Box Seat" is in this sense the centerpiece of part 2; not only the longest work in this section, but, more significant, it is the piece that realizes most completely the terms of modern urban life. (It is also close to the numerical center of the forty-page section, beginning on the nineteenth page.) As the title suggests and the imagery of the story repeats almost obsessively, the inhabitants of Washington are boxed in to their middle-class lives, bolted into upright chairs that are, in turn, secured into place: "There is a sharp click as [Mrs. Pribby, the prudish landlady] fits into her chair and draws it to the table. The click is metallic like the sound of a bolt being shot into place" (60). Though Dan wants to believe that Muriel, a tenant of Mrs. Pribby and the woman he loves, is a different kind of person, she too, "clicks into a high-armed seat" (61) and refuses to submit to his sexual advances or to his idealistic views. Likewise, at the theater, where the black middle class goes for entertainment, the imagery of forced enclosure abounds: "Each [seat] is a bolt that shoots into a slot, and is locked there" (64), "The seats are slots. The seats are bolted houses" (64), "From either aisle, bolted masses press in" (65).

Muriel hopes that the theater will provide a distraction from some unnamed trouble she refuses to discuss with Dan—and which the story refuses to disclose as well. Dan tries to raise the issue with her: "[I] wanted to talk to you—to see you and tell you that I know what you've been through—what pain the last few months must have been" (61). However, referring to the pain indirectly as "that," Muriel asks Dan not to discuss it; when he attempts to elevate her suffering by idealizing it—"But Muriel, life is full of things like that. One grows strong and beautiful in facing them. What else is life?" (61)—she changes the subject to the "show at the Lincoln this week" (61). It is significant that Muriel regards the theater as an escape from her trouble since the "box seats" of the Lincoln Theater clearly offer the same constraints she tolerates at Mrs. Pribby's. What Dan (and many readers) fail to take into account, however, is that this is precisely what Muriel wants. There are many hints that Muriel's trouble is that she has been raped, an occurrence that would meet with ambivalence in *Cane*. Though such a sexual violation would threaten Muriel's middle-class respectability, sexual respectability is a virtue the book scorns. Moreover, *Cane* has shown a conflicted attitude toward the violation of women; from Karintha to Carma, Fern, Louisa, Avey, and on to Carrie K. in part 3, women are desired and yet feared by *Cane*'s men, who fancy themselves the champions of women most especially when they cannot express their own sexual desires. It may be that Muriel lives with Mrs. Pribby in her guarded world because she doesn't feel safe anywhere else. Dan himself demonstrates "an obstinate desire to possess her" (63), and Muriel thinks of rape when she sees him enter the theater: "Looks like Dan. He mustnt see me. Silly. He cant reach me. He wont dare come in here. He'd put his head down like a goring bull and charge me. He'd trample them. He'd gore. He'd rape!" (65).

In fact, Dan also characterizes himself as sexually domineering when he articulates his philosophy of sex; tellingly, his proposition to "silly women arguing feminism" (67) like Muriel and her friend Bernice is presented as verse:

Me, horizontally above her.
Action: perfect strokes downward oblique.
Hence, man dominates because of limitation.
Or, so it shall be until women learn their stuff. (67)

His vision offers the most conventional emblem of sexual hierarchy as "natural"—the missionary position—yet renders it in strangely mechanical language, a point he himself observes in the prose that follows the verse proposition, where he claims that the technological age is natural because it emerged from the nontechnological eras that preceded it: "[. . .] I hereby offer [the proposition] to posterity as one of the important machine-age designs. P.S. It should be noted, that because it *is* an achievement of this age, its growth and hence its causes, up to the point of maturity, antedate machinery. Ery . . . " (67). (This is not a brilliant defense of the machine age, by any means, but it is a revealing if tautological attempt on Dan's part to unify the past and the present.) His "proposition" is, of course, simply a coarse sexual overture despite the fact that he punningly elevates it to the status of scientific theorem in his own mind. Men should be on top of women during intercourse, he proposes, because in that position the phallus can make "perfect strokes" in "downward oblique" movements that resemble the regularity and efficiency of pistons in a machine. This arrangement must prevail until "women learn their stuff"; Dan justifies male dominance by suggesting that women are inadequate. It is, of course, Dan who feels inadequate, his only gift "to posterity" will be this ridiculous proposition, not procreation. His rhetoric in both the "poem" and the gloss is as stiff and mechanical as his vision of sex: "Hence," "so it shall be," "I hereby offer," "P.S. It should be noted" are phrases suggestive of business correspondence or technical reports. These are hardly lyrical utterances, and yet the formatting indicates that this is a poetical moment for him. Indeed, the curious phonetic bit "Ery," which he utters just before trailing off, is a fragment of a word, a suffix echoing the ending of "machin*ery*"; this verbal particle is at once an onomatopoeic groan of frustration (emotional and sexual) and an effort to rhyme. "Maturity [. . .] machinery [. . .] Ery": the last syllable casts about awkwardly for a rhyming word, making a sound resembling Rhobert's gagging more than song. Like John uttering "Glorious Dorris" in his dream, Dan habitually reaches for poetry to ordain his romantic fantasies.

If this is love poetry, then Muriel's fear of sexual vulnerability is justified. Not only does Dan, whom she privately admits to loving, want to violate her, but she will presently be imposed upon by Mr. Barry, the performing dwarf, who will sing her a love song, hand her a suggestively bloody rose, and make a spectacle of her in the very place she went to get away from her troubles. That Dan's "love poem" is a pretentious, misogynistic hodgepodge of poetic pomposity and scientific jargon is just one more indication that Muriel isn't safe—even with someone who loves her. Dan's poem is absurd, but it is nevertheless menacing; Mr. Barry's song is "high-pitched" and, though the words are sentimental, he too is "threatening" (69). As he offers her the rose, which she feels she must accept with a smile because the audience expects her to play her part, his eyes express hatred: "Hate pops from his eyes and crackles like a brittle heat about the box" (69). The imagery here overtly recalls Tom Burwell's lynching ("Stench of burning flesh soaked the air. Tom's eyes popped" [36]), just as the imagery of Dan's proposition ("perfect strokes downward oblique") brings to mind the axes of "Seventh Street" hacking away middle-class pretensions and setting the black blood flowing. Muriel's escape to the show turns out to be one more encounter with violence and hatred.

Women are particularly vulnerable because gender roles in *Cane* are so rigidly conventional. Men imagine themselves as prophets and leaders; indeed, many of the male characters and narrators are rehearsals for Kabnis in part 3, who will explicitly attempt the role of orator. Women, on the other hand, are nearly mute. Esther, Louisa, Dorris, Muriel, Bona, and Carrie K. each have a few, mostly ineffective words, but Karintha, Becky, Carma, Fern, Avey, and even "Nora" (the woman in "Calling Jesus" whose name Toomer removed from the title and the text of that vignette) remain utterly silent while male narrators speak for them or their male counterparts talk incessantly at them. Predictably, these men idealize female bodies, not female speech, and hope to contact an authentic culture through those bodies. However, despite their sexual desire for African American women, men in *Cane* are repeatedly depicted as impotent: they want a cultural connection rather than a sexual one, a myth rather than a woman. These contradictory desires not only render them sexually ineffective but deeply ambivalent about black women.

Consequently, for all his grandiose delusions of potency—"Break in. Get an ax and smash in. Smash in their faces. I'll show em. Break into an engine-house, steal a thousand horse-power fire truck. Smash in with the truck. I'll show em. Grab an ax and brain em. Cut em up. Jack the Ripper. Baboon from the zoo" (59)—and all Muriel's fears about his potential for violence, especially sexual violence ("He'd rape!"), Dan "shrivels" when he actually comes into contact with a black woman's body. The woman in question is significantly not sexual in conventional terms. This is not Karintha or Avey or Dorris, the romantic heroines of male fantasy, but a "portly Negress" (65), who embodies for Dan an authentic and unifying African American presence:

He shrivels close beside a portly Negress whose huge rolls of flesh meet about the bones of seat-arms. A soil-soaked fragrance comes from her. Through the cement floor her strong roots sink down. They spread under the asphalt streets. Dreaming, the streets roll over on their bellies, and suck their glossy health from them. Her strong roots sink down and spread under the river and disappear in blood-lines that waver south. Her roots shoot down. Dan's hands follow them. Roots throb. Dan's heart beats violently. He places his palms upon the earth to cool them. Earth throbs. Dan's heart beats violently. He sees all the people in the house rush to the walls to listen to the rumble. A new-world Christ is coming up. Dan comes up. (65)

Dan shrinks beside the portly Negress, not man enough for her because she herself embodies both male and female power, maternal and paternal capability. On the one hand, she appears to be an earth mother: the streets (and, we assume, Dan) roll over on their bellies asleep and dreaming, like babies napping after nursing. But on the other, she is repeatedly described in phallic terms: her "huge rolls of flesh" and "shoot[ing]," "sink[ing]," "throb[bing]" roots more aptly describe the mythic father. Dan's shriveling is directly related to her expansiveness.[24]

In his fantasy he imagines following her roots all the way back to the South, where Northern bloodlines unite with ancestral ones; and he imagines being reborn through his earth mother as a black prophet and savior. The shriveling he experiences in the real world is transformed into an erection of sorts in his fantasy, where imagery deftly replaces the sexual reference (the impotent phallus) with a reference to birth (the Christ child): only in dreams can "Dan [come] up"; only in myth can a savior be born of woman alone—the Blessed Virgin or, here, the androgynous Negress. Inevitably, his own delusions of grandeur are too much for him, and Dan comes back to reality to discover that he makes no difference at all. It is sadly appropriate, then, that his actual engagement with a member of the audience is not with the deified black woman but with a man: "He treads on a man's corns. The man grumbles" (65). Dan cannot follow the black woman's imagined roots back to fields of cane; instead, he will end up in a row with a man whose "corns" emblematize in small what ails Dan. Corn is no longer a symbol of the South; it's simply one more symptom of constricting city life, no grander than Rhobert's rickets.

Nevertheless, despite the failure of the dream, Dan continues to imagine himself as Muriel's redeemer. He explicitly opposes himself to contemporary black culture as it is performed in the theater, calling jazz "[o]ld stuff" (66) and offering even older stuff in its place: "I sing your praises, Beauty! I exalt thee, O Muriel! A slave, thou art greater than all Freedom because I love thee" (66). His "song" is anachronistic at best—and not just in its archaic diction and style. His inflated poeticisms are anachronistic in a more disturbing way: the unspoken apostrophe to Muriel (the irony of an unspoken apostrophe is crucial) appropriates African American history for figurative language; he is a "slave" to love even as his beloved is a "slave" to convention. This unself-conscious invocation of slavery as a state of mind rather than a historical circumstance is precisely the kind of poetic license *Cane* most fears, and yet the book's own impulse to poetize and idealize is the very thing that will inevitably destroy the past it so longs to preserve.

The profanation of song culminates in "Box Seat" when Dan's agitated thoughts coincide with Mr. Barry's unspoken "words" ("Words form in the eyes of the dwarf"). Just before Muriel touches the rose, an act that precipitates Dan's actual outburst, Mr. Barry's and Dan's thoughts appear in the text as a silent duet in verse, with Dan's part italicized:

Do not shrink. Do not be afraid of me.
Jesus
See how my eyes look at you.
the Son of God
I too was made in His image.
was once—
I give you the rose. (69)

Each demands acceptance despite his flaws—indeed, because of them—the dwarf for his physical deformity and Dan for his position as social outcast. Each invokes God to make his case. Mr. Barry insists that he was made in the image and likeness of God, and Dan compares himself to Jesus, who not only cured lepers but performed the role of "social leper" himself. Indeed, Christ's divinity is what kept him apart from others, and Dan feels superior to people like Mrs. Pribby who would ostracize him. They sing the same tune, each in his own key; Mr. Barry appeals to Muriel in a pleading, lovesick manner (conventional to the love song genre of his act), while Dan delivers a bombastic proclamation hardly appropriate to the moment. The intertwining of their "lyrics" culminates in Dan's declaration, "JESUS WAS ONCE A LEPER!" (69). Having asserted his likeness to Christ, "Dan steps down" (69), a decidedly the-atrical gesture. Dan longs to express an authentic identity that he believes urban, middle-class life has suppressed. But that being a redeemer is just one more performance, that his outburst is delivered in a theater, indicates the impossibility of authentic identity in the part 2 world. Cru-cially, he attempts to reveal himself in song, as though the elevated lan-guage of lyric will convey something that he hasn't been able to commu-nicate in ordinary talk, but his song is just one more deformed thing, and worse, just one more performance.

Having spouted off, Dan now withdraws from his fantasy of being a poet, prophet, and redeemer, of joining physically with Muriel or the portly black woman to produce a new race. The text hints that his verbal discharge has functioned as a substitute for sexual release: "He is cool as a green stem that has just shed its flower" (69). Yet even this clumsily imported pastoral image only confirms that his "deflowering" is deplet-ing rather than productive. Unlike the dwarf's bloody rose, which at least represents a battered engagement with life, Dan's cool, green, flowerless stem suggests the solitary, unproductive calm of defeat.

When Dan walks away from the fracas he himself has instigated, he turns his back on the violence invoked in "Seventh Street" and "Box Seat" as redemptive. Instead, he retreats to an interior world where social and sexual conflicts are eluded in fantasy. All around him reality presses in: "The alley-air is thick and moist with smells of garbage and wet trash. In the morning, singing niggers will drive by and ring their gongs . . ." (69). But Dan escapes these real-world surroundings; tellingly, just the mention of the black garbage men's *songs* is enough to transport him into dream. The "singing niggers" are followed by the familiar ellipsis, signal of imaginative transport, and we can guess that they have been transformed in Dan's mind into cane-lipped singers of the past. Thus, Dan reenters his imaginary place "populated" with personified houses—"Eyes of houses, soft girl-eyes" (69)—the unnaturally natural realm that part 2 consistently tries, and fails, to body forth.

"Bona and Paul," like "Theater" and "Box Seat," takes place in theat-rical settings: a gymnasium, the *Pure Food Restaurant,* and the Crimson Gardens nightclub. In each setting, race is again presented as a spectacle: Paul's "nigger" rhythms during the military drill in the gymnasium (72), Art's white rendition of jazz in the restaurant (75), and Bona and Paul's erotic dance at the nightclub, a dance in which "pink-faced people have no part" (79). Here, the performance of black identity is specifically related to the popular musical culture witnessed elsewhere in part 2. And again, though there is a strained effort to associate each setting with poetry, the music-hall environment proves to be an unreliable repository of African American culture.

Thus, Bona says to Paul, "I thought you were a poet—or a gym director" (79), as if a poet were no more than someone who shouts orders (as a matter of fact, this is an apt description of Dan's "poetry") and concerns himself wholly with the physical realm. If song has degenerated to dance in part 2 generally, dance has degenerated even further to gymnastics and drills in "Bona and Paul." The movements of the men practicing a military drill are "rhythmical and syncopated" (72), and the "dance of [Paul's] blue-trousered limbs" during practice "thrills" Bona (72) much like Dorris's impromptu dance thrills John. Likewise, the basketball match between men and women prefigures Bona and Paul's dance at the Crimson Gardens, offering an opportunity for physical contact. Though the match has been read as a uniquely egalitarian encounter in *Cane*, "The basketball game is a kind of utopian moment, for within the game there is gender equality and contact between the races" (Scruggs and VanDemarr 181), this is hardly the kind of cultural ritual *Cane* has been seeking.

Complicating the demise of ancestral culture is that it is Paul's white friend Art who plays jazz at the restaurant: "Art sat on the piano and simply tore it down. Jazz. The picture of Our Poets hung perilously" (75). "Tore it down" is more than a colloquial expression for furious piano playing; it also registers the destruction of a prior musical form that has been replaced by jazz, as the fragile picture of the old masters suggests. Clearly the painting hangs over the piano as the older generation hovers over the younger, but it now hangs "perilously" because the past is in a precarious relation to the present. Yet this scene remains ambivalent about whose past and whose present. "Our Poets" was a familiar designation for a gallery of nineteenth-century American "Schoolroom Poets"—like Bryant, Holmes, Longfellow, Lowell, and Whittier—whose portraits hung in classrooms.[25] These genteel white poets obviously do not represent the black ancestral culture. A white man playing jazz that threatens to topple white literary poetry offers an emblem of something more complex than the African American present superseding the African American past. It reveals that cultural tradition and ancestry are complicated by a history of interracial contact.

This problem arises again in Paul's fantasy of his past. His imaginary South conforms to the pastoral idyll invoked throughout *Cane*: sun, wheat, pines, songs, Negresses, "lush melodies of cane and corn" (73). But it also includes "the fact of racial intermingling," here envisioned as the lovely and loving union of the black mother and the white father:

> Paul goes to his [room]. Gray slanting roofs of houses are tinted lavender in the setting sun. Paul follows the sun, over the stock-yards where a fresh stench is just arising, across the wheat lands that are still waving above their stubble, into the sun. Paul follows the sun to a pine-matted hillock in Georgia. He sees the slanting roofs of gray unpainted cabins tinted lavender. A Negress chants a lullaby beneath the mate-eyes of a southern planter. Her breasts are ample for the suckling of a song. She weans it, and sends it, curiously weaving, among lush melodies of cane and corn. Paul follows the sun into himself in Chicago. (73)

"Curiously weaving," indeed. Like the intermixing of white and black in the preceding passage, where Art's jazz displaces the old white poetry, Paul's daydream of the South imagistically interweaves North and South (they share slanted gray roofs poetically tinged with lavender), sun and son, return and decline, sex and song, and, most important, black and white. The song that carries the "lush melodies of cane and corn" to Paul in Chicago is engendered by the mating of the white Southern planter and the black slave—a union pointedly not pictured here as rape. Clearly, in Paul's mind, the intermixing of black and white is the solution to the problem of racial identity. This is his explanation for passing for white: only in blending the two races until difference is lost will harmony be achieved.

The Crimson Gardens nightclub provides the setting for the finale of part 2 and the rearticulation of the racial ideal introduced in Paul's daydream. Paul and the narrator seem to think that the nightclub offers a metaphor for the mingling of blackness and whiteness: in the twilight of the Crimson Gardens, flower petals lose their distinctive shades, blending in the mythical hour of dusk to purple shadows (like the lav-

ender rooftops of the North and the South) that do not admit of difference. Here, the "Gardens [are] purple like a bed of roses would be at
dusk"; "white faces are the petals of roses" and "dark faces are the petals of dusk" (80). Yet this potentially "natural" (and thus appealing)
metaphor is rendered grotesque when the flower blossoms figure forth
not just the commingling of opposites—specifically, of white and black,
Bona and Paul—but a coagulation of interracial blood lines to form a
blood clot rather than a new race. Hence, the Crimson Gardens is literally crimson: white faces may be the "petals of roses" and black faces the
"petals of dusk," but this imagery is not finally able to extricate itself
from the vision of Mr. Barry's battered face and bloody rose. Couples are
repeatedly referred to as clots: "Art and Helen clot [on the dance floor]"
(79) and "[Bona and Paul] are a dizzy blood clot on a gyrating floor"
(79). The efforts of part 2 to set black blood flowing in a regenerative
way will cease once and for all in "Bona and Paul," where blood imagery
is consistently described as clotting rather than flowing.

If Paul is the last hope for part 2, the imagery reveals how fragile that
hope is. From the beginning he is a racially liminal figure, a "candle that
dances in a grove swung with pale balloons" (72)—that is, an idealized
light-skinned black man amid ridiculous white people. Yet the candle
flame is no less ephemeral than the balloons, even if it is a less pejorative figure, and both the image of Paul as a dancing candle and his white
friends as bobbing balloons situate them in a carnival realm where performance replaces a more stable notion of identity. Whether Bona and
Paul are performing for each other in the gymnasium during a basketball game or dancing with other couples at the nightclub, the story can
offer no location that relieves them of the necessity of acting out their
identities.

This is what prevents the African American energies celebrated at the
beginning of part 2 in "Seventh Street" from flowing: black identity is
no longer authentic and can only be performed. Inevitably, in the terms
Cane has set out, when African Americans move north, they are severed
from their ancient heritage—removed from the land in which they are
rooted and estranged from the cultural forms in which their spirituality
is preserved. Thus, Bona and Paul's dance, which is meant to function as
sexual foreplay, generative of a new race, appears dangerously, literally,
like a heart attack: "The dance takes blood from their minds and packs
it, tingling, in the torsos of their swaying bodies. Passionate blood leaps

back into their eyes. They are a dizzy blood clot on the gyrating floor" (79). Given the frequent splitting of part 2 characters into body and mind—John in "Theater" or the persona in "Prayer"—this description can be read as an effort to release the couple from the mental inhibitions that fracture so many of the inhabitants of the North. Yet, that very hope only renders more disturbing the fact that their sexual energies clot rather than flow. Nevertheless, the narrator seems confident that their tingling is an "instinct" (79) that will lead them "away from Art and Helen" (79), outside to the gardens, and even further into "natural" sexual consummation. Instead, however, Paul returns to the nightclub in order to tell the black doorman what he should be telling Bona. In a typical scene of verbosity and impotence, the long-winded oration of a man who considers himself a poet-prophet takes the place of a flesh-and-blood encounter:

> "I came back to tell you, to shake your hand, and tell you that you are wrong [to think that Paul simply seeks a sexual encounter with Bona]. That something beautiful is going to happen. That the Gardens are purple like a bed of roses would be at dusk. That I came into the Gardens, into life in the Gardens with one whom I did not know. That I danced with her, and did not know her. That I felt passion, contempt and passion for her whom I did not know. That I thought of her. That my thoughts were matches thrown into a dark window. And all the while the Gardens were purple like a bed of roses would be at dusk. I came back to tell you, brother, that white faces are petals of roses. That dark faces are petals of dusk. That I am going to gather petals. That I am going out and know her whom I brought here with me to these Gardens which are purple like a bed of roses would be at dusk."
>
> Paul and the black man shook hands.
>
> When he reached the spot where they had been standing, Bona was gone. (80)

Part 2 ends with just so many flowery words that come to nothing.

Perhaps this is why, by certain of Toomer's accounts, part 2 doesn't end here at all. If, as he told Waldo Frank, *Cane* "ends" for Toomer at "Harvest Song," the last poem in the volume, then part 2's structural and conceptual conclusion that the dream of cultural harmony is only a dream, that black blood cannot purify whitewashed blood either by re-vivifying African Americans or by uniting blacks and whites, then we can begin to understand why Toomer looked *back* not just one page to "Harvest Song," but back a whole epoch to the agrarian South, for a symbolic terminus to part 2. Naturally, that finale would have to be a song.

It is ironic that the final poem in part 2 is "Harvest Song" (71), a *song* with long, rhythmic lines and cadenced repetitions, a poem coming from a reaper who has "been in the fields all day" and whose images clearly belong to part 1: oats, grain, fields, dust, hills, scythes, dusk, wheat, corn, songs, reapers, and, most significant, "sweet-stalked cane." "Harvest Song," on the facing page of "Prayer," seems to follow the fourth poem's ellipsis. If the white space surrounding "Prayer" reflects the godless void of outer space, as "Beehive" and "Storm Ending" have already shown, then one way that "Harvest Song" answers that visual silence is with the sheer density of its words. Long biblical lines exceed the right margin of the page and crowd into bulky verse paragraphs. This formal allusion to biblical poetry is one kind of answer to the spiritual poverty of the modern world: the empty heavens, the trapped spirit, the muted poetry. The question is how does part 2 harvest song out of silence, words out of white space? How does it recover nature, the past, the South, and lyric after demonstrating that all of this has been lost? Most important, how does "Harvest Song" conclude part 2?

Toomer said that *Cane* was a swan song, an elegy for the glorious African American past; of all the pieces in the volume, "Harvest Song" most explicitly performs this elegiac function.[26] Its moment is not merely the end of day ("sundown" and "dusk") but the end of the season, harvesttime. The singer who works the land is called a "reaper" rather than a farmer or sharecropper, and he clearly represents the Grim Reaper. Through a pun on the word "cradled," the reach of his scythe extends beyond the crops, beyond even his own life, to the lives of the next generation. He says "[a]ll my oats are cradled" to indicate his work is done. "Cradled" here literally means "cut down with a scythe," but it also generates more positive connotations, and we might picture his oats *nestled* safely away after harvesting. As "Kabnis" will shortly demonstrate, the baby "cradled" in the treetop is at risk: the wind will blow, and he'll come tumbling down. Similarly, "cradled" in "Harvest Song" uneasily locates birth and death in one word, hinting that the death of the past will entail the death of the present and future.

Further evidence of a wider cultural decline is that he harvests everything *but* the book's symbolic crop: cane. Oats, wheat, and corn represent the dry, unappetizing grains that crack between his teeth but leave
his throat dry. As we would expect, the dry throat, his own and those of
his "brothers," cannot produce the saving song. His harvest song is as
silent as theirs: "it would be good to hear their songs," but he can't. Since
he, in turn, "fear[s] to call" to them, the field holler, "Eoho," appears only
in the parentheses, which surround it in silence, or following the ellipsis,
which locates it in fantasy.

Cane, too, enters the poem only in one of these parenthetical moments of fantasy:

> It would be good to hear their songs . . reapers of the
>   sweet-stalk'd cane, cutters of the corn . . even though
>   their throats cracked and the strangeness of their voices
>   deafened me.

In a now-familiar signal of the intrusion of lyrical voice, the ellipses
frame the only mention of cane in the poem. Sugar cane, with its quench-
ing sweetness, is not the crop he harvests. Cane, songs, brothers, the land,
the South, the past can only be imaginatively seen: "I am a blind man
who stares across the hills, seeking stack'd fields of other harvesters."
Cold, blind, deaf, without capacity to taste, the reaper is insensible to
everything but memory, a faculty that renders his pain "sweet" because
he can imagine it so without the intrusion of reality. At the beginning
of the poem, he says he "fear[s] knowledge of [his] hunger," but by the
end, memory rather than reality encloses him. Because memory has
been given up wholly to illusion in *Cane*, he need no longer fear: "My
pain is sweet. [. . .] It will not bring me knowledge of my hunger."

If "Song of the Son" is part 1's Song of Songs, a lyrical paean to love
and hope, then "Harvest Song" is part 2's Leviticus, a text of instruction
rather than celebration, an expression of the need for sacrifice in order
to purify and protect sinners. Leviticus, with its emphasis on ritual sacrifice as a means of atonement, legitimates priests, who are needed to
perform these rituals. This instinct, too, for a prophetic, redemptive figure who will save African American culture from its own historical development, first articulated in part 1, gains strength in part 2. The narrators and characters of "Avey," "Theater," "Box Seat," and "Bona and

Paul" conceive of themselves as high priests of culture—and in this they are all rehearsals for Kabnis. That their prophetic utterances are at best doggerel and at worst discordant snatches of songs indicates why part 3 turns completely away from lyric and embraces instead the "ugly words" of Kabnis's oration.

4
Misshapen, Split-Gut, Tortured, Twisted Words

Cane, Part 3

IF POEMS ARE MISSHAPEN and tortured in part 2, language itself is twisted in part 3, composed of ugly words that preclude poetry entirely. Fragments of folk songs break up the prose, but part 3 does not offer a single complete poem. Instead, the final section of *Cane* is comprised of "Kabnis," a quasi-dramatic work in six numbered sections,[1] which tells the story of Ralph Kabnis, a Northerner teaching in Sempter, Georgia, who yearns to be a poet for the African American South, much like his counterpart in "Song of the Son," but here poetry will not take shape. Kabnis associates the absence of poetry with the impossibility of beauty. Yet beauty is impossible not because it doesn't exist but because its existence makes him more acutely aware of the ugliness that constitutes life in the South:

> Kabnis is about to shake his fists heavenward. He looks up, and the night's beauty strikes him dumb. He falls to his knees. Sharp stones cut through his thin pajamas. The shock sends a shiver over him. He quivers. Tears mist his eyes. He writhes.
> "God Almighty, dear God, dear Jesus, do not torture me with beauty. Take it away. Give me an ugly world." (85)

Like God, who "doesn't exist, but nevertheless He is ugly" (85), beauty exists only to torture Kabnis by hinting at something unattainable beyond the squalor and violence of reality. He imagines himself a Tantalus figure, observing beauty that he cannot reach: "Dear Jesus, do not chain me to myself and set these hills and valleys, heaving with folk-songs, so close to me that I cannot reach them" (85). Significantly, he imagines being chained to himself and not to some outside force that withholds beauty; able to perceive beauty but not to realize it, Kabnis is a dream of beauty in a reality of ugliness (83–84), and he seems constantly intent on waking himself out of the dream in order to spare himself reality's disappointments and keep himself alert to its dangers. At the same time, nonetheless, he holds out a hope that his dream might redeem that reality. Such a hope leads to a sense of personal, not just historical, failure, evidenced in his images for the real and the ideal. If he is capable of apprehending beauty, then being chained to *himself* ought not keep him from it; likewise, if the beauties of the South are "so close to [him]," why can't he touch them? In fact, they are "so close [...] *that* he cannot reach them," suggesting again his particular failure. Even worse, unlike his counterparts in part 2, it is *real* beauty Kabnis can't grasp—not imagined beauty. Kabnis "returns" to the South, where real beauty still exists, but he can't reach it because it inheres in a world of overwhelming ugliness. This marks a significant change from part 2, where poet-sons can only imagine beauty in a world bereft of it: "Avey"'s narrator in his songs and poems, the "Beehive" speaker in his pastoral fantasy, John in his daydream, Dan in his messianic delusions. These Northern prophets blame forces outside themselves for their failure to realize their visions, whether industrialization, materialism, middle-class mores, or the women who embody these evils. Though Kabnis realizes the larger forces that prevent him from attaining and articulating beauty, he nevertheless consistently depicts the failure to transcend those forces as his own weakness.

But Kabnis's "failing" is the failure of poetry itself in a world immune to lyrical transformation, and his poetic gift is a weakness precisely because it leaves him vulnerable to a fleeting beauty that cannot be recuperated in song. In part 1 of *Cane* the poet is the prophet, as lyric expresses truth and translates it to myth; in part 2 the poet yearns to be the prophet, but lyric exposes a truth that cannot be transmuted; in part 3 the poet has become an object of ridicule to himself and to others, and there is no place for poets or poetry. His lyricism and vision only render him acutely sensitive to the noise and violence of the South.[2]

Thus, Kabnis must curb the lyrical impulse in himself even as he recognizes it in the South. For lyric is part of what makes the nighttime Southern landscape, "heaving with folk-songs," beautiful. It is notable that Kabnis is struck "dumb" by the scenery, the familiar trope of awe suggesting something ominously more than wonderment in a story about the loss of poetic language. Kabnis rouses himself from the mute spell with the antilyrical, cacophonous grunts and groans that will characterize part 3's prose and forces himself to look at all the ugliness, which *is* in reach: "There is a radiant beauty in the night that touches and . . . tortures me. Ugh. Hell. Get up, you damn fool. Look around you. Whats beautiful here? Hog pens and chicken yards. Dirty red mud. Stinking outhouses. Whats beauty anyway but ugliness if it hurts you?" (85). *What's beauty anyway but ugliness if it hurts you* would make an appropriate epigraph for "Kabnis" and indeed for all of *Cane.* In a world where white people scorn and violate African Americans and where African Americans are taught to hate themselves, observing beauty, however rare it is to find, can only lead to disappointment, or worse, to violence. Thus, for instance, when Kabnis stops to admire the moonlight on the courthouse tower, he inevitably sees a horror: "[The courthouse] is dull silver in the moonlight. White child that sleeps upon the top of pines. Kabnis' mind clears. He sees himself yanked beneath that tower" (85). The courthouse bathed in moonlight ought to be doubly beautiful—both as an object in itself and as a representation of Justice; but these ideals must be "cleared" away to make way for the real thing that white Southern courthouses signify: injustice, whose most fanatical form is lynching.

Understandably, Kabnis views his own capacity to apprehend beauty as a weakness, a fragile face set "uncertainly" upon the "bull-necked" body of the world (83). This paradox of beauty and ugliness, dream and reality is precisely what Kabnis wishes he could articulate in poetry but can't: "God, if I could develop that in words. [. . .] If I could feel that I came to the South to face it. If I, the dream (not what is weak and afraid in me) could become the face of the South. How my lips would sing for it, my songs being the lips of the soul" (83–84). If he could face the ugliness of the South and by doing so transform it into the beauty he senses there, then he would be able to compose songs that express the paradoxical soul of the South. But Kabnis doesn't believe in souls ("Soul. Soul hell. There aint no such thing" [84]), and the plaintive song of the South that so moved Toomer during his visit to Georgia is heard by Kabnis as "shouting"—suggesting again that he cannot extricate beauty and ugliness. Even the physical description of Kabnis on the first page of the story reveals that his lips will never be the lips of the South's soul: "Kabnis' thin hair is streaked on the pillow. His hand strokes the slim silk of his mustache. His thumb, pressed under his chin, seems to be trying to give squareness and projection to it. Brown eyes stare from a lemon face" (83). In *Cane*'s iconography of race, Kabnis's straight, thin hair, weak chin, and light complexion signify that he must also have thin lips. The chorus of the cane cannot be carried on by a body that manifests the loss of connection to the African past.

How far *Cane* has come from its mission to preserve the voices of the past in the voice of its own poetry. If Kabnis is the culmination of all the other poet-sons in the book and if part 3 offers to reconcile parts 1 and 2 by bringing a Northern black man to the South to discover his roots there, then *Cane* seems to acknowledge here at the end that it cannot accomplish what it set out to do. Both the "Song of the Son" speaker and Toomer himself describe the project of *Cane* as a song—"An everlasting song, a singing tree" (14), " 'Cane' was a swan-song. It was a song of an end" (*Wayward* 123)—yet Kabnis will insist that song has degenerated to shouting and that poetry is no longer possible. In fact, what remnant of song persists in part 3 is not merely ineffective or dissonant; it is consistently associated with violence, especially with the lynching fire. For instance, while Kabnis's friends recount stories of lynching to him, singing and shouting accompany their tales like a Greek chorus (90–93). Throughout the story, the wind sings a lynching song: "White-man's land. / Niggers, sing. / Burn, bear black children / Till poor rivers bring / Rest, and sweet glory / In Camp Ground" (83, 87, 105). Further, song is imagined as lynching—"Her song is a spark that travels swiftly to nearby cabins. Like purple tallow flames, songs jet up" (98); and lynching as song—"Their [the imagined lynchers'] clammy hands were like the love of death playing up and down my spine" (93).

Understandably, then, though Kabnis longs to be the singer of the South at the outset of his story, by the end he repudiates poetry and declares that he is an orator not a poet: "I was born and bred in a family of orators, thats what I was" (111). He takes pains to distinguish oration from other genres:

I said orators. O R A T O R S. Born one an I'll die one. [. . .] I've been shapin words after a design that branded here. Know whats here? M soul. Ever heard o that? Th hell y have. Been shapin words t fit m soul. Never told y that before, did I? Thought I couldnt talk.

I'll tell y. I've been shapin words; ah, but sometimes theyre beautiful an golden an have a taste that makes them fine t roll over with
y tongue. (111)

Though I am drawing a distinction between Kabnis's original poetic vo-
cation and his claim to be an orator here, he is distinguishing between
preachers—whom he terms "wind-busters"—and orators.[3] Still, preachers, like poets, who are also associated with the wind in "Kabnis" and
elsewhere in *Cane*, are blowhards, talking about things that have no substance, fashioning lies out of thin air. Orators, in contrast, shape solid
truths from language as wheelwrights "[chop] things from blocks of
wood" (111). He admits that some of these words have a golden taste,
like honey—but part 2 has already demonstrated how quickly honey
turns bitter in *Cane*. Thus, he relinquishes beautiful language in favor
of rough-hewn words that express the bull-necked world he lives in:

Those words I was tellin y about, they wont fit int th mold thats
branded on m soul. Rhyme, y see? Poet, too. Bad rhyme. Bad poet.
[. . .] Ugh. Th form thats burned int my soul is some twisted
awful thing that crept in from a dream, a godam nightmare, an
wont stay still unless I feed it. An it lives on words. Not beautiful words. God Almighty no. Misshapen, split-gut, tortured, twisted
words. (111)

That those abandoned beautiful words are poetry seems likely, especially
given his explicit rejection of poetry in this second part of his oration.
Hearing the assonance of "mold" and "soul," he draws attention to the
off rhyme as proof that he could write poetry—but only bad poetry. If
he's a poet, he's a poet of dissonance, one who feeds the ugliness in himself with ugly words, as these passages with their grunts, gutturals, and
dialect distortions testify.[4] Part 1 teaches us that poetry is the source of
ancient truths, that ancestral voices echo in the songs of their sons, that
the beauty of the past adheres in traditional poetic forms. When Kabnis
renounces the notion that African American life is beautiful, he must
also deny his own lyric impulses. He spells out the word "orators" as
though chiseling each letter from a resisting block. O R A T O R S becomes a word that will never rise into song.

The form that's branded on his soul is modeled on reality rather than on myth and derives from the tale of Mame Lamkins and her baby, one of the lynching stories Halsey and Layman tell Kabnis to dispel his belief that the South is "not half the terror [Northerners] picture it" (89). As Rudolph P. Byrd asserts, "[t]he twisted awful thing" is "history" (24) and thus the "form" of part 3 must be prose rather than poetry, the form associated with fact. Lynching, not lyric, shapes Kabnis's soul, and it requires ugly words: "Misshapen, split-gut, tortured, twisted words" that conform to historical reality.

And yet song accompanies the story of Mame Lamkins, not lovely folk songs now but church singing that has escalated, "almost perfectly attuned to the nervous key of Kabnis" (92), to shouting. As the preacher's voice "rises to a crescendo note" and "[t]he sister begins to shout," Kabnis asks to hear the story of Mame Lamkins, which he thinks "can be no worse than the shouting," correlating song and lynching as opposed to part 1's correlation between song and salvation. Layman, a sometimes preacher whose name registers one more doubt about religion in *Cane*, gives this account:

> She was in th family-way, Mame Lamkins was. They killed her in th street, and some white man seein th risin in her stomach as she lay there soppy in her blood like any cow, took an ripped her belly open, an th kid fell out. It was living; but a nigger baby aint supposed t live. So he jabbed his knife in it an stuck it t a tree. (92)[5]

Obviously, the child that "fell out" of Mame's belly is akin to the one who "fell out of [Karintha's] womb" and to all the other aborted images of renewal in *Cane*: the ruined infants like Karintha's child or Esther's "pink meshbag filled with baby toes"; the doomed conjunction of death and life in the phrase "[b]urn, bear black children" (83, 105); the ravaged beauty of "Face," "Portrait in Georgia," and Carrie K.;[6] the disappointed aspirations of Esther, Tom, John, Dan, Paul, and so many others; and the miscarriage of hopeful imagery in "Seventh Street," "Beehive," "Storm Ending," "Her Lips are Copper Wire," and numerous other places. Most crucially, as we shall see, the specter of aborted birth will vex the last lines of the book.

Misshapen, split-gut, twisted, tortured: Kabnis's ugly words articulate violation and atrocious violence, the deformation of beauty, the destruction of promise, and the negation of renewal. The image of Mame's baby, split from her gut and impaled on the tree, is a terrible conflation of Christ's nativity and crucifixion, the infant crucified before his birth and thus before he can become a spiritual leader and redeemer.[7] Here is the emblem of defeated aspirations in *Cane*, the explanation for why so many would-be messiahs fail: racism destroys them before they even begin.[8] It destroys through blatantly violent acts like lynching. However, it also operates through internal mechanisms like fear and self-hatred. Kabnis explicitly links the form that's branded on his soul with these various forms of racism in America in his outburst during the party in the shop the night before Lewis leaves the South:

> Layman was feedin it back there that day you thought I ran out fearin things. White folks feed it cause their looks are words. Niggers, black niggers feed it cause theyre evil and their looks are words. Yallar niggers feed it. This whole damn bloated purple country feeds it cause its goin down t hell in a holy avalanche of words. (111)

Both whites and blacks are implicated in the country's downfall because racism corrupts everyone. Kabnis's figure for the pervasive power of racism is, crucially, something equally ubiquitous: language. Even evil looks and violent acts are forms of language in Kabnis's vision of America destroyed in a torrent of words. Hence, the form that's burned on Kabnis's soul is itself a figure for language, a branding iron's searing sign, a figure whose literal connotations (the historical branding of slaves like livestock) are as horrific as its metaphorical ones. This equation between language and evil must spell the end of poetry since poetry in *Cane* is the medium of truth and beauty.

It is notable that Father John's "oration" the next day even more literally identifies language as the crux of racism. Uttering only "death" and "sin" until the last paragraphs of the story, he finally delivers a full thought when Carrie K. offers to listen to him despite Kabnis's objections: "Th sin whats fixed [...] upon th white folks [...]—f tellin Jesus—lies. O th sin th white folks 'mitted when they made th Bible lie" (117). "Fixed" again hints at branding (and impaling), and what Father John has waited so long to say is that white people are marked with the sin of corrupting the Word of God. Their interpretation of the Bible perverted God's word in a justification of slavery.[9] Though Kabnis dismisses

Father John's speech as old news, calling him an "old black fakir" (117, punning on "faker," another instance of the susceptibility of language to distortion), Father John's accusation is of a piece with his own. Both point to the abuse of language as a constituent feature of racism. For Kabnis, who claims to come from a long line of orators, corrupted language is at once a reflection of and a response to a corrupted world. He will not be the poet-son who returns to take up the soft carol (14) of his ancestors but the orator-son who spews forth the ugliness and viciousness of their lynchers, ironically contributing to the torrent of verbal abuse that has silenced the singers and threatens to destroy the country. In fashioning the image of his words after the murdered baby, then, Kabnis at once figures forth the lynching of African American promise and the related destruction of language.[10]

The ramifications of corrupted language are best observed in the ongoing tension in *Cane* between poetry and prose. In part 1, we may recall, the meaning of Karintha as a "November cotton flower" shuttles between its ominous overtones in the prose story and its positive connotations in the sonnet. Similarly, Kabnis's picture of America as a rotting corpse, bloated and purple, recalls the bursting, purple plum in "Song of the Son." There it was an ambivalent figure of generation; here, it unequivocally portrays America as a land of death rather than birth, decay rather than renewal. The difference between the poem's hopeful if precarious imagery of slave culture coming to fruition in its descendants—

O Negro slaves, dark purple ripened plums,
Squeezed, and bursting in the pine-wood air,
Passing, before they stripped the old tree bare
One plum was saved for me, one seed becomes

An everlasting song, a singing tree [. . .] (14)

—and Kabnis's utterly hopeless portrayal of America as a bloated, purple corpse is the difference between poetry and prose in *Cane*. As we have seen, the lyric poetry in the book is capable of discovering fragile beauty in bull-necked reality. But Kabnis cannot lyricize life; in rejecting poetry and resisting beauty, he has forfeited the formal resources of lyric, especially the musicality of rhythm and rhyme that can establish an aural connection to the ancestral past. Constrained by the hideous form that's branded on his soul, the form of racism, violence, and aborted possibility, he cannot ignore the constant threat that racism poses, nor can he transform death into renewal, as the speaker in "Song of the Son" is able to do in poetry.

One reason for the differences in these figures of America is that Kabnis and his counterpart conceive of the past differently. The son in part 1 embraces his ancestors, giving immediacy to his connection to them through apostrophes ("O land and soil," "O soil," "O Negro slaves" 14), acknowledging his relationship to them ("Thy son [. . .] I have returned to thee"), and declaring their continuing vitality ("An everlasting song," "What they were, and what they *are* to me"). All of this is possible because he *hears* them, "[c]aroling softly," the proof that "it is not too late yet" and the means by which he will immortalize them. In contrast, Kabnis does not perceive the souls of slavery as sustaining ancestors but as menacing ghosts. In the first section of part 3, he can't sleep for fear of the spirits of lynched men (86). What they are to him is one more horror: "There must be many dead things moving in silence. They come here to touch me. I swear I feel their fingers . . . " (86). To Kabnis, the slaves "die[d] in silence" and their ghosts move in silence still; hence, he cannot hear the consoling echoes of their songs but only feel the eerie tingle of their touch—which is, of course, his own fear. Indeed, his inability to hear the ancestors is one more indication that he is not a poet. Lacking that sacred aural connection to the past, Kabnis is not sustained but haunted by it and seeks out instead the "mute," "tongue-tied" old slave as a representative of a past that cannot be lyricized (106). Sitting in darkness, spouting ugly words, Father John bodies forth the form that's branded on Kabnis's soul.

And yet even as Kabnis seeks such external corroboration for what he feels inside, he wants to exorcise the twisted form on his soul. His language for this removal is significantly ambiguous, indicating how inextricably he is linked to the culture he abhors: "I want t feed th soul—I know what that is; th preachers dont—but I've got t feed it. I wish t God some lynchin white man ud stick his knife through it an pin it to a tree. An pin it to a tree" (111). It's easy to miss Kabnis's distinction here between the soul, which he wants to feed, and the form that's burned into his soul, which he is forced to feed with ugly words. That is, "soul" is not the antecedent of "it" in these lines. "It" is the awful thing in his soul that he wishes some lyncher would pluck out. He makes this same distinction earlier, and there, too, it is difficult to discern. He says just before this that he is "shapin words after a design that branded [on his soul]" but then that he's been "shapin words t fit m soul [. . .] sometimes theyre beautiful." That is, the words that fit his soul can be beautiful, but those that fit the form that's branded on his soul are entirely ugly. These strained subtleties are precisely the problem, for how can Kabnis finally separate his soul and what's affixed to it? The corruption of the soul is a permanent condition; it cannot be removed without tearing out the soul, too. The repetition of "an pin it to a tree" registers this inseparable doubleness.[11] Indeed, a white lyncher would be the last person to distinguish between a black man's soul and what taints it; and Kabnis's wish reveals that self-destruction is the only way he can imagine to purge the imprint of racism. The necessity of self-destruction is something Kabnis has learned in one of the lynching stories. When Kabnis asks Halsey and Layman "cant something be done" about lynching, Layman responds, "Sho. Yassur. And done first rate as well. Jes like Sam Raymon done it." But what Sam Raymon *did* about lynching was kill himself before the mob could murder him (90). If this is the only antidote to lynching, then it makes sense that Kabnis takes Mame Lamkins's lynched baby as a figure for racism and for himself because he recognizes racism has already shaped him. Having abandoned his hopes to be a poet of golden-tasting words, then, he aspires to become the orator of ugly words. But he fails even at this.

To everyone else in the story, Kabnis is sometimes an idle chatterer, sometimes a blowhard, but never an orator. Though the other characters remark on his garrulousness, they never take his words seriously. For instance, when he explains to Layman and Halsey why he disapproves of the church singers' "shouting," Halsey responds that "[Yankees like Kabnis] always were good at talkin," meaning that he talks too much (91). Later, Halsey compares Kabnis's aspirations to the enterprise of moonshine liquor makers, "th boys what made this stuff have got th art down like I heard you say youd like t be with words" (95), an analogy that equates writing with an ignoble activity and poetry with inebriation. Even worse Kabnis himself suffers in the comparison since, unlike the moonshiners, he hasn't yet produced anything. He is especially ridiculed for talking incessantly to Father John, who is believed to be deaf. Halsey says that Kabnis "blows off t [Father John] every chance he gets" (104) and twice teases that Father John can't talk because "Kabnis wont give him a chance" (106), at which the prostitutes Cora and Stella laugh knowingly. In a comment that suggests Kabnis's verbosity compensates for sexual inadequacy (a chronic condition in *Cane*), Stella says, "it ud be a sin t play with him" because "[h]e takes it out in talk" (109).

At the farewell party for Lewis, Kabnis sports a robe that looks like "a gaudy ball costume" (106) in a self-mocking gesture that characterizes his failed ambition: "Kabnis, with great mock-solemnity, goes to the corner, takes down the robe, and dons it. He is a curious spectacle, acting a part, yet very real" (107), simultaneously in earnest about being a prophet-orator and contemptuous of his own failed ambition. He delivers himself of diatribes easily enough but can't speak effectively when he needs to. A month earlier, on the night that Kabnis is fired from his teaching job, he tries to rouse himself three times to resist Halsey's taking over his fate and turning the aspiring writer into a wheelwright. When Halsey tells Hanby, the school president, to leave Kabnis alone because he is going to take care of Kabnis and teach him the wheelwright's trade, "Kabnis wants to rise and put both Halsey and Hanby in their places. He vaguely knows he must do this, else the power of direction will completely slip from him to those outside" (96), but he doesn't speak. Moments later, Kabnis recognizes that it is Lewis, the reformer from the North, who can help him, but again he fails to speak or act: "Kabnis has a sudden need to rush into the arms of this man. His eyes call, 'Brother.' And then a savage, cynical twist-about within him mocks his impulse and strengthens him to repulse Lewis" (98). In another moment, Kabnis is moved a third time when a woman's voice sparks the whole countryside into "a soft chorus" (98). Kabnis tries to hold on to the song, asking the others urgently if they hear it, too. But they distract him with worries about Lewis being lynched, and Kabnis is finally subdued. The power of direction leaves Kabnis, who becomes passive and childlike; in fact, Halsey bathes him before taking him away: "He bustles and fusses about Kabnis as if he were a child. Kabnis submits wearily. He has no will to resist him" (99). These three moments of self-denial constitute a betrayal tantamount to Peter's denials of Christ. In submitting to Halsey and becoming a wheelwright, in resisting Lewis and abandoning his greater aspirations, in ignoring the song that for once is a *song* and not a shout, Kabnis has denied what's redemptive in himself, the part of himself that dreams of being a spiritual leader.

It is significant that each of these denials involves lynching imagery.

When he allows Halsey to speak to Hanby for him, Kabnis feels "tortured" and "a feverish, quick-passing flare" comes into his eyes. His arms jerk "upward in futile protest" as though he is being hanged (96). When he refuses to ally himself with Lewis, the narrator describes him as "a promise of soil-soaked beauty; uprooted, thinning out. Suspended a few feet above the soil whose touch would resurrect him" (98). The uprooted flower is a predictable enough formulation in *Cane*: Kabnis could realize his promise if only he would take root in the South. Beauty must be "soil-soaked," nourished by the Southern land. However, the rest of the image veers away from this naturalizing logic toward something more sinister. The language becomes pointedly violent: "Suspended a few feet above the soil" is one more image of lynching. The soil might resurrect Christ, the Son of God, but Kabnis knows that if he were lynched, like Mame Lamkins and her baby, he would not return from the dead. Finally, the song Kabnis hears ignites the countryside almost too literally: "Like purple tallow flames, songs jet up. They spread a ruddy haze over the heavens. The haze swings low" (98). The fiery imagery and the echo of "Swing Low, Sweet Chariot"—a song about dying—are more reminders of violence and death.

This imagery, and the history it evokes, explain why Kabnis is so ineffectual. He would like to be a leader and speaker for African American people, but he's terrified, and with good reason. Lewis, the real reformer, is threatened—a note tied to a rock and thrown through a window says, "You northern nigger, its time fer y t leave. Git along now" (92)—and though this warning comes from other black people, it testifies to the level of fear in Sempter. The stories of lynching, and the pervasive atmosphere of racism that they reflect, have made Kabnis as twisted and tortured as the world around him. The "savage, cynical twisting-about within him" that mocks his impulse to embrace Lewis is the same twisted thing that festers in his soul. Such ugliness not only prevents him from being a poet, but it also thwarts him in his role as orator. By the end of the story, Kabnis will drop his last pretense of being an orator, the gaudy robe,[12] and turn to the belated task of repairing wagon wheels in an age of automobiles,[13] a trade for which he's particularly ill suited (102).

Kabnis acknowledges the absurdity of working on wagons with Halsey in language that suggests such a fate is one more kind of lynching: "Great God Almighty, a soul like mine cant pin itself onto a wagon wheel an satisfy itself spinnin round" (115).[14] But what the wheelwright's shop does offer Kabnis is "The Hole," the cellar where the blind and deaf old slave lives: "I got my life down in this scum-hole. The old man an me—" (115). Readers who regard "Kabnis" as a positive ending to *Cane* interpret his identification with Father John here as an indication that Kabnis is confronting and accepting his African American heritage—especially the terrible aspects of the past that he has been distancing himself from throughout the story.[15] However, his identification with the old slave derives from self-hatred, not from a sense of solidarity with the past, and he remains conflicted about Father John to the end. Though he links himself to Father John in this moment of self-loathing, he spends the rest of the scene attempting to distinguish himself from him. His difficulty in doing so is a sign of his failure to establish continuity between the past and present; that is, Kabnis does not see himself in relation to Father John but rather as dangerously conflated with him.

Having asserted his connection with Father John in a moment of despair, then, Kabnis immediately attempts to sever that link by denouncing him in grossly racist terms, terms that inevitably invoke lynching: "You sit there like a black hound spiked to an ivory pedestal" (114). Yet his harangue is deeply self-hating, and he recognizes his similarity to Father John: "Youre dead already. Death. What does it mean t you? To you who died way back there in th 'sixties. What are y throwin it my throat for?" The old slave is defunct since slavery ended in the 1860s, he argues, but his "devilish word" now issues from Kabnis's throat. He wishes the feeling of hell in his soul would come forth and lynch the old man, expelling it from himself and annihilating Father John in one violent exorcism: "You know what hell is cause youve been there. Its a feelin an its ragin in my soul in a way that'll pop out of me an run you through, an scorch y, and burn an rip your soul" (114). But lynching the old slave will hardly eradicate the racist culture's sins against the soul, even sixty years after the Emancipation, nor will it free Kabnis from his bondage to that past. He taunts Father John—"Do y think youre out of slavery? Huh?"—telling him that he dwells in a cellar where they "used t throw th worked-out, no-count slaves," but such invective toward the old man cannot separate Kabnis from him: "Why I can already see you toppled off that stool an stretched out on th floor beside me—not beside me, damn you, by yourself, with th flies buzzin an lickin God knows what they'd find on a dirty, black, foul-breathed mouth like yours" (115). Not only does Kabnis initially picture the two of them dead together, but even when he corrects himself and insists that Father John will be alone, his imagery reveals the inevitable connection between them: Father John's mouth may be literally dirty, black, and foul from age, infirmity, and situation, and even metaphorically filthy because of the wicked things he utters, but this description fits Kabnis with his ugly words at least as well as it fits Father John.

Kabnis again has difficulty keeping himself separate from Father John when he tries to explain to Carrie K. why he castigates the old man. Referring to himself in the third person and using "he" to refer both to himself and to Father John renders his speech ambiguous: "Ralph says things. Doesnt mean to. But Carrie, he doesnt know what he's talkin about. Couldnt know. It was only a preacher's sin they knew in those old days, an that wasnt sin at all" (116). Kabnis calls himself Ralph, as if to distance himself from his own ranting, and then tells Carrie that "he," now abruptly shifting reference to Father John, doesn't know what he's talking about when he says "Sin." The ambiguous pronoun reference registers for a moment that *Ralph* doesn't know what *he's* talking about. This confusion lingers through the rest of Kabnis's speech, undermining his sense of superiority to the past. What the past meant by sin, Kabnis says, is merely the kinds of offenses that preachers warn against, presumably stealing, cheating, lying, adultery, and other standard misdeeds. But the only real sin is "whats done against th soul"—and by this he seems to mean the kinds of things that "rip your soul" rather than offenses of the external world. Racism, of course, is the paramount sin of this sort, and Kabnis considers himself its greatest victim: "Th whole world is a conspiracy t sin, especially in America, an against me. I'm th victim of their sin." In an effort to distinguish himself from the old man once more, to prove he's more an embodiment of sin than Father John is, he urges, "I'm what sin is. Does he look like me? Have you ever heard him say th things youve heard me say? He couldnt if he had th Holy Ghost t help him" (116). These are strange boasts, indeed, coming from a young Northerner who never experienced slavery, an uninspired orator who spends his breath denouncing an old slave. Far from discovering, like the son in part 1, "what they were and what they *are* to me," Kabnis "returns" to the South to discover a history that makes him feel completely isolated and victimized. Like the town blacks whose threat to Lewis signifies self-hatred and fear, Kabnis can only sputter abuse at a past that horrifies and threatens him—precisely because he cannot finally separate himself from it. But his identification with Father John is not a sustaining connection, as his references to victimization, dying, and lynching attest.

Significantly, then, Kabnis's relation to the past is consistently figured not as continuity but as regression. Thus, his failure to reconcile past and present as a race leader is signaled here at the end, as it has been throughout, as infantile regression. When he tries to ridicule Father John once more after the old man speaks, Carrie interrupts him and "draw[s] the fever out" of him with her cool hands (117). As Lewis predicted, Carrie will nurture Kabnis, and her mothering will offer a welcome relief from himself even as—or precisely because—it stifles him: "Carrie presses his face tenderly against her. The suffocation of her fresh starched dress feels good to him" (117). The starched dress recalls all the women in *Cane* who have been criticized by the male narrators for their submission to white middle-class mores, and "suffocation" hardly needs glossing. Carrie mothering Kabnis is only the final image among many of Kabnis's regression to an almost infantile passivity. As we have already seen, Halsey bathes him to sober him up "as if he were a child" (99), and Lewis envisions Carrie K. taking care of Kabnis: "He wonders what Kabnis could do for her. What could she do for him? Mother him" (104).

Kabnis regresses not merely to his own past, of course, but to the cultural past, which he has not been able to renew. He "ascends" from The Hole, the symbolic repressed past of slavery, to the more recent past of wagons and wheelwrights, of African Americans frightened into silence and submission by numerous forms of white racism. The son has come to the South in time to hear the last echoes of the souls of slavery, here literalized in Father John, but he has found those echoes to be torturous and hideous. Unable to carry forth the past in song, because he is unable to isolate its beauty from the surrounding ugliness without lyric, he submits to the past and falls silent there. Silence and dejection characterize Kabnis at the end of the story:

Kabnis rises and is going doggedly towards the steps. Carrie notices his robe. She catches up to him, points to it, and helps him take it off. He hangs it, with an exaggerated ceremony, on its nail in the corner. He looks down on the tousled beds. His lips curl bitterly. Turning, he stumbles over the bucket of dead coals. He savagely jerks it from the floor. And then, seeing Carrie's eyes upon him, he swings the pail carelessly and with eyes downcast and swollen, trudges upstairs to the work-shop. (117)

Though this scene still registers Kabnis's discontent with Halsey's and Carrie's way of life,[16] his petulance only increases the overwhelming sense of defeat. Kabnis goes "doggedly" to work in the shop, a beaten man. Even the parodic vestige of his greater aspirations, the robe, must be removed and hung, suggestively, on a nail.[17]

One other detail of Kabnis's exit is critical. It is worth pausing to consider his revulsion when he looks at the tousled beds since so many of the Kabnis figures in *Cane* link sexual and verbal prowess in their fantasies. The narrators of "Fern" and "Avey," the speakers of "Georgia Dusk" and "Her Lips Are Copper Wire," and loquacious lovers like Dan Moore and Paul all equate verbal communication with sexual intimacy, artistic creation with procreation, and yet all fail at both. An even more thoroughly isolated and unregenerative lover than these characters, Kabnis is in bed masturbating when the story opens: "He slides down beneath the cover, seeking release" (83).[18] His first speech is a monologue of sexual fantasy as he murmurs to an imaginary lover: "Near me. Now. Whoever you are, my warm glowing sweetheart, do not think that the face that rests beside you is the real Kabnis" (83). Ironically, he assures an imaginary woman that the real "Ralph Kabnis is a dream," not the abject man who lies beside her in bed. His convoluted sense of unreality and inadequacy, emblematized in his autoerotic fantasy, is immediately associated with verbal impotence: "God, if I could develop that in words. Give what I know a bull-neck and a heaving body, all would go well with me, wouldnt it, sweetheart?"[19] In "Kabnis," as in the rest of *Cane*, sex is associated with impotent delusions of grandeur (think of Esther, the narrators of "Fern" and "Avey," John, Dan, and Paul) or with violence ("Karintha," "Carma," "Portrait in Georgia," "Blood-Burning Moon," "Storm Ending," "Her Lips Are Copper Wire," and the implication of rape in "Box Seat") because African American dreams and desires are so frequently met with violence, as in "Blood-Burning Moon." The impotent figures in *Cane*, Kabnis most of all, are men who know instinctively that their dreams and desires can get them lynched. Thus, dreams turn inward, festering in fantasies but never realized in actuality. *Cane*'s image of the black messiah, much like Esther's fantasy of King Barlo, is a virile and eloquent man—one of Toomer's stereotypical images. But such a figure is never realized in the book. Kabnis scowls when he looks at the rumpled beds because he sees the wreck of his own sexual and artistic ideals there. This is what he's come to: spending himself on prostitutes in the back cellar of a wheelwright's shop. It is extremely ironic that "Kabnis" concludes with a sunrise figured as the birth of a "[g]old-glowing child," for how could such a child be imaginatively conceived? Certainly not in the fantasy of Kabnis and his illusory "warm glowing sweetheart," not in the midnight encounter of Kabnis and Cora (which we are led to understand is all talk), and not in final alliance of the virginal, sexually repressed Carrie and the ancient Father John. These are safe but sterile pairings.

Significantly, as Kabnis turns away from his vision of failure, he stumbles over a bucket of dead coals, a defeating enough image in its own right. Scruggs and VanDemarr regard it as a sign that "[t]he poet's light has gone out [. . .]" (206), but it is also a bitter allusion to Booker T. Washington's famous bucket: the dictum "Cast down your bucket where you are" was the keynote of Washington's Atlanta Exposition address, in which he enjoined African Americans to remain in the South, accommodate whites, and aspire to physical rather than intellectual labor.[20] His rationale was that "[i]t is at the bottom of life we must begin, and not at the top" (100). In becoming a wheelwright, Kabnis "begins," in Washington's terms, at the bottom of life, not at the top—though, of course, this is the ending, not the beginning, for Kabnis, and the dead coals represent his own burned-out hopes and passions.[21] Still, it pains him to accept this fate, and he takes the bucket up with a savage jerk. Carrie pacifies him with a glance, like a mother subduing her child, and he continues on his way, "downcast" and "trudg[ing]." This is the last we see of Kabnis in the story, and it is a vision of utter defeat.

If we recall for a moment Mertis Newbolt turning the pages of her Bible in search of a text that articulates her shifting moods, we will note that "Kabnis" fails to embody Christ's Sermon on the Mount, the third part of the Bible that Mertis reads. Part 1 of Cane seemed written in the spirit of the Song of Solomon and part 2 in the spirit of Leviticus, yet part 3 appears sadly unrelated to the hopeful, forgiving Sermon on the Mount. Still, it was Kabnis's dream to be a savior, speaking eloquently to his people, leading them to redemption with assurances that the poor, the suffering, the meek, the innocent would be rewarded. But Christ's focus on prophets who "are persecuted for righteousness' sake" ("Natalie

Mann" in *Wayward* 272) suggests why Kabnis abandons his mission. Though Kabnis would like to be the savior on the mount, thronged by his faithful followers, the persecution of prophets is precisely the thing that prevents him from fulfilling this role. The Sermon on the Mount may offer a powerful vision of forgiveness and eternal reward, but even Christ acknowledges that the prophet will be reviled and persecuted before he attains the kingdom of heaven. If even the Son of God fears lynching, as Christ clearly does, then how can Kabnis, a mere mortal who doesn't believe in heaven, face such a fate?[22] With reason, he turns his back on all of his dreams and submits to being one of the meek who must still await the coming of the savior.

But Kabnis's finale is not the end of the story, much less the end of *Cane.* A lyric strain, like the one that assumed control over Karintha's tale when it got too grim and Carma's before it turned tragic, emerges in the final paragraphs of "Kabnis" and restores *Cane*'s optimism—or attempts to. Readers have debated whether the sunrise at the end of the book constitutes a "promise song":[23]

> Light streaks through the iron-barred cellar window. Within its soft circle, the figures of Carrie and Father John.
>
> Outside, the sun arises from its cradle in the tree-tops of the forest. Shadows of pine are dreams the sun shakes from its eyes. The sun arises. Gold-glowing child, it steps into the sky and sends a birth-song slanting down gray dust streets and sleepy windows of the southern town. (117)

Negative imagery, "iron-barred," "cellar," "slanting down," "gray," "dust," and "sleepy," vies with positive imagery, "Light," sun rise, "Gold-glowing child," and "birth-song," in this final vision of dawn. This is the first sunrise in a book of countless sunsets, and the figure of the sun as a gold-glowing child seems redemptive compared to the cold, white moon baby who has dominated the story until now.[24] As the golden child, heir to the souls of slavery, ascends into the sky, he promises to displace the white one who had been figuratively suckling at the breast of African America from the beginning of the story:

> rock-a-by baby . .
> Black mother sways, holding a white child to her bosom.

when the bough bends . .
Her breath hums through pine-cones.
cradle will fall . .
Teat moon-children at your breasts,
down will come baby . .
Black mother. (84)

Here, back on the second page of "Kabnis," the familiar nursery rhyme appears interpolated with prose commentary that destroys the rhythm of the lullaby and, consistent with the interruption of poetry throughout *Cane*, exposes the reality behind the idealized image of the black mother in the South: she's forced to nourish a white baby. Yet the nursery rhyme explicitly invoked at the beginning of the story and alluded to again at the conclusion of "Kabnis" ("the sun arises from its cradle *in the treetops*") itself ends with the baby crashing to earth: "When the bough breaks / The cradle will fall; / And down will come baby, / Cradle and all." At the beginning of the story the song hints that the white baby will be overthrown by the black mother—not only because we know the baby will fall but because the prose lines hint that the wind in the boughs is the black mother's breath and that she is calmly biding her time until the bough breaks; in contrast to the white baby, the African American child escapes the fall from the treetops. Instead, the black child "arises" and "steps into the sky" (117). If the dark night of African American history has been dominated by whites—the cold, white moon suckling in the black sky—then the ascension of the gold-glowing child marks a new dawn for African Americans. This is the "son"-rise the book has been yearning for, and it seems to come, like the "Song of the Son" speaker, just in the nick of time—in the closing sentence of *Cane*. But how is the sun's ascent different from Kabnis's "ascent" to the shop? The allusion to the ominous nursery rhyme disturbs the hopeful conclusion, and the incessant diction of descent ("slanting," "down," "gray," "dust," "sleepy," and, in this context, "southern") encumbers the symbolic sunrise. *Cane*'s last flourish, "the end" in small capitals centered on the page directly beneath the sunrise, adds one more irony to a hopelessly inconclusive conclusion.

Yet the ending of "Kabnis" is less perplexing in its ambiguity than in its lyricism. This is a voice we've heard elsewhere in "Kabnis," both in the lyrical texture of the prose, as in these last paragraphs, and in snippets of poetry that punctuate the prose text. Kabnis may have abandoned his dream of singing for the South, but other voices in the story persist in striving to carry song along. Indeed, in a sense, "Kabnis" opens with poetry. Ralph Kabnis is trying to read himself to sleep in the first sentence of the story (a suggestively cynical use of literature for a writer), but "[n]ight winds in Georgia are vagrant poets whispering," and he is stirred by their poetry:[25]

White-man's land.
Niggers, sing.
Burn, bear black children
Till poor rivers bring
Rest, and sweet glory
In Camp Ground. (83)

However, this first specimen of lyric reveals that poetry will suffer the formal and conceptual dissonance typical of poetry in part 2. Vestiges of "Deep River" and like spirituals about crossing over the river Jordan to heaven echo only faintly amid lines that twist the hopeful spiritual into a bleak work song: whites own the world, while blacks fill it with song; whites burn African Americans, while blacks bear more children to be burned. This follows a familiar pattern in work songs, contrasting a line about white privilege with a line about the exploitation of blacks, a pattern of disappointment and defeat that spirituals can transcend with recourse to a just God and a compensating afterlife.[26] Contributing to the corruption of the spiritual, the third line here concentrates the dynamic between sex and violence that is so prevalent in *Cane* until sex becomes violence. "Burn" simultaneously connotes sexual fervor, especially the volatile desire of whites like Bob Stone for women like Louisa, and the consequences of such desire for black men like Tom Burwell; sexual "burning" leads to both literal burning and to "bearing" black children, who themselves will burn—under a sawdust pile because their mothers have to abandon them or in a lynching pyre because they have overstepped the racist boundaries or, like Kabnis, they will smolder inwardly with unrealized dreams. No wonder the wind's song unsettles Kabnis

(83); part 3 invariably associates song with violence and death, and each fragment of song bears the marks of this burden.

For instance, the "White man's land" fragment appears three times in the story, each time introducing the uneasiness that Kabnis experiences when he first hears the song. The vagrant wind poets consistently disturb the nighttime peace. At the beginning of section 1, as we have seen, they keep him awake "against his will" (83), and at the end of that section, they sing while he sleeps, insinuating that there will be no real rest until death (87). The third recitation of this song is introduced by a highly lyrical narrative voice that emerges at key moments throughout the story. Opening section 5, this lyric strain attempts to set the scene for nighttime renewal through imagery of sex and childbirth:

> Night, soft belly of a pregnant Negress, throbs evenly against the torso of the South. Night throbs a womb-song to the South. Cane- and cotton-fields, pine forests, cypress swamps, sawmills, and factories are fecund at her touch. Night's womb-song sets them singing. Night winds are the breathing of the unborn child whose calm throbbing in the belly of a Negress sets them somnolently singing. Hear the song. (105)

The imagery offers a vision of the night sky as a pregnant black woman lying against her lover, the land of the South. The throbbing of the baby in her womb—that is, the sun hidden in the darkness of the night—is a procreant rhythm that renews not only the idealized cane fields but also forests and swamps. Cotton and trees flourish, eventually filling factories and mills with harvested crops. The whole countryside sings in its sleep, and we are challenged to listen to its song. But the song that follows this injunction is the stanza of "White-man's land," which, as we know, offers quite a different picture of the South from the one the lyrical prose has been painting. How are we to reconcile the optimistic invocation with the gloomy song? The point is precisely that we can't.[27]

The lyrical strain in the prose is articulating just the sort of romantic view of the South that has been associated with lyric from the first page of Cane. We have seen lyric lose its power over the course of the book, adroitly negotiating reality and myth in part 1, faltering in the face of unrelenting reality in part 2, and all but extinguished in part 3. Both "Kabnis," the short story that includes no poems, and Kabnis, the man who is committed to antipoetical ugly words, announce the death of poetry. Hence, the fragments of song in "Kabnis" can only embody the necessity of ugly words. The corrupted stanzas from "Deep River" and "Rock-A-Bye, Baby," as we have seen, regard ugly words like "sin" and "death." Similarly, the refrain from "My Lord, What a Morning," turns hope into despair. As Halsey realizes that Kabnis has bolted from his house in fear of being lynched, the choir sings "My Lord, what a mourning, / My Lord, what a mourning, / My Lord, what a mourning, / When the stars begin to fall" (93). In a song about Judgment Day, "morning" becomes "mourning" to an unredeemed world.

By the time we have reached part 3 of *Cane*, lyric is no longer an idealized form. The fragments of song that remain know their place, formally and thematically embodying dissolution. Prose, the genre of oration and ugly words, assumes the role of oracle once fulfilled by poetry. For example, the prose that follows "White man's land" affirms Kabnis's sense that everything is marked by racism. The streets of Sempter seem lined with lynched bodies: odd bits of rope "dangle" and "four figures sway beneath iron awnings" (105). These are not in fact corpses but living men, who are on their way to Halsey's shop for the party, yet the language reveals the potential for violence everywhere. The prose and the bits of song both register the atmosphere of racial violence; however, the lyric strain that erupts in the prose—and that we can distinguish from the normative prose in "Kabnis"—persists in romanticizing the South. In the context of the rest of the story, and the rest of *Cane*, its poetical account of the countryside is absurd. The tale of Mame Lamkins cries out against the glorification of the "pregnant Negress." Similarly, the notion that sawmills and factories are "fecund" strains the metaphor of the sun revivifying the natural world. Indeed, sawmills and factories are where cane, cotton, and pine wood are taken after they have been killed, as the many "wraiths" of smoke coming from sawdust piles, chimneys, and factory stacks throughout the book attest (4, 8, 15, 36, 41, 84, 93). The "*breathing* of the *unborn* child" is one more incongruous detail that hints, like "Rhobert," at gasping for breath in a suffocating environment. That the lyric strain seems unwilling to recognize the corruption of the actual song, that it describes a world that neither the song nor the prose observes, demonstrates why this impulse must be rejected: even when it's beautiful, it's ugly. Black women's ravaged beauty, black men's unfulfilled dreams, the past of slavery, the present of factories, cities, electricity—poetry can make any of this *sound* good, as we have observed in "Karintha," "November Cotton Flower," "Song of the Sun," "Carma," "Avey," "Seventh Street," "Her Lips Are Copper Wire," and "Bona and Paul." But if the cadences of lyric do not ring true, as they increasingly do not, the book argues, then lyric is no longer a viable form. To ignore the dangers of a racist world because it can be idealized in poetry is to risk becoming a victim of that world. What's beauty anyway but ugliness if it hurts you?

Thus, the aesthetic and romantic ideals associated with lyric at the beginning of the book no longer adhere in the snippets of song in "Kabnis"; however, a maverick lyric strain that erupts in the prose refuses to abandon those ideals. This is a lyricism estranged from formal poetry and its ritual invocation of the past, a lyricism that turns away from reality but cannot make a connection with a mythic alternative precisely because it is bereft of the lyric forms that embodied "the mighty voices of the past" (*Selected Essays* 4). Such a turning constitutes the sort of "impotent nostalgia" that grips Kabnis in a moment when he misses his life in New York (86). Ironically, he eases his homesickness for the North by indulging an even deeper nostalgia: "He forces himself to narrow [his thoughts] to a cabin silhouetted on a knoll about a mile away. Peace. Negroes within it are content. They farm. They sing. They love" (86). Land, song, and sex: here are the constituents of the pastoral doctrine, which Kabnis yearns to believe in even though nothing in his experience supports it. Kabnis, of course, will abandon such illusions by the time he gives his oration at Halsey's party. But these are just the illusions that the lyric strain cannot relinquish.

Predictably, too, the renegade lyric voice emerges at moments of aborted contact with the ancestral past, typically accompanied by the telltale ellipses that signal the irreparable breach between myth and reality. Similarly, the compulsive apostrophes we hear at these moments betray the effort to invoke an unanswering golden age. In addition to the paean to night at the beginning of section 5 and to dawn at the end of the story, this effort can be heard when Kabnis hears the woman singing, when Lewis christens Father John, again when he recognizes Father John as his ancestor, and when the prostitutes, Stella and Cora, prepare to leave the morning after the party—all moments that the lyricism wants to prolong and mythologize. Hearing them en masse demonstrates how strangely formulaic this strain is:

Her song is a spark that travels swiftly to near-by cabins. Like purple tallow flames, songs jet up. They spread a ruddy haze over the heavens. The haze swings low. Now the whole countryside is a soft chorus. Lord. O Lord . . . (98)

Slave boy whom some Christian mistress taught to read the Bible. Black man who saw Jesus in the ricefields, and began preaching to his people. Moses- and Christ-words used for songs. Dead blind father of a muted folk who feel their way upward to a life that crushes or absorbs them. (Speak, Father!) Suppose your eyes could see, old man. (The years hold hands. O Sing!) Suppose your lips . . . (106)

Lewis, seated now so that his eyes rest upon the old man, merges with his source and lets the pain and beauty of the South meet him there. White faces, pain-pollen, settle downward through a cane-sweet mist and touch the ovaries of yellow flowers. Cotton-bolls bloom, droop. Black roots twist in a parched red soil beneath a blazing sky. Magnolias, fragrant, a trifle futile, lovely far off . . . His eyelids close. A force begins to heave and rise . . . (107)

As they kneel there, heavy-eyed and dusky, and throwing grotesque moving shadows on the wall, they are two princesses in Africa going through the early-morning ablutions of their pagan prayers. Finished, they come forward, stretch their hands and warm them over the glowing coals. Red dusk of a Georgia sunset, their heavy, coal-lit faces . . . (113)

All of the ellipses in these passages are Toomer's. It is significant that each eruption of the lyric strain trails off into an ellipsis, after which the more realistic prose voice resumes, creating a striking contrast between the narrative norm and these moments of rapture. Readers have commonly read Toomer's ellipses as a form of modernist rupture, not romantic rapture, associating them with the energy and innovation of a new poetics, a modernist, jazz poetics.[28] But only in "Seventh Street," where the elliptical breaks are literalized as an ax cutting through convention, can such an argument be considered, and it is telling that everyone who argues for the disruptive form of *Cane* cites "Seventh Street" (and usually only "Seventh Street") as evidence. Yet even there, the literalness

of the device, the blunt correspondence between "Split it! In two!" and
" . . ," undermines its disruptive potential. The ellipsis is more redun-
dant than disruptive. In every other instance in the book, and there are
many, the opening ellipsis signals the intrusion of nostalgia—whether
pastoral idyll, romantic fantasy, or spiritual yearning—and, as in the passages above, the closing ellipsis signals the petering out of such illusions. Consequently, songs, sunsets, rice-fields, cane, cotton-bolls, soil,
the South, and even Africa comprise these lyrical moments—not jazz,
not modernity, and certainly not a vision of renewal.

Nevertheless, the lyric strain holds sway at the end of "Kabnis," insisting on a different story from the one Kabnis or the conventional narrative would tell, a tale of harmony between the past and the present,
represented in the tableau of Father John and Carrie K., and between
blacks and whites, figured in the gold-glowing child; a tale of resolution
and renewal. Indeed, many readers embrace just such an ending, attest-
ing to the tremendous appeal of the lyrical strain.[29] But this is a "birth-
song" we should regard with suspicion just as Cane has come to regard
all lyric with suspicion.

The ending of "Kabnis," and thus of Cane, is not simply the surrender
of the son to his past (whether one considers this a positive or negative outcome for Kabnis) and not simply the dawn (of a new or of just
another day). These thematic quandaries rest on a formal dispute about
the status of lyric in Cane. Can a lyricism committed to the past but
lacking past forms constitute the "everlasting song" that will preserve the
continuity of past and present? The structure of Cane argues that it cannot. The absence of poetry as a distinctive form in part 3 of the book
completes the process of degeneration suffered by lyric in part 2. Though
a residual lyric strain indulges profoundly nostalgic impulses, it speaks
without the authority of past forms and therefore without authority
about the past. Given Cane's investment in lyric as a privileged form, the
absence of poems in part 3 ought to register with readers more ominously than it does. Likewise, given Kabnis's explicit denunciation of poetry, the lyric strain at the end of the story ought to generate more skepticism than it does. Yet so persuasive is this lyricism that even readers
who view Kabnis as a failure hold out hope for the ending of his story
because of the last paragraphs.[30] This is the seductive power of poetry
that Kabnis has been suspicious of all along. This is a language that obscures the realities of African American life and conjures sunrises, circles

of light, newborns, and songs in their place. It is not, of course, that sunrises, births, and songs don't exist for African Americans in the South; it is that those sustaining elements of life are more than matched by sunsets, deaths, and ugly words. The final paragraph's refusal to acknowledge this resounds as the ultimate condemnation of lyric in *Cane*. Poetry itself has been extinguished; the poetic impulse that remains cannot be countenanced because it does not operate in concord with the past.

Toomer's suggestion to Waldo Frank after the manuscript of *Cane* was in the mail that the work really "ends (pauses) in Harvest Song" (*Reader* 26) reveals the magnitude of the book's investment in lyric.[31] In saying that *Cane* "plunges" from the "awakening" of "Bona and Paul" into Kabnis's dark night of the soul, Toomer characterizes "Kabnis" as the spiritual low point in *Cane*'s trajectory; one only "emerges" in "Karintha" and "swings upward" in "Theater" and "Box Seat." Toomer's retrospective outline of the book, that is, does not posit an optimistic ending for "Kabnis." Much as the lyric strain attempts to lure "Kabnis" from tragedy to transcendence, Toomer seems to want to wrest *Cane* from its bleak conclusion in "Kabnis." Where better to end *Cane*, given the book's notion of lyric, than in a poem? Yet Robert B. Jones and others have demonstrated that reading *Cane* in this manner—beginning with "Bona and Paul" and ending with "Harvest Song"—not only confirms the sense of tragedy and failure implicit in "Kabnis" but more explicitly confirms the failure of poetry: "In an extended metaphor of the poet as reaper, ["Harvest Song"] describes the poet's inability to transform the fruits of his labor into art" (*Prison-House* 62).[32] The end of lyric in *Cane* is rightly represented by a poem about the failure of poetry.

But the failure of poetry, like the defeat of Kabnis, should not be interpreted as the failure of *Cane*. Though "Harvest Song" anticipates the end of poetry, and though "Kabnis" bears it out, the loss of poetry is *Cane*'s formal equivalent to the loss of an idealized time and culture. As we well know, Toomer believed that culture "was walking in to die on the modern desert," and thus he wrote *Cane* as "a swan-song [. . .] a song of an end." *Cane* was meant to be a song of death, then, and its most powerful figure for this elegiac mission would be the death of song.[33]

Late Minstrel of the Restless Earth

Poet and Poetry after *Cane*

IF TOOMER'S VISION OF African American modernity in 1922 required the death of lyric, his subsequent understanding of worldwide modernity also necessitated an antilyrical poetry. He continued to equate lyric poetry with the past, especially the African American past, and was suspicious of indulging his lyric impulses. Added to this, he was developing a new aesthetic program that had more affinities with Kabnis's ugly words than with the Son's soft carol. Like Kabnis, Toomer was becoming an O R A T O R, even as he continued to write poems, and he wanted his writing to speak to the modern world, not sing to the past.

When he wrote to *The Liberator* in August of 1922, while still composing *Cane*, Toomer had equated artistic creativity and racial identity:

> Within the last two or three years, [. . .] my growing need for artistic expression has pulled me deeper and deeper into the Negro group. And as my powers of receptivity increased, I found myself loving it in a way that I could never love the other [aspects of his ethnic heritage]. It has stimulated and fertilized whatever creative talent I may contain within me. A visit to Georgia last fall was the starting point of almost everything of worth that I have done. I have heard folk-songs come from the lips of Negro peasants. I saw the rich dusk beauty [. . .]. And a deep part of my nature, a part that I had repressed, sprang suddenly to life and responded to them. (*Reader* 16)

By the time *Cane* appeared in 1923, however, Toomer's art had ceased, and he was questioning his identity: "During the winter of 1923, owing to a complex of causes, my writing stopped; and my disharmony became distressingly prominent. So it became clear that my literary occupations had not worked deep enough to make of me an integrated man" (*Wayward* 128). As is well known, he began a process of self-exploration that led him away from the New York literary world and into the spiritualist realm of George Ivanovich Gurdjieff: "I became a champion of something nonliterary, nonartistic [. . .]" (*Wayward* 129). He never again wrote a book like *Cane* and consequently lost his publishers and readers.[1]

Critics have lamented Toomer's turn away from *Cane*'s lyrical evocation of African American life, noting that his didactic, spiritualist later writings lack both the artistry and the interest of *Cane*: "The lyricism of *Cane*, its seductive prose and verse rhythms, the spectacular union of sense with sound, of meaning with ambiguity, is supplanted by a voice riddled with jargon and platitudes, a voice with discordant features, a voice shouting a thesis" (Byrd 181).[2] But that discordant voice had already emerged in the second and third parts of *Cane*, a fact commentators (and even Toomer himself) have overlooked in comparing the writing in *Cane* to what came after. Regarding *Cane* as a volume of pure lyricism, Toomer claimed he could no longer work in a lyrical mode because he associated it with a way of life that no longer existed. As we recall, "*Cane* was a swan-song. It was a song of an end. And why no one has seen and felt that, why people have expected me to write a second and a third and a fourth book like *Cane*, is one of the queer misunderstandings of my life" (*Wayward* 123). In another autobiographical piece, he identifies "the end" of *Cane*'s way of life as modernity and commits his own efforts to the present, not the past:

> The modern world was uprooted, the modern world was breaking down, but we couldn't go back. [. . .] [S]uch peasantry as America had had—and I sang one of its swan songs in [*Cane*]—was swiftly disappearing, swiftly being industrialized and urbanized by machines, motor cars, phonographs, movies . . "Back to nature," even if desirable, was no longer possible, because industry had taken nature unto itself. [. . .] So then, whether we wished to or not, *we had to go on*. We had to go on and accept the task of creating a *human world* that was at least as conducive to man's well-being and growth as the world of nature was conducive to the growth of plant and animal life. The creation of a human world, this was our task.

Those who sought to cure themselves by a return to more primitive conditions were either romantics or escapists. (*Wayward* 129)

Familiar as these passages are in the narrative of Toomer's journey from celebrated black writer to disregarded philosopher, it is important to note the particulars of his chronicle. Most remarkable, he ignores the second and third sections of *Cane,* which indeed did confront modernity, now casting the whole volume as an elegy for a period and a people to which we can never return. To represent that past in any mode but elegy (a labor he has already performed) is to indulge unproductive romantic illusions of escape from modernity—"Back to Nature." In these comments, Toomer reveals that the desire of *Cane*'s many speakers to create a connection with the places and cultures of the African American past had been in fact his own "romantic and escapist" fantasy informing the book. Yet in repudiating the futile desire to return to the past, Toomer here implies that African American culture itself must be repudiated. In a disturbing equation of African American life not merely with "primitive conditions" but with "plant and animal life," he insists that his new work is to create "a *human world*." We understand, of course, that he uses "human" here in contrast to the various individual identities— black, mulatto, white—*Cane* had explored; nevertheless, in trying to make the distinction between specific racial identities and a common humanity, he equates plant and animal life with the racialized past of *Cane* and human life with a postracial modernity. (He will make a similar move in his long poem on national identity, "The Blue Meridian," where conquered Native Americans become the "fertilizer" for later cultures: "But pueblo, priest, and Shalakos / Sank into the sacred earth / To fertilize the seven regions of America" [*CP* 54].)

Such extremity in the autobiographical account of his changing interests (repetition, italics, and overstatement) suggests how emphatically Toomer wanted to shift his energies in 1923—and perhaps how difficult it was for him to do so, having to give up not just notoriety and success but a rich and fecund motivation for writing he had only recently discovered. Darryl Pinckny and others have suggested that Toomer's writing suffered after this change because philosophy and poetry, didacticism and lyricism didn't mix: "The problem, the sadness of Toomer, was that his lyrical gift could not hold his free-fall into philosophy" (qtd. in Gates 224).[3] Others claim that this was not merely a formal problem but a racial one: that once Toomer disavowed his identification with African America, he lost his lyrical gift.[4] I would like to make a subtly but significantly different point: that *given Toomer's assumptions about lyric,* assumptions I have argued are dramatized in *Cane,* abandoning "the past" and rejecting a specifically African American identity would inevitably entail abandoning lyric, a form Toomer equated with the African and African American past.

In an unpublished manuscript of aphorisms assembled in 1938, in fact, he carefully dissociates his new life's work from poetry:

> Since then I have become psychological, to include ever more of that labyrinth [of the self]—and this is the simplest explanation I can give to those who expect poetry from me, get psychology, morality, and something of religion, and are puzzled. (*Wayward* 432)

His aphorisms on poetry come in a late section of the proposed volume, section 5, "Two Forces Behind Human Values," which measures "the force of beauty" against "the moral force" (431). The force of beauty produces only "small verse," while the moral force drives toward the "Great Work," the work of higher consciousness and spiritual enlightenment. Embedded in these distinctions is a notion of lyrical forms as primitive, belonging to a past that must be transcended. (Ironically, Toomer frequently employs a voice from the ancient past, the Bible, for making his proclamations about his *new* work: "Seek ye [the Great Means to the Great End], and all these other things will be added unto you" [433].) Yet though readers should no longer expect poetry from him, he persists in viewing himself as a poet: "I am not less poet; I am more conscious of all that I am, am not, and might become" (433). By the end of section 5, Toomer has fully divided the poet from poetry: "I count it good that any poet stops writing his own small verse, [. . .] and becomes a student of the Great Work" (433). Thus, he retains the *figure* of the poet but eschews poetry itself, reiterating the very ambivalence about poetry that *Cane* had expressed. And also like *Cane,* the aphorisms attempt to preserve the role of poet even as they argue that actual poems cannot do the Great Work—in *Cane,* the work of African American cultural renewal, in Toomer's later writing, the work of spiritual enlightenment.

And, yet, Toomer did continue to write "his own small verse," assembling poems for publication in 1931 and rearranging the manuscript for a few years before copyrighting it in 1934 as "The Blue Meridian and Other Poems." He also projected two other volumes, "Day Will Come (also entitled "Rise") and "As Hands Unturned." And he completed still another volume, "The Wayward and the Seeking," around 1940, which contained fifty new poems (Jones, *Prison-House* 157–58). He wrote hundreds of poems over a period of thirty years, evidently finding a use for poetry even when publishers rejected it and his own philosophy called its value into question.

Byrd has skillfully explained why Toomer maintained the image of himself as a poet even as he grew more and more skeptical of poems:

> In the outline of a lecture delivered to the Catholic Poetry Society of America on 15 April 1947, Toomer declared that the "writing of poetry, and to [a] less extent, the reading," leads to "restoration, renewal, rejuvenation, [and] oneness." He asserted that the reading of poetry written by poets who "possess their possessions"—that is, verse by poets who, through some sustained, Herculean effort, have achieved a high level of consciousness—is a "means of moving" and bringing others into their "possessions" or higher consciousness. Such poetry [. . .] transmits powerful, inspirational influences, "opening and enlarging" the "heart and consciousness" of all who read it. This species of poetry, whose properties are symbolic, dramatic, and restorative, is the product of the poet's "momentary fusion and wholeness" with himself and the spiritual forces of the universe. During these intense and rare intervals of knowledge and integration, poetry is born, and "for this time [. . .] the poet possesses and is possessed by his possessions." Through such inspired verse, the poet [. . .] shares his "possessions" and in so doing brings others to a "similar level" of thought and feeling. Poetry thus becomes a prod, a catalyst for higher development, as well as a record of the effort to achieve it. This particular function of poetry [. . .] is "more important than aesthetic pleasure." (152)

Important here is Byrd's qualification, "This species of poetry," which distinguishes the kind of poetry Toomer valued after 1923 from the kind he wrote before. This new species of poetry is "symbolic, dramatic, and restorative" rather than lyrical, subjective, and reflective of lived experience. It is fashioned out of spiritual abstractions, which Toomer believes are universally inspiring, and not out of the languages, cadences, and materials of the literary tradition or of people's lives. Poetry's didactic function, as a "prod" to spiritual development, supersedes its aesthetic function, most especially, as we shall see, its lyricism.

Such an artistic program annulled everything readers admired in *Cane*. "As the Eagle Soars," for instance, first published in 1932, offers long, prosy, aphoristic lines that work against "aesthetic pleasure":

> It takes a well-spent lifetime, and perhaps more, to crystallize in
>   us that for which we exist.
> Let your doing be an exercise, not an exhibition.
> Man is a nerve of the cosmos, dislocated, trying to quiver into
>   place.
> A true individual is not conformative but formative.
> We move and hustle but lack rhythm.
> We should have a living spirit and the ability to spiritualize
>   experience.
> We do not suffer: seldom does our essence suffer, but pride,
>   vanity, egotism suffer in us.
> My breathing is the Great Breath broken into nostrils.
> Whatever is, is sacred. (*Collected Poems* 48)

Arid abstractions ("that for which we exist," "your doing," "spiritualize experience") replace sensual figurative language, and a voice that emits orders and truths supplants the compelling lyric "I" of "Evening Song" or "Song of the Son." One of the rare, but unrealized figures in the poem, the eagle in the title, suggests that people should strive to live "as the eagle soars," but nothing in the poem actually contextualizes or develops this figure, and it remains not a "restorative" image of higher consciousness but just one more accusation, by contrast, of our collective spiritual plodding. In fact, each line of the poem is insulated in its complacent totality of thought; there is no formal or thematic reason for one line to follow another here except, perhaps, for the brief but inclusive adage, "Whatever is, is sacred," which ends the poem by encompassing everything else in a final abstraction.

As Byrd suggests, it is not clear why we would consider such work poetry (181–82). The question is why did Toomer consider these lines, which do not differ from his aphorisms or essays, poetry?[5] He seems to have been caught between his lyrical talents, training, and taste on the one hand (he was still giving volumes of Emily Dickinson and William Blake to new friends during this period [Kerman and Eldridge 187]) and his programmatic devaluation of lyric on the other. What he wanted was a poetry devoid of lyricism, his new project requiring the poet as seer even as it repudiated the distraction and smallness of poetry's lyric effects.[6] Thus, while *Cane* and these later works appear to have little in common, they share the notion of lyric poetry as a primitive form that died out with primitive cultures. Likewise, a vestigial lyric strain would occasionally recur in his later poems much as it had haunted the last two sections of *Cane*. And, again like *Cane*, when the lyric impulse emerges after 1923, it voices Toomer's struggle with racial identity and modernity.

Toomer's major poetic work after *Cane* is "The Blue Meridian," a poem about national identity and spiritual development that he had begun as early as 1921, when he wrote "The First American." Parts of what eventually became Toomer's 800-line epic were published in 1932 (as "Brown River, Smile") and 1936 (as "Blue Meridian") before it appeared posthumously in 1970 as "The Blue Meridian" complete (*Collected Poems* 108). That is, he worked on the poem for thirty years, striving to create an American epic that would settle the paired questions of identity and modernity and lead his countrymen to higher consciousness. The few critics who have looked closely at "The Blue Meridian" differ about the specifics of its structure but agree that the poem envisions the development of America from "sleeping" (50) to "waking" (62) to full wakefulness and awareness of cosmic unity (the verb changes from "waking" to "Awakes" [74], indicating a completion of the waking process).[7] This journey from sleep to awareness corresponds to Gurdjieff's four states of human consciousness: the sleeping state, waking consciousness, self-consciousness, and cosmic consciousness.[8] In the poem, Toomer equates these four stages of development with a problematic narrative of United States history.[9]

Whatever other ways the poem can be divided, it is structured by three meridians: "*Black Meridian*," associated with African Americans (50–61), "*White Meridian*," with Euro-Americans (62–74), and "*Blue Meridian*," with New Americans, who have transcended race in their attainment of cosmic consciousness (74–75).[10] Even though italicized stanzas about each meridian punctuate the poem, the sections that follow them are wide-ranging in their subject matter, not limited to African Americans, whites, and enlightened beings respectively but oscillating between accusations of human shortcomings and exhortations to achieve more, between national history and personal narrative. Like Whitman's "Song of Myself," Toomer's epic aspires to speak for the one and the all because the one is the all. Whitman:

> I celebrate myself, and sing myself,
> And what I assume you shall assume,
> For every atom belonging to me as good belongs to you. (ll. 1–3)

And Toomer:

> Uncase, unpod whatever blocks, until,
> Having realized pure consciousness of being,
> Knowing that we are beings
> Co-existing with others in an inhabited universe,
> We will be free to use rightly with reason
> Our own and other human functions—
> Free men, whole men, men connected
> With one another and with Deity. (65)

This epic persona, who speaks for the entire nation as he speaks for himself, is crucial to the poem's argument that "We are [all] beings" (65) and can transcend racial, national, regional, sexual, and class differences as we achieve higher consciousness and recognize the unity of all things (64–65).

The poem is deeply indebted to Whitman, as Toomer turns from his early lyrical influences to an epic progenitor.[11] Given his ambivalence about lyric poetry, Toomer's shift to epic answers not merely his desire to compose a "Great Work" about national identity and higher consciousness but also his need to avoid creating just another "small verse" or, as Waldo Frank had termed it, another "mere direct lyric." Indeed, "The Blue Meridian" posits a history of poetic forms that parallels the other narratives it proposes about mankind's progress from primitive races to enlightened beings, from the natural world to modernity, and, ultimately, from sleeping to awakening. The hortatory, oracular lines of the epic poet who has transcended race supplant the racially specific lyric forms of America's prehistory.

Each initial description of the different races in "The Blue Meridian" entails a reference to their songs, and, as we might expect, song receives the greatest emphasis in the poem's "history" of African Americans. Whites, in contrast, are characterized by their industrial energies:

> The great European races sent wave after wave
> That washed the forests, the earth's rich loam,
> Grew towns with the seeds of giant cities,
> Made roads, laid silver rails,
> Sang of their swift achievement,
> And perished, displaced by machines,
> Smothered by a world too huge for little men,
> Too empty for life to breathe in. (52)

The passage acknowledges that Euro-Americans "[s]ang of their swift achievement," but those songs are ancillary to building cities and rail-roads: lyrical records of accomplishment, not accomplishments in themselves. Black history, on the other hand, is a chronicle of song:

> The great African races sent a single wave
> And singing riplets to sorrow in red fields,
> Sing a swan song, to break rocks
> And immortalize a hiding water boy.
>
>> I'm leaving the shining ground, brothers,
>> I sing because I ache,
>> I go because I must,
>> I'm leaving the shining ground;
>> Don't ask me where,
>> I'll meet you there,
>> Brothers, I am leaving the shining ground.
>
> But we must keep keep keep
>   the watermelon.
> He moaned, O Lord, Lord,
> This bale will break me—
> But we must keep keep keep
>   the watermelon. (53)

Not only are the second and third stanzas quoted here delivered in the form of song (alluding to spirituals, blues, and work songs—even if, as in *Cane*, their forms are corrupted), but the entire passage equates African Americans with song. The passage curiously envisions one "wave" of African immigration (the slave trade is emphatically ignored)—as opposed to the multiple "wave after wave" of European immigration. While the white waves, like tidal waves, "washed the forests" of "the earth's rich loam," spreading and transforming that natural richness into "giant cities," "roads," and "silver rails," the African wave is a mere "riplet" of song in "red fields." That is, without acknowledging why one group would storm the continent with its "achievement[s]" and the other would toil sadly in the fields, the poem depicts Africans as a defeated people who came to America singing "sorrow songs" that were always, inevitably elegiac: "Sing a swan song." The phrase "swan song" is, of course, Toomer's own term for *Cane,* yet this part of "The Blue Meridian" goes even farther than *Cane* in insisting on the death of the "great African races." Black history is a tale of woe, from the spirituals of the slaves to the work songs of the chain gangs, and these songs can only "immortalize a hiding water boy." Wagner reminds us that "[t]he little water-carrier who hides away somewhere is one of the most pathetic and best-known characters in these black convict songs" (276), and the water boy functions as one more image of failure in this stanza.

The next two stanzas let us hear the broken voices of first the spirituals and then of the blues and work songs, and to emphasize defeat those lyrical forms are broken as well: the first song mimics a spiritual about leaving this hard life and getting over to "there"—some better place that cannot be imagined ("Don't ask me where"). This falls far short of the main theme of spirituals, which is heavenly reward for earthly suffering; the spirituals knew where Camp Ground was. The second song, in turn, imitates both the blues (especially in the repeated first line and the refrain "He moaned, O Lord, Lord") and work songs ("This bale will break me"), but here in an even more mocking way. Invoking a familiar icon from racist coon tales, the watermelon-stealing black, the bluesy section seems to answer the spiritual: we can't leave the shining ground because "we must keep keep keep the watermelon," as if the stereotypical love of watermelon exceeds the love of freedom. Taken together, the two fragments of folk song suggest that African Americans can only suffer and submit not merely to the injustices of racism but to racist stereotypes themselves. After all, "[they] sing because [they] ache." When the African American aching is over, the lines imply, black song will be ended, too.

Though there is no "red meridian," the poem next introduces the "great red race," equating the Native Americans with song much as it had African Americans. The history of Native people is once again a tale of primitive song and ritual:

> The great red race was here.
> In a land of flaming earth and torrent-rains,
> Of red sea-plains and majestic mesas,
> At sunset from a purple hill
> The Gods came down;
> They serpentined into pueblo,
> And a white-robed priest
> Danced with them five days and nights;
> But pueblo, priest, and Shalakos
> Sank into the sacred earth
> To fertilize the seven regions of America.

> Hé-ya, hé-yo, hé-yo,
> Hé-ya, hé-yo, hé-yo,
> The ghosts of buffaloes,
> A lone eagle feather,
> An untamed Navajo,
> Hé-ya, hé-yo, hé-yo,
> Hé-ya, hé-yo, hé-yo. (53–54)

This section registers more regard for Native Americans than the previous one had for African Americans, yet the representation of Native people is equally dismissive and stereotypical. Though they are inhabited by gods and engaged in sacred rituals, still they "[s]ank into the sacred earth / To fertilize" America for later settlers. Their song is rendered as a "primitive" Indian chant, its English lines equating the "untamed Navajo" with not merely buffaloes and eagles but with the "*ghosts* of buffaloes" and a "*lone* eagle feather," that is, with extinct or nearly extinct native wildlife. The history of conquest is forgotten here just as the history of slavery was forgotten in the previous section. And though the poem idealizes Native spirituality and offers Native culture as a model for New Americans—"We are waiting for a new people, / For the joining of men to men / And man to God"—it simultaneously denies the existence of indigenous people:

> When the spirit of mankind conceived
> A New World in America, and dreamed
> The human structure rising from this base,
> The land was as a vacant house to new inhabitants,
> A vacuum compelled by Nature to be filled. (54)

Taken together, these three depictions of the "old peoples," Euro-Americans, African Americans, and Native Americans, indicate that song played a crucial role in ancestral life—though white, black, and Native song functioned differently in each culture. Still, the past seems defined by song, the lyric impulse an expression of primitive societies. Yet even as these sections relegate song to the past, a quatrain that cannot be clearly identified with a particular racial group calls for a renewal of lyric:

> Late minstrels of the restless earth,
> No muteness can be granted thee,
> Lift thy laughing energies
> To that white point which is a star. (53)

Though the late minstrels suggest the roving ("restless") singers of old, their "laughing energies" locate them in a specifically American minstrelsy: blackface performers who presented racist imitations and sang African American folk songs and spirituals. Why the poem would single out such figures as redemptive is a vexing question, which a second appearance of the "late minstrels" stanza helps to clarify. Now it follows a stanza that depicts the minstrel as comic relief in a tragic world:

> Yet, in this crashing world
> Terrorized by bullet-athletes,
> I unbolt windows and ten-cents greet
> A happy simple thing—
> An organ grinder with a jaunty hat,
> With wayward roaming feet,

And his monkey,
Sauntering along a spring street,
Diddle-lidle-le, diddle-lidle-le.

Late minstrels of the restless earth,
No muteness can be granted thee,
Lift thy laughing energies
To that white point which is a star. (60)

The speaker regards the organ grinder's song as a "happy simple thing" in a world troubled by unhappiness and complexity. He exhorts such minstrels, belated as they are, not to be mute, urging them to "lift" their songs in the expectation that those songs will lift our spirits. Yet it is hard to imagine "Diddle-lidle-le, diddle-lidle-le" having a restorative effect; rather, when we actually hear the "late" songs—"We must keep keep keep the watermelon," "Hé-ya, hé-yo, hé-yo," "Diddle-lidle-le, diddle-lidle-le" —we detect the poem's deep ambivalence toward its minstrels. The speaker wants to renew and celebrate these racialized lyrics even as he disparages them in his own minstrel-style mimicry of the songs. It is not clear just what he means by telling the minstrels to aim their songs at "that white point that is a star." The distant point of light may suggest the North Star that led slaves to freedom or even the Star of Bethlehem that signaled the birth of Christ; and white is typically Toomer's color for transcendence.[12] In any case, the speaker directs the minstrels' songs beyond "this crashing world" to that celestial point, as if in supplication to a higher force. He appears divided between invoking the songs of the late minstrels as healing *precisely because they are "late,"* because they are voices of the past, and insisting that their songs must be redirected toward a future vision of national spiritual enlightenment. The unusual instance of rhyme in this section (athletes, greet, feet, street) is thus at once mocking and nostalgic. Conventional lyrical forms—like minstrel songs, Native American chants, spirituals, blues, and work songs— belong to earlier times that were "happy," "simple," and "jaunty," times that can now be sounded only in hollow mimicry.

And yet, the speaker's own relation to song is more complex than such a history of lyric suggests. He listens to an array of records from different cultural registers, and though he transcends them when he hears his own song, these prior songs seem to lead him to that transcendence:

Upon my phonograph are many records
Played on sides in sacred and profane extremes;
Sometimes I hear Gregorian chants
Or Bach's "It Is Consummated";
Sometimes I hear Duke Ellington
Or Eddy Duchin sing popular contemporary;
And some rare times
I hear myself, the unrecorded,
Sing the flow of I,
The notes and language not of this experience,
Sing I am,
As the flow pauses,
Then passes through my water-wheel—
And those radiant others, the living real,
The people identical in being. (67–68)

The speaker recognizes others—presumably late minstrels as well as Gregorian chanters, Bach, Duke Ellington, and Eddy Duchin—as "identical in being" when he is attuned to the "flow of I," when he can "[s]ing I am." His song clearly supersedes theirs—"The notes and language [are] not of this experience"—and in this supersession allows him to recognize the unity of all things. The speaker has attained cosmic consciousness, and his "unrecorded" song ought to be the new national epic if "It is a new America, / To be spiritualized by each new American" (50, 55, 66, 69); yet, that higher song remains unrecorded because it cannot be translated to his countrymen. Its notes and language belong to a transcendent realm, which only the speaker experiences. Gurdjieff maintained that cosmic consciousness could not be represented in language (Byrd 81), but, as we have seen, the poet's task is to translate higher consciousness into a poetry that can at least prod our understanding. The poet-speaker's problem, then, is to transform the song "I am" into something we can all hear without recurring to "Diddle-lidle-le." How can the "flow of I" be sung without recourse to outmoded lyric forms? Having recognized the unity of all things, the speaker must incorporate the past in himself as a means of transcending it.

The birth of this New American poet—"The man of blue or purple" (72) who has outgrown cultural differences and belongs to the blue meridian—requires the death of "late" minstrels, who we now realize are not merely belated but deceased. Positioned between stanzas reiterating the history of "The great African races" and "The great red race," the emergence of the poet seems to require the end of such racial identities:

> Earth is earth, ground is ground,
> All shining if loved.
> Love does not brand as slave or peon
> Any man, but feels his hands,
> His touch upon his work,
> And welcomes death that liberates
> The poet, American among Americans,
> Man at large among men. (71)

There is no explicit subject for "loved," and "Love" appears to be a force in its own right, not requiring particular people to feel it; if love ruled, the poem says, no one would be a slave (an indirect reference to the stanza about African Americans directly preceding this one) or peon, and everyone's work would be appreciated. The lack of an agent for "loved" effectively obscures who has lacked love in the past, who has enslaved and devalued whom. Out of these vague democratic tenets, the poet emerges, "American among Americans," a latter-day Representative Man, who has been liberated by the death of those specific racial identities that had resulted in slavery and peonage.

But in the next reiteration of Native American history, the "great red race" no longer merely "fertilizes" later generations but is "resurrect[ed]" (71) in them. The blue man, who has grown "[b]eyond the little tags and small marks" (72) of racial identity, is the New American who unites all differences to transcend them:

> We are the new people,
> Born of elevated rock and lifted branches,
> Called Americans,
> Not to mouth the label but to live the reality,
> Not to stop anywhere, to respond to man,
> To outgrow each wider limitation,
> Growing towards the universal Human Being;
> And we are the old people, witnesses

That behind us there extends
An unbroken chain of ancestors,
Ourselves linked with all who ever lived,
Joined with all future generations;
Of millions of fathers through as many years
We are the breathing receptacles. (72)

"Americans" are "new people," who can take their place in "An unbroken
chain of ancestors" as long as they are "Growing towards the universal
Human Being." This is unity rather than history—we are connected to
our past simply because we are connected to all things—a vision of humanity that embraces "all who ever lived" and "all future generations"
without acknowledging the particularities of African American, Native
American, Euro-American (or of the unmentioned Asian American and
Hispanic American) experiences. The poem moves quickly from its vision of unity to the "*Blue Meridian*" (74), a personified cosmic force who
dances rather than sings: "*He dances the dance of the Blue Meridian /
And dervishes with the seven regions of America, and all the world*" (74).
Likewise, the conclusion of the poem does not sing but employs only
Toomer's new poetics, the antilyrical lines of the Great Work. It calls for
lifting "waking forces" not songs, addressing itself at last "beyond" the
lyric specificity it has been working to overcome: "Beyond plants are
animals, / Beyond animals is man, / Beyond man is God" (75).

Nearly all of Toomer's post-*Cane* poetry would abide by the poetics
he worked out in aphoristic remarks on poetry and dramatized in "The
Blue Meridian." Yet the ambivalence we hear in "The Blue Meridian"'s
treatment of lyric must have persisted, for the late poems occasionally
indulge the very lyricism Toomer had repudiated. "Rolling, Rolling," a
poem he wrote when he fell in love with Emily Otis in 1929 (*Wayward*
186), is a paean to love:

Rolling, rolling,
Emily, Emily.

Rolling away to Santa Fe,
Over the golden rails,
From white buildings to adobes,
From boulevards to trails,

Rolling away to Santa Fe,
My darling Emily. [. . .] (84)

Here, conventional romantic feelings find expression in conventional poetic forms, as Toomer employs rhyme and meter ("Rólling awáy to Sánta Fé / Óver the gólden ráils"; *rails/trails*) to capture the speaker's lilting emotions. Too, repetition of her name and location provide rhythmic recurrence, and the apostrophe to "darling Emily" bespeaks a poem that is unabashedly traditional and lyrical. Another late poem, "To Gurdjieff Dying," is written in sonnet form:[13]

Thou Venerene ascending to desire,
Knowing the Buddhic law but to pervert
Its power of peace into dissevering fire,
Coiled as a serpent round the phallic Tau
And sacramental loaf, yet still alert
To turn the nether astral light athwart
The beam ethereal, wherefore now art thou
Snake and seducer, Son of the Elder Liar?

Thou hast deformed the birth-bringings of light
Into lust-brats of black imaginings,
Spilling Pan-passions in the incarnate round
Of hell and earth. Lords of the Shining Rings
Skilled in white magic, may your skills abound!
Save even Gurdjieff from his hell forthright. (103)

Toomer's contradictory feelings about the master whom he had devotedly followed, bitterly broken with, and later returned to are captured in the contradictory impulses of the poem.[14] Archaisms of diction and syntax ("Thou Venerene," "The beam ethereal"), an allusion to *Romeo and Juliet* ("wherefore [. . .] art thou"), and the sonnet form itself suggest the need to invoke the grandeur and beauty of the past in order to elegize Gurdjieff. Yet the poem's caustic accusations and phrasings render the gesture to tradition deeply ironic. The "ugly words" of modern poetry ("phallic Tau," "lust-brats of black imaginings") resist archaic euphonious and euphemistic phrasings ("Son of the Elder Liar," "Lords of the Shining Rings"). Despicable as Gurdjieff is, the speaker begs the "white magic[ians]" to forgive him his "black imaginings": "Save even Gurd-jieff from his hell forthright." The troubled form of the poem adroitly represents the speaker's ambivalence about Gurdjieff's death, but the fact that Toomer employs a sonnet so late in his career, and on such an important occasion, testifies to a regard for lyric poetry that philosophy could not completely overcome.

This anguished struggle between Toomer's gift for what he wrongly considered his "own small verse" and his commitment to the "Great Work" is recorded in "Not For Me" (*Collected* 93), a poem from 1938 in which the poet-speaker asks the higher powers to "sanction" his writing by keeping him focused on what is essential: "Of the thousand things that mind could write, / Guide it to the essential, hold it, / Single and intent upon the essential." As we have seen, "the pure essence of life" (93) was not the stuff of lyric poetry. Once Toomer considered his individual being a "broken instrument" (93) and attempted to write from the Human Being, his poems became antipoetical tracts. He believed modernity required such measures, first, because traditional lyricism had died out with the old peoples, especially with African Americans, and the times demanded a modern form. Second, the only corrective for modern ills was higher consciousness, and lyric poetry hindered the path to enlightenment with its sensual evocations of this world and its backward-looking forms. Yet Toomer remained a late minstrel of the restless earth, attempting to create a modernist poetics that would open and enlarge the "heart of consciousness" but never quite abandoning the lyrical call of the swan's song.

Notes

CHAPTER 1

1. Sherwood Anderson told Toomer after reading *Cane* that Toomer was the only Negro "who seems really to have consciously the artist's impulse" (*C* 160). Waldo Frank's introduction to the first edition claims that Toomer is distinctive in literature dealing with African Americans in the South because he is a poet first: "A poet has arisen in the land who writes, not as a Southerner, not as a rebel against Southerners, not as a Negro, not as apologist or priest or critic: who writes as a *poet*" (*C* 138–39). Allen Tate called *Cane* "the genuine thing" (*C* 161). See also contemporary reviews of *Cane* by Robert Littell and Gorham B. Munson. In "The Same Difference: Reading Jean Toomer, 1923–1982," Henry Louis Gates Jr. surveys *Cane's* reception thoroughly, explaining the book's significance for two distinct, and often opposed, literary movements (the Harlem Renaissance and the Black Arts movement). In 1975 Warren French compared *Cane* to *The Waste Land* in an extended discussion written as an "Afternote" to an essay by Blyden Jackson. Nellie McKay compares the book to *Ulysses* (86). Cary Nelson argues for reading *Cane* alongside *Spring and All* (180, 219), and Michael North devotes a chapter to the comparison (147–74). North also implies a correspondence between *The Waste Land* and *Cane* at several points (147), as does Linda Wagner-Martin (20).

2. Munson's perceptive 1925 remark that "*Cane* is, from one point of view, the record of [Toomer's] search for suitable literary forms" (*C* 172) anticipates much recent critical interest in the book's formal innovation. I discuss this work at length later in chapter 1.

3. In 1966 Arna Bontemps refers to early readers who were "generally stumped" by *Cane's* form: "Poetry and prose were whipped together in a kind of frappé. Realism was mixed with what they called mysticism, and the result seemed to many of them confusing" (25). In 1968 Edward Margolies acknowledges the unsettling form but insists on *Cane's* thematic coherence: "*Cane* is very nearly impossible to describe. At first glance, it seems a hodge podge of verse, songs, stories, and plays,

yet there is a thematic unity celebrating the passions and instincts of black persons close to the soil as opposed to the corruption of their spirit and vitality in the cities" (39). Michael Soto quotes numerous reviews that respond negatively to the mixed-genre form in his excellent 2001 essay on *Cane*'s publication history.

Alain Locke called *Cane* a collection of short stories in his influential 1925 collection *The New Negro*, and Robert Bone (1958) and Darwin Turner (1971) initiated a debate about whether *Cane* is a novel (Bone 81) or a collection of disparate works (Turner 14). On this debate, see also Arthur P. Davis, who calls it a "mélange" and a "potpourri" while arguing for its "tonal unity" (46). Much recent writing explores the notion that *Cane*'s generic multiplicity is a formal expression of Toomer's interest in multiracial identity. Alan Golding made this equation as early as 1983, claiming that "Toomer's drive to make the pieces of *Cane* balance or cohere enacts on the formal level his struggle to reconcile both the contradictory spirits of North and South and the black and white within himself" (198). In 1993 Robert B. Jones makes a parallel claim but in reference to much broader concerns: "[Toomer's formal] innovations represent the author's attempts to find literary equivalents for his idealism. Moreover, these literary experiments may be traced to Toomer's reified consciousness, specifically his efforts to reconcile his divided self, as well as self and world, within a unified philosophical system" (48). In 1994 Michael North locates another source for *Cane*'s formal hybridity, claiming that *Cane*'s mixed form unites the African American past and the multiethnic present: "It is in this freedom from fixed forms, in this boldness of expression, that Toomer is faithful at once to the African American experience he discovered in the South and to his vision of the new American" (167-68). In still another approach to the relationship of form to identity, Joel Peckham (2000) argues that "[i]n *Cane*, Toomer attempts to enact a disruption of social boundaries through literary form by exploding the genre borders of fiction, lyric poetry, and drama" (275) because "Toomer found in his multiethnic biological makeup a possible model for the transgression of societal boundaries" (276-77).

4. Even as Robert Bone argues that Toomer used "words as a plastic medium" and was the only Harlem Renaissance writer to participate in modernism on "equal terms" with Stein, Hemingway, Eliot, and Pound, he nevertheless puts Toomer's experimental form in service of a "higher realism": "While his contemporaries of the Harlem School were still experimenting with a crude literary realism, Toomer had progressed beyond the naturalistic novel to 'the higher realism of the emotions,' to symbol, and to myth" (80-81). In fact, many invoke the form of the novel to give coherence to *Cane*'s unruly parts. Bernard Bell, for instance, approaches it "as a poetic novel, the disparate elements and illusive meanings of [which] coalesce into an integral whole and provide a poignant insight into the sensibility of a modern black artist" (*Afro-American Novel* 98). In his introduction, Frank insists that "This book *is* the South"—meaning the black South—precisely because it did not attempt to offer a thorough or factual account of the South. In responding artistically (rather than historically or politically) to "the essences and materials of his Southland," Toomer achieved an accuracy of representation that exceeded realism

(*C* 138). Frank's catchy formulation was echoed like a refrain in other reviews; see Gregory and Littell (*C* 166, 169).

Frank's remark contains an even deeper paradox. He claims that *Cane*'s authenticity is achieved not through verisimilitude but rather through poeticalness: "The fashioning of beauty is ever foremost in his inspiration: not forcedly but simply, and because these ultimate aspects of his world are to him more real than all its specific problems" (*C* 139). Frank assumes that writing as a poet entails eschewing history and politics in favor of beauty (and assumes these are mutually exclusive concerns). It is the apprehension of beauty, then, that produces the higher realism he praises. As I discuss in detail later in chapter 1, when Frank says "poet," he means a special kind of prose writer; thus, his claims about *Cane*'s authenticity are consistent, if circuitously so, with the claims of those who regard the volume as prose and thus as an unproblematic depiction of black life.

5. In addition to Golding, North, and Peckham, Geneviève Fabre and Michel Feith's recent anthology *Jean Toomer and the Harlem Renaissance* (2001) includes a majority of essays analyzing Toomer's formal efforts to resist conventional racial representation. See excellent essays by Fabre and Feith, Werner Sollers, Charles-Yves Grandjeat, Monica Michlin, Fabre, Wolfgang Karrer, Martha Jane Nadell, Michael Soto, and Diana I. Williams. Charles W. Scruggs and Lee VanDemarr also discuss "a new form uniquely suited to the complicated world—'mixed-blood' America and the Negro's unknown peasant past" (118). Another recent contribution to this discussion is Catherine Gunther Kodat's "To 'Flash White Light from Ebony': The Problem of Modernism in Jean Toomer's *Cane*."

6. By far the most persuasive work on Toomer's interracial project is that of George Hutchinson, who rejects the familiar formulations about Toomer's racial identity and demonstrates that Toomer's work from the *Cane* period reveals "a strong impetus toward deconstruction of a traditional American racial ideology and the 'birth pangs' of a new one" ("Racial Discourse" 231). In Hutchinson's account, Toomer is not trying to reconcile black and white but to reject the very terms of American racial discourse; thus, for instance,

> [t]he achievement of "Kabnis," its very language, derives from the sort of tension Kabnis feels—not merely the tension between black and white but, most important, the tension between "black/white" discourse and the dream of an alternative, new "American" discourse that would be completely divorced from the old. (240)

Hutchinson's work must make us cautious about assigning simple racialized meanings to particular literary forms—for instance, assuming that *Cane*'s lyrical impulses are black and its realistic impulses white (as Peckham does).

Additionally, Hutchinson's groundbreaking study, *The Harlem Renaissance in Black and White*, identifies an interracial subjectivity and its attendant literary forms that have been marginalized in our accounts of the period. This position is meticulously argued and documented, and it would be impossible to debate Hutchinson's claims that the Harlem Renaissance was a time of interracial cultural exchange that defies our familiar racialist categories of understanding. Though Hutchinson has been the most important influence on my thinking about the period, I am convinced that *Cane* is engrossed with more narrow definitions of race than Hutchinson might allow, even if only to reveal their inadequacy. Though *Cane* includes many instances of interracial struggle (Fern appears to be Jewish and African American; Becky is a white woman who has two sons by a black man; Kabnis is clearly a mulatto, and the sunrise that concludes his section emblematizes the promise of what Toomer called "racial intermingling" [*Reader* 16]), the book remains heavily invested in a distinctly African American ideal.

The resolution to my apparent (and, in any case, slight) disagreement with Hutchinson may be in Hutchinson's own account of Toomer's projected second book. There, "Toomer apparently envisioned the hero as emerging from his underworld experience [the experience Kabnis cannot overcome], an articulate embodiment of the 'new race'—like Toomer himself—expressing himself in a 'classic American prose,' a fusion of diversely appropriated idioms" ("Racial Discourse" 237). Our agreement deepens later in the essay when Hutchinson describes *Cane* as "an embodiment of a phase that both he and the United States were about to pass out of, while his projected next book would indicate the future" (242–43). That is, if *Cane*, like America in the 1920s, is caught in limiting racialist definitions that prevent Kabnis from effectively articulating and experiencing a complex notion of racial identity, then my reading of the problem of lyric in *Cane* offers one more way to elucidate that impasse.

In another excellent study of *Cane*'s attitude towards race, Charles Harmon argues that

> *Cane* does not seek to dispose of race[. . . .] Rather than seeking to dispense with the whole project of a naturalized identity—as poststructuralism does—*Cane*, like its author, is obsessed with the topic and attacks not identity in general, but racial identity specifically. While the achievement of an unambiguous sense of cosmic belonging remains a main goal of *Cane*, all forms of racial or ethnic solidarity are finally represented in *Cane* as unable to help individuals achieve that goal. At the end of the day (which, in *Cane*, is the beginning of a new day), *Cane* finally places itself in the service of a distinctive (yet strikingly familiar) form of mystical individualism, in which lone subjects seek (and find) unmediated fusion with the universe. (92)

Harmon's essay demystifies what he aptly terms "the lure of identity," which always "brings with it various negative effects" (93).

7. For a sampling of arguments on each side of this debate, see Bell (*Afro-American Novel*), Bone, Fisher, and Turner, who read the ending of *Cane* negatively,

and Baker (*Afro-American Poetics*), Bontemps, Byrd, Goede, Ikonné, Lieber, McKay, and Perry, who read it positively.

8. Charles T. Davis makes a similar point in another context: "What is being lost, as the poet looks and ruminates, is song, along with other vestiges of the slave culture, not simply music itself but the ability to make music" (192).

9. Bernard Bell published "A Key to the Poems in *Cane*" in 1971, in which he argued that the poems are "all functional, serving to elucidate or to set the stage or to provide a transition between the sketches" (253). Thus, even an essay dedicated to the poems regards them as "serving" the prose. Further, he gives only the poems of part 1 detailed treatment, dispatching part 2 poems in a single paragraph that conflates them with the earlier poems: "In contrast to the ten poems in Part One, there are only five in Part Two. However, they are characterized by the same dramatic tensions between either the body, emotions and intellect or man and modern social conventions" (257). That is, Bell reads all the poems in *Cane* as sharing thematic concerns and does not consider their formal distinctions or how the particular form of a poem manages these shared thematics. Even in essays not devoted solely to *Cane*'s poetry, part 1 poems typically receive attention while part 2 poems do not. See Heiner Bus, "Jean Toomer and the Black Heritage," who offers no discussion of part 2 poems after a lengthy discussion of part 1 poems.

10. Bone and Huggins, for instance, analyze *Cane* without treating the poems; Byrd goes carefully through the text without looking at any poem except "Harvest Song." Payne says he does not discuss the poems because they appear to him to be of a piece: "I have spent little time describing these [poems], because characteristically they repetitiously describe a woman or a setting in nature while attempting to evoke a mood" (51); he then quotes excerpts from three separate poems as a block to demonstrate *Cane*'s "lyric celebration of life and land" (52), a generalization that would not bear up if each poem were treated singly. In contrast, McKay treats each piece in *Cane* in detail, though she typically conceives of the poems as "bridging" (112), "extending" (93), "reinforc[ing]" or "intensif[ying]" (103) the prose pieces: for instance, "[t]he second short poem that follows 'Karintha' is 'Reapers,' which like 'November Cotton Flower' has a direct relationship to the narrative" (96–97). Robert B. Jones must be credited with giving all of Toomer's poems their due: he edited (with Margery Toomer Latimer) *The Collected Poems of Jean Toomer*, perhaps the first step in recognizing the significance of poetry in Toomer's oeuvre, and offers the first in-depth analysis of *Cane*'s prose poems in *Jean Toomer and the Prison-House of Thought* (33–49). Scruggs and VanDemarr accord the poems an equal status with the prose, and their meticulous close readings offer some of the best analyses of *Cane*'s poetry.

11. North views Toomer's use of conventional lyric forms as a failure of imagination, given that the task he set for himself in *Cane* was to create a modern literature that would be faithful to the African American past without reproducing its forms: "However, the formal structure of most of the poems in the collection—and

certainly those in the first section of the book—suggests that Toomer could not imagine how to make the imagist aesthetic of breaks and discontinuities serve this function" (172). Peckham effectively makes the same argument by omission; his commitment to associating "lyric" with disruption ("Poetic language [. . .] is inherently disruptive because it is ambiguous and therefore challenges traditional bourgeois norms of thought and association," 287) forces him to avoid considering any of the actual poems in *Cane* since "Song of the Son" or "Georgia Dusk" would undermine his claim that lyric is always revolutionary.

12. Scruggs and VanDemarr usefully qualify the meaning of *Cane*'s circular structure: "the central assumption of a cyclical history is that it needs to 'ascend' in order to offer hope; to begin anew a history of exploitation and murder is the Gothic terror of repetition" (187). While Toomer may have attempted to create a structure of cyclical renewal in the three parts of *Cane,* the "awakening" to racial difference in part 2 turns out to be a nightmare: "Paul, Kabnis, John, Dan, and the singer of 'Harvest Song' all occupy the same place on the circle, a point of Gothic repetition and sameness where the protagonist awakes from the dream to find it a nightmare" (187–88).

13. Scruggs and VanDemarr assume that Toomer is referring to the prose works in part 2 as "complex":

> *Cane* alternates between story and lyric, sometimes within the same narrative, and Toomer regarded the stories in the middle section as his most complex and experimental works. The return to "simple forms" in the aesthetic reading concludes with the tableau of Father John embracing Carrie K. and the author sending his text out into the world. (186)

However, the "simplicity" of the final tableau is not self-evident, and one scene does not, in any case, account for Toomer's claim that the book moved back to simple *forms* since the form of "Kabnis" is not significantly different from other quasi-dramatic pieces in part 2, like "Theater" and "Box Seat."

14. While I regard the snippets of folk songs as fragments of a lost culture, most readers consider such textual moments as evidence of cultural resiliency. Clary, for instance, asserts: "Woven into the sketches, the songs perpetuate pastoral conventions that symbolize the spiritual resiliency of the black community" (76). Likewise, Bell employs almost exactly the same terms, regarding the "songs as symbols of spiritual resiliency" (*African American Novel* 98). Our disagreement is crucial to my argument that the poems express a powerful idealizing impulse, so powerful, in fact, that readers have consistently been seduced by even the merest scrap of lyric. One notable exception is Vera M. Kutzinski, who shares my suspicion of the lyric voice in *Cane*: "The text's purportedly sensual lyricism, much like the 'radiant beauty' of the southern landscape, has to it an eerie, nightmarish quality that unsettles its readers (or at least this reader) more than it communicates an abiding sense of 'spiritual fusion' and 'harmony'" (166).

15. Turner says that "Song of the Son" "might have been a prologue to *Cane*" (*Minor Chord* 25). McKay also reads it as a mission statement for *Cane*: "The unambiguous intent of the poet is to convey his personal commitment, through his song, to the restoration of the glory of his history. In the evocation of heritage and past, he hopes to save the cultural remnants from oblivion and make them immortal [through art]" (89). One could cite any number of critics who read "Song of the Son" as *Cane*'s raison d'être; see, for instance, Charles T. Davis (191), Innes (320), Lieber (37).

16. See also Griffin (154), Scruggs and VanDemarr (195), Blake (533), Lieber (50), and MacKethan (434).

17. For accounts of Toomer's efforts to become a spiritual leader, see Kerman and Eldridge, chapters 3, 4, 5, and 6, and Larson's discussion of Toomer in the chapter entitled "Endgame" (120–65).

18. Scruggs and VanDemarr demonstrate that Toomer sometimes conceived of *Cane* as a book about the South, thinking of "Washington as in some sense *part* of the South" (123). Yet when he returned from Spartanburg and wrote the stories set in Washington, he now "saw Washington as a representative modern city." This shift in attitude toward Washington, as well as the inclusion in part 2 of a story set in Chicago, enabled Toomer to assert that the book moved "[r]egionally, from the South up into the North, and back into the South again" (*Reader* 26).

19. "For M. W." may have been a poem to Mae Wright, which Toomer sent her during their brief courtship. She describes receiving a poem from him that was "mainly descriptive of the natural beauties of Harpers Ferry and which he said was reminiscent of our summer there" (O'Daniel, "Interview" 39). The poem "Tell Me," which Toomer did not include in *Cane*, fits this description. If "For M. W." is a poem, then his intention to include it in a prose section indicates another subtle but significant shift in his plans for the book: a move away from organizing the volume by genre.

20. Jones's second chapter, "*Cane*: Hermeneutics of Form and Consciousness," offers an excellent discussion of Toomer's style and draws helpful distinctions among lyric poetry, prose poems, lyrical narratives, and prose narratives (33–62).

21. The first two quotations are from Payne (42, 43), the next two from Arthur P. Davis (46); Bontemps calls it a "frappé" (25), Wagner-Martin a narrative sequence (19), Duncan "an elaborate jazz composition" (323), Scruggs and VanDemarr a "hybrid short story cycle" (1), Nicholls uses the term "pastiche" (*Conjuring the Folk* 25), and Peckham uses the metaphor of montage to understand *Cane*'s structure (275).

22. See pages 3–7 and chapters analyzing Toomer's commitment to African American concerns: chapter 1, "Sparta"; chapter 3, "Cultural Politics, 1920"; and chapter 4, "Whose America?"

23. In *Authentic Blackness: The Folk in the New Negro Renaissance*, J. Martin Favor thoughtfully argues that Toomer conceived of racial identity as performative rather than essential. When "negroid ideals" are invoked in *Cane*, they are instances of racial performance rather than essential types. In Favor's reading, *Cane* foregrounds

the variety and instability of racial identity by representing intraracial differences: Northerners visiting the South, rural folk moving into cities, middle-class blacks interacting with the lower classes, and light- and dark-skinned people offering competing notions of blackness. Thus, for Favor, Toomer employs versions of supposed "authentic blackness" in order to call racial essence into question. See chapter 1, "Discourses of Black Identity: The Elements of Authenticity" (1–23), for a thorough discussion of the issue of authenticity in African American letters, and chapter 3, "'Colored; cold. Wrong somewhere.': Jean Toomer's *Cane*" (53–80), for an intriguing analysis of racial representation in *Cane*.

24. Hutchinson argues that "Toomer's consistent trope (from the 1910s through the 1930s) [was] of a river signifying the dissolution of the 'old' races into the 'New World' soul" ("Racial Discourse" 232), an observation that is not at odds with my reading of the portly Negress. In the passage I quoted, the river of her blood lines runs *back* from North to South, moving in the direction of her unmixed racial origins.

25. The question Diana Fuss urges us to ask is "if this text is essentialist, *what motivates its deployment?*" (*xi*). *Cane*'s valorization of African race memories and the African American folk is motivated by Toomer's desire to "harvest what the past has stored" as a way of "giving the Negro to himself" (*Reader* 90). By this he means to draw out sustaining aspects of the African American past and create an account of black culture and identity that African Americans can embrace with pride and promise. Very shortly, his project would change dramatically, and he would recognize more potential in resisting group identification, but in 1922 he felt pulled "deeper and deeper into the Negro group" (*Reader* 16).

26. As Fuss rightly points out "the constructionist impulse" (the desire to stipulate that "essentialist" categories are culturally, especially linguistically, constructed rather than ontologically true) "rather than definitively counteracting essentialism, often simply redeploys it through the very strategy of historicization" (20).

27. Around 1929 Toomer would term himself an essentialist, and though he means something different from the word's contemporary critical connotations, his explanation of the label is relevant to current debates about his position on race:

> As for writing—I am not a romanticist. I am not a classicist or a realist, in the usual sense of these terms. I am an essentialist. Or, to put it in other words, I am a spiritualizer, a poetic realist. This means two things. I try to lift facts, things, happenings, to the planes of rhythm, feeling, and significance. I try to clothe and give body to potentialities. (*Wayward* 20)

The move to raise specific "things" (individual characters, for instance) to a higher plane of significance is a move to abstract types or concepts from material conditions. Such abstraction applied to character would produce an essential type as it certainly does at points in *Cane*. It is also significant that Toomer titled his late manuscript of aphorisms and maxims "Essentials," a reminder that his spiritual interests inevitably led him away from historical specificity toward transcendent ideals.

28. Though my argument about Toomer's formal and racial essentialism opposes "essentialism" and "hybridity," these two categories also reinforce one another. We could not have a sense of hybridity without a sense of essentialism. Yet that does not preclude their functioning as opposites. For discussions on the relation between essentialism and hybridity, see Fuss and Favor.

29. For a persuasive discussion of Whitman's influence on Toomer and on the Harlem Renaissance, see Hutchinson, "The Whitman Legacy and the Harlem Renaissance."

30. Exactly the same points must be made about Frank's collection of short stories, *City Block,* and Frank's emphatic contributions to the writing and publication of *Cane.*

31. *A Boy's Will* (1913), Frost's first book of poetry, was published two months after *North of Boston* in America in 1915. *Mountain Interval,* Frost's third volume, was published in America in 1916, and Toomer certainly read it as well.

32. In the verse dialogues, Frost wanted to dramatize the impasse of two people talking, especially a man and a woman, about a tragedy for which neither of them is responsible and which their conversation can't resolve: "To write a poem in which something terrible happens and no one is to blame—as in 'Home Burial' with the different responses of husband and wife to the death of their young child—Frost felt as a challenge [. . .]" (Pritchard 100).

33. Frost develops his theory of the sound of sense in a letter to John T. Bartlett, where he says that "[t]he best place to get the abstract sound of sense is from voices behind a door that cuts off the words" (664).

34. See Bond's discussion of Stein's mock sonnet from "Patriarchal Poetry" and Williams's quibbles with the form in his letters (7–10).

35. It should go without saying that African American poets often invoked traditional Anglo-European forms ironically. One of the best examples of poetic conventions deployed ironically is Countee Cullen's sonnet "Yet Do I Marvel," in which the elaborate sonnet structure, allusions to Christian doctrine and *Paradise Lost,* and references to Greek myths combine to prove the speaker's high-cultural credentials while simultaneously challenging the assumptions (and exposing the hypocrisy) of that very culture (*My Soul's High Song* 79). Still, along with its shrewd attack on white high culture, the sonnet's lyricism articulates the black poet's gift of song. Langston Hughes gives anecdotal evidence for the widespread assumption that African Americans were innately poetical when he recalls being voted eighth-grade class poet because he was one of only two black students in the class: "my classmates, knowing that a poem had to have rhythm, elected me unanimously—thinking, no doubt, that I had some, being a Negro" (*The Big Sea* 24).

36. In fact, in "The Sorrow Songs" DuBois makes this claim explicitly, transcribing the melody and lyrics of a song passed down in his family for two-hundred years: "Do bana coba, gene me, gene me! / Do bana coba, gene me, gene me! / Ben

d' nuli, nuli, nuli, nuli, ben d' le." He says, "we sing it to our children, knowing as little as our fathers what its words may mean, but knowing well the meaning of its music" (539).

37. Hajek recapitulates Bowen's argument about call-and-response, Coquet posits call-and-response as the key structure, and countless critics invoke call-and-response in reference to *Cane*. Boutry traces blues structures in the book, while Duncan argues for jazz structures. Gayl Jones, however, treats the "Karintha" quatrain as both blues and ballad.

38. Though Bowen applies the call-and-response structure too liberally to *Cane*, her notion that the volume seeks a communal voice, epitomized by that structure, is compelling. It is telling, however, that the tendency to idealize formal moments as call-and-response structures leads to an idealization of voice in *Cane*, and many of her specific readings, of "Her Lips Are Copper Wire" or Dan Moore's interior monologue in "Box Seat," ring false with optimism. Finally, it is curious that Bowen valorizes call-and-response (and thus blues) in *Cane* since she carefully traces allusions and connections to conventional Anglo-European poetic traditions like metaphysical poetry (15) and the Romantic lyric (15).

39. Again I want to emphasize that the blues tercet rhyming AAa is not the only form used by blues people. However, it is universally recognized as the "blues stanza." See, for example, Taft, where all of the songs take this form; Oliver (6); or discussions of blues, which frequently contract the first two lines when quoting lyrics, giving evidence of the established structure of the blues stanza:

Honey, let's go to the river and sit down (twice)
If the blues overtakes us jump overboard and drown. (Tracy 23)

Sachheim takes issue with such abbreviations, precisely because the practice implies "the confining yet more or less ubiquitous notion that the blues constitute essentially a single form" (viii), that single form being the AAa tercet.

40. In fact, it is significant that *Cane* only once alludes to the blues, when Kabnis says (speaking of his own lineage) that there "Aint much difference between blue and black" (108), an allusion to the blues song "(What Did I Do to Be So) Black and Blue." And, the only character in the book associated with jazz is Paul's white roommate Art (75).

41. For an excellent discussion of modernism's suspicion of traditional lyric forms and concomitant valorization of prose, see Timothy Steele, *Missing Measures: Modern Poetry and the Revolt against Meter*, especially chapter 2, "'The Superior Art': Verse and Prose and Modern Poetry." In *Holiday* (1923), a novel about African Americans that Frank was writing while Toomer wrote *Cane*, Frank did find a use for lyric. Here, interludes of free verse break up the prose, sometimes signaling a shift between white and black perspectives, sometimes expressing the longings of the main characters, a wealthy white woman who desires liberation from her staid

life and a poor black man who seeks freedom from his constricted world. Frank certainly observed the potential in juxtaposing prose and poetry in reading his friend Toomer's work, but his own use of the combination suggests simple equations between prose and reality, poetry and fantasy that do not aspire to Toomer's far more complex orchestration of forms.

42. In fact, "the Chicago poets" are not all poets, either; they include Masters, Dreiser, Sandburg, Anderson, and Frederick Booth, only two of whom wrote poetry.

43. Frank and Toomer typically omitted the apostrophe in contractions like "don't" both in their correspondence and in their published writings. Frank's letters to Toomer are excerpted in the Norton Critical Edition of *Cane*. The passages I quote appear on pages 153 and 159.

44. In his own study of U.S. culture, however, Frank had neglected to include African Americans.

45. In attempting to distinguish "our" America (the younger generation's nation) from the America dominated by a commercial, conformist middle class (the heirs of the Puritans), Frank imagines a line of spiritual descent from the "buried" Mexican and Native American cultures to contemporary immigrant cultures. In the chapter on Chicago, for example, a "race" of immigrant farmers follows the vanishing Americans:

> The Mississippi and his legion of waters make [the prairie] fecund. Nations of Indians called it their world and their mother. Buffalo roamed over it like the winds. And then the white man. Buffalo and Indians vanished. But the loam of the plains was ready like a wanton woman. Here was a race who could plant endless wheat and corn, a race of insatiate desire. The prairie would have fruit to dower and dominion the world. Here at last was a race of lovers to satisfy the prairie. (117)

Native Americans are at once the finest model of American identity and doomed to lose their identity, through extinction or assimilation, a situation that renders Frank's attitude toward them purely elegiac. Such an elegiac stance toward the ethnic past is clearly relevant for *Cane*. See Walter Benn Michaels's discussion of just this issue in *Our America: Nativism, Modernism, Pluralism* (136).

CHAPTER 2

1. Since no poem in *Cane* extends beyond one page in length, I will give the page number of each poem in parentheses after the title and will not repeat it each time I quote from the poem. "Song of the Son" appears on page 14.

2. In fact, these stanzas anticipate a famous song about lynching, "Strange Fruit," in which the purple, bursting bodies of the lynching victims hang from the limbs of Southern trees—an image of nature perverted that quickly achieved iconic status in American popular culture when Billie Holiday sang it:

Southern trees bear a strange fruit,
(Blood on the leaves and blood at the root)
Black body swinging in the southern breeze,
(Strange fruit hanging from the poplar trees.)

The poem "Strange Fruit" was written and set to music by Lewis Allan. Novelist Lillian Smith heard Billie Holiday sing it and used the title for her best-selling story of 1944. The poem appears in Lewis Allan, *The Eye of the Storm and Light Verse for Heavy Hearts,* 15.

3. Battenfeld also observes the speaker's seduction by lyric: "The speaker of the poem, seduced by the power of language, misses the violence suggested by this image. In his love of the song, and his desire to possess the song, he forgets the singer whose voice has been cut off by a lynch mob" (1246).

4. For a list of poems Toomer planned to include, see Robert B. Jones's introduction to *The Collected Poems of Jean Toomer* (xxxi–xxxii), and for publication history of the poems, see Robert B. Jones and Margery Toomer Latimer, *The Collected Poems of Jean Toomer* (105). "And Pass" was first published by Darwin Turner in *The Wayward and the Seeking* (1980) and later in *Collected Poems* (1988).

5. DuBois also spells it "mourning," and for similar reasons, in *The Souls of Black Folk:* "The seventh [of ten 'master songs' of 'undoubted Negro origin'] is the song of the End and the Beginning—'My Lord, what a mourning! [. . .]'" (539–40).

6. In fact, the sun sets on nearly every page of *Cane,* and celestial "risings" typically occur at night, not morning. Thus, Karintha's skin is the color of dusk on the *eastern* horizon, suggesting sunrise, yet the designated time is "[w]hen the sun goes *down*" (3). Likewise, "Carma," "Fern," "Avey," "Box Seat," "Harvest Song," and "Bona and Paul" occur at sunset; "Song of the Son" and "Georgia Dusk" employ sunset as a figure of cultural decline and renewal respectively; and "Blood-Burning Moon" inverts the association of dawn with rising and night with setting: "*Up* from the skeleton stone walls, *up* from the rotting floor boards and the solid hand-hewn beams of oak of the pre-war cotton factory, dusk came. *Up* from the dusk the full moon came" (30, emphasis added). In the last paragraph of "Kabnis" (notably, the last page of the book) sunrise finally occurs, yet the description is again cast in the language of decline: "The sun arises. Gold-glowing child, it steps in to the sky and sends a birth-song *slanting down gray dusk* streets and *sleepy* windows of the *southern* town" (117, emphasis added).

7. Thomas Fahy makes a different but compatible, and important, point about folk songs in *Cane*: that folk songs function to enslave African American women and that, as I also contend, African American men are failed folk singers in the volume: "The music of Toomer's male characters unwittingly communicates their frustrating failure to form lasting heterosexual relationships" (50–51). Especially in part 2, according to Fahy, the men's "broken song [. . .] communicates the impact of [their] exclusion from both past and present" (51).

8. Robert B. Jones uses a similar phrase, "the continuum of verbal art in *Cane*"

(38), to describe not merely the range of formal possibilities in the volume but also to indicate that gradations of differences between adjacent forms are often slight.

9. Toomer was originally named Nathan after his father, who deserted him and his mother when Toomer was a few weeks old. His maternal grandfather took them in but insisted on changing the child's name to avoid reference to the absent parent. He was then called Eugene after his godfather, and Toomer began spelling it "Jean" in early adulthood after reading Romain Rolland's *Jean-Christophe* and identifying with the alienated hero (Scruggs, "Fugitive" 85). Still, Toomer employed the name Nathan for fictionalized autobiographical characters and later in life attempted to reclaim that name as his own (Kerman and Eldridge 28–30, 231, 285). In "Natalie Mann," Natalie, as her name indicates, is Nathan's female counterpart, and thus she, too, is a fictional aspect of Toomer. It's significant that Toomer creates characters in "Natalie Mann" who are able to do what Toomer himself cannot accomplish in *Cane*: set the contemporary portrait of "Karintha" to folk tunes. Perhaps it is also significant that it takes two of them, one to read the text and one to create a musical background for it, to achieve this ideal and that one is male and the other female. These are two of the many dichotomies (written/oral, male/female) Toomer was not finally able to reconcile in a persuasive way in his work.

10. See Monica Michlin's "'Karintha': A Textual Analysis" for an excellent reading of the story. Michlin's argument about the contention of genres in "Karintha" agrees with my claim that the entire book depends upon generic distinctions not generic blendings:

> It appears that the discordant symphony of voices that arise page after page in "Karintha" ultimately serves to negate the wishful lyricism and celebration of the book's epigraph as the narrative voice keeps differing from itself (from prose to poetry, from archaic to modernist styles, from lyrical to staccato bitterness) in Toomer's effort to differ from past writing on blackness and to differ from both black and white. (96)

11. Michlin also observes that the narrator's "deliberate selection of vague phrases [. . .] can be understood as the voice's shying away from cruder terms out of hypocrisy or the fear of censorship" (102).

12. Michlin cleverly remarks that "pyramidal" puns on "pyre" (103). For readings of "Karintha" that do not acknowledge the death of her baby, see Duncan ("It is [Karintha's] soul as well as her womb that is ripened bearing holy fruit, flowering none too soon" 326) and Chase ("Like the baby that 'fell out of her womb,' [Karintha] exists in a haze of sweet smoke. In the rural South, poor, with nothing to *do*, she is very much free to *be*" 260).

13. Even if one reads the anonymous lyric as being about Karintha's baby, the song assimilates the tragedy of the child into a Christian mythology, emphasizing the resurrection of the soul.

14. Françoise Clary similarly observes that the shift away from ordinary lan-

guage to the "iconic representation" typically found in lyrical moments is a move that "neutralizes reality" (73).

15. Jones offers a slightly different spectrum of genres: poems, prose poems, lyrical narratives, and prose narratives (37).

16. One exception to this is "Cotton Song" (11), a work song reminiscent of the African American oral tradition (a call-and-response structure, with nonverbal, heavily stressed sounds like "Hump" and "Eoho" voiced to cadence workers' movements, and biblical references). I discuss this poem at length later in chapter 2.

17. Of course, in a social or political reading, the literal fact of their dark skin is anything but *simple:* they are the ones who have to harvest the crops precisely because they are dark-skinned men in a white racist society. "Reapers," like many pieces in *Cane*, orchestrates the various aesthetic, spiritual, social, and political connotations of "black" with subtlety and irony.

18. These two poems on facing pages are the eighth and ninth of sixteen pieces in the first section of *Cane*.

19. In a fine reading, Bus argues that "Cotton Song" creates a parallel between work-song activity and the spiritual quest, that is, between work songs and spirituals (58–59).

20. Richard Eldridge has pointed out Toomer's ironic use of "the courtly tradition" of "itemiz[ing] various physical attributes" in "Face" (225). However, he may underestimate the extent of the irony:

> Toomer plays with the tradition in ironic ways, though with a beauty perhaps far more profound than that usually found in poems of the courtly tradition. The beauty of the woman [in "Face"] is not derived from her static association with ideal and therefore spiritually "superior" attributes. Instead, her beauty is an inward growth of one who has loved and suffered for it, a beauty not of innocence, but of the deepest experience like that expressed in the *Pietá* or the *Caritas Romana*. (225–26)

I read the portrait as a revelation of the destruction of beauty, not as a vision of inner beauty formed through suffering. See Fahy for a discussion of the blazon form in the "portrait" poems that accords with my reading.

21. Given that the woman's hair is "silver-gray," the destruction of beauty is even more complicated than my reading above suggests. Silver hair indicates that the woman in the portrait is already old—and thus not a typical subject for the blazon, which enumerates the qualities of youthful beauty. Yet, the first three lines of the poem—"Hair— / silver-gray, / like streams of stars"—indicate that the blazon form may be invoked to reclaim or discover the older woman's beauty. Her hair is not grizzled and dull but silvery and shiny like stars. When the poem shifts direction in the next image—"Brows— / recurved canoes / quivered by ripples blown by pain"— the expectation that the poem will offer a beautiful portrait (an expectation that has been raised in line 1, questioned in line 2, and reasserted in line 3) is finally

defeated. This is a minor observation but reveals Toomer adeptly managing and undermining the expectations of traditional form.

22. Among others, Eldridge reads "Portrait in Georgia" as a description of a white woman, whose physical features incite scenes of lynching: "The effect is one of uniting passionate desire with ugly violence. Each physical attraction brings the black man closer to the consummation of death instead of love" (234). While I recognize the value of his reading, I hesitate to assume that the woman in the poem is white because the imagery suggests something more ambiguous than the familiar white woman/black man iconography of lynching. The other moments in *Cane* that refer to lynching—"Blood-Burning Moon" and the story of Mame Lamkins in "Kabnis"—do not concern this familiar American plot. On the contrary, Tom Burwell is lynched for fighting with a white man over a black woman, and the black Mame Lamkins and her baby are lynched because she hides her husband from whites. Lynching in *Cane* seems associated with the destruction of whatever is black and beautiful (whether an attractive African-America woman or the love between African Americans) rather than with black desire for whiteness. What Eldridge's reading cleverly exposes, nevertheless, is the tortured confusion of black and white, desire and violence, in *Cane*. Michaels captures this confusion particularly well: "The description of *her* body is simultaneously the narrative destruction of *his* body, which is to say that the description of a black man's love for the white woman is simultaneously the description of the destruction of the black man by his love for the white woman" (61). In a fascinating discussion of *Cane*'s exploration of racial boundaries, Hutchinson argues that the poem "superimpos[es] the images of the white woman, the apparatus of lynching, and the burning flesh of the black man," imagery that embodies the racist culture's most extreme method of "maintain[ing] a racial difference the poem linguistically defies" ("Racial Discourse" 233–34).

23. The critique of Christianity as an alien, white religion is even more overt in a longer version of the poem Toomer composed for a short story, "Withered Skin of Berries," not published in his lifetime:

Court-house tower,
Bell-buoy of the Whites,
Charting the white-man's channel,
Bobs on the agitated crests of pines
And sends its mellow monotone,
Satirically sweet,
To guide the drift of barges . .
Black barges . .
African Guardian of Souls,
Drunk with rum,
Feasting on a strange cassava,
Yielding to new words and a weak palabra
Of a white-faced sardonic God—

In an image that recalls H.D.'s famous Imagist poem "Oread"—"Whirl up, sea— / whirl your pointed pines" (*Collected Poems* 55)—the pine-covered landscape is imagined as an ocean. The white tower of a white institution (here the courthouse tower but also suggestive of a church spire) emerges from this sea of green, like a signal buoy, to guide blacks, who are journeying in an alien land (this may account for the defamiliarizing imagery of land as sea), into the "white-man's channel." That "[b]ell-buoy" puns on "bellboy" hints at the likely result of cultural contact between the Africans and the white Americans: blacks will be put into service to whites. The poem appears in the text of "Withered Skin of Berries" in *The Wayward and the Seeking* (161).

24. I take this account of the conservatism of the Greek chorus from *The New Princeton Encyclopedia of Poetry and Poetics* (201). For a fuller discussion of the social function of the chorus, see Webster.

25. The invitation to "Come along" echoes Robert Frost's "The Pasture," a similarly idealizing invitation to enter the traditionally lyrical and bucolic world of his first book, *A Boy's Will.* The second stanza captures the mood:

I'm going out to fetch the little calf
That's standing by the mother. It's so young,
It totters when she licks it with her tongue.
I sha'n't be gone long.—You come too. (3)

26. Similarly, the cane field in "Blood-Burning Moon" will function as a mythic healing ground even for the white Bob Stone: "He crashed into the bordering cane-brake. Cane leaves cut his face and lips. He tasted blood. He threw himself down and dug his fingers into the ground. The earth was cool. Cane-roots took the fever from his hands" (34).

27. For a detailed analysis of imagery associating Louisa with the moon, see Mellard (49–50).

28. "The Day of Judgment" appeared in the 1867 *Slave Songs of the United States* (53). "Stars in the Elements" is from *Religious Folk-Songs of the Negro* (1927), published only a few years after *Cane,* and appears in a section devoted to "Hymns of Judgment" (162–63).

29. The erotic imagery in the description of Tom's lynching (his "erect" head and his popping eyes, suggesting sexual consummation) expresses white fears of black sexual potency. Of course, the excessive violence of the lynching ritual—hanging, castration, and burning—reveals the fear that killing a black man is not enough to check his sexual power. Throughout *Cane* Toomer focuses on the burning component of lynching, the literal boiling and "popping" of the body during lynching serving as a metaphor for the self-hatred and rage that consume many of his male characters.

30. For an excellent discussion of figuration in the Song of Songs, especially the

figurative play between beloved and landscape, see Robert Alter's chapter "The Garden of Metaphor" (185–203) in *The Art of Biblical Poetry.*

CHAPTER 3

1. Benson and Dillard (80–81), Baker (*Journey* 32), Byrd (39), Martin (12), and others have noted the pun on "robot." Arthur P. Davis considers the spelling of "Rhobert" affected, as if to suggest a French pronunciation, a sign of Rhobert's bourgeois pretensions (47). Griffin suggests that the "'h' inserted in his name [. . .] illustrate[s] his wearing a 'h'ouse; it has become significant to his identity" (66).

2. Rice analyzes the change in the *imagery* of song in part 2 (as opposed to the forms of lyric), though he also gives excellent readings of the poems themselves ("Incomplete Circle"). Golding also makes such a distinction: "The sterile North bears less poetry literally and metaphorically" (208).

3. "Gulp" derives through a series of associations from the Dutch word *gulpen,* meaning to "swallow, guzzle, to issue in streams." It is also related to the Middle Swedish word *glup,* which means "throat" ("Gulp," *Oxford English Dictionary,* 1989 ed.).

4. Technically, of course, the drone's work is to inseminate the queen and populate the hive. However, the notion that drones are parasitic nonworkers is quite popular, both in literature employing the beehive as a figure for human society and in apiary lore.

5. While it's true that part 1 poems depict Southern experience and part 2 poems Northern experience, this is not finally what distinguishes them. The crucial difference is not that the first vision is all beauty and glory and the second is all defeat and reality but that part 1 poems can do the work they set out to do, whether to reveal the ugliness or the beauty, while part 2 poems consistently cannot. In "Portrait in Georgia," the braided chestnut hair that's coiled like a lyncher's rope is part of a coherent if terrible metaphor associating the recognition of black beauty with its destruction; however, in "Storm Ending" the thunder that blossoms gorgeously like bell-flowers, like bells, like faces, like a face bitten and bleeding, like a honeycomb, like some terrible encompassing thing the whole earth must fly from, as we shall see, isn't coherent.

6. Nicholls also argues that the urban denizens of part 2 seek an escape into pastoral fantasy; the speaker of "Beehive," for instance, "abstracts himself from the [urban] scene into an agrarian landscape" ("Modernization" 162).

7. The use of synesthetic imagery may have even subtler and more reaching significance. Synesthetic imagery is a device associated with Symbolist rather than Imagist poetics. The Symbolist longing to retreat from the modern industrial world, a world increasingly committed to scientific realism, is antithetical to the Imagist project of precision and clarity. The characteristic inwardness, dreaminess, and privacy of Symbolist poetry may help explain the tendency of part 2 poems to veer from Imagist realism toward Symbolist impressionism. The poems in part 2 consis-

tently demonstrate the futility of poetry in the Northern industrial environment. As song weakens in this section, the revelatory powers associated with poetry in part 1 falter. "Beehive" and "Storm Ending" fail to perform their Imagist function in *Cane* because they retreat from documentary realism to private symbolism, a retreat that signals the defeat of lyric in this particular book.

8. See, for example, "Seventh Street" (41) and "Rhobert" (42).

9. Only Rice seems to notice the metaphorical distortions in the poem ("Incomplete Circle" 450).

10. Wagner-Martin, who recognizes a comic tone in the poem (22), and Rice, who reads the electrical imagery negatively (450), are rare exceptions to the general consensus that "Her Lips Are Copper Wire" is a successful love poem—and one of the most masterful poems in the book.

11. Mark Whalan makes one of the most careful and persuasive arguments for reading "Her Lips" as a paean to technology. In "Jean Toomer, Technology, and Race" he distinguishes between Anglo-European celebrations of technology (the Futurists, for instance) and the African American suspicion of industrial advances that would likely leave black people unemployed. Toomer, Whalan argues, ignored "the impact upon African Americans of machinery in the workplace" and was thus free "to speculate on how technology's twin attributes of power and radical novelty might be useful in reconceptualising the increasingly inflexible categorisation of race within the United States" (467). Thus, he concludes that the "bodies in 'Her Lips Are Copper Wire' achieve a liberatory form of interpersonal communication, and freedom from white discursive structures of the black body, achieved through the new communicative possibilities of technology" (468). Here and elsewhere, Whalan's work brings needed historical detail to the study of Toomer; however, like other readers he doesn't observe the poem's extremely troubled invocation of technology.

12. Fahy also remarks on the imperatives: "The speaker's use of second person places a formal distance between himself and the woman he is addressing [. . .]. As a matter of fact, in all these love songs no dialogue occurs—the men only describe and command" (59).

13. See Tim Armstrong, *The Technology of Modernism*, especially chapter 1, "Electrifying the Body."

14. In fact, the electrical imagery doesn't require the wet setting in order to suggest electrocution. The filaments in a tungsten bulb are never insulated, and thus one does not "remove the tape" in order to produce light. The insulated wires are those that carry the charge from the source to the bulb, where the exposed filaments together produce radiance. If the tape on the insulated wires were removed, the lamp would shock and short out. This may sound like a pedantic objection to the imagery, but if the lovers are like insulated electrical wires (as opposed to uninsulated tungsten filaments), then undressing/removing the tape would not be incandescent but fatal.

15. Copper is a soft, malleable metal, and applying these traits to the poem could generate a more positive reading; however, the word "wire" obstructs such a reading. Toomer's comment on copper in "Reflections of an Earth-Being" makes an analogy between copper sheets and flower petals that seems to assert a congruity between the natural and industrial worlds that many would like to read in "Her Lips." Indeed, there he also associates the smell of electricity with "the smell of earth after a spring shower" (*Wayward* 43) in a suggestive parallel to the poem's combination of electricity and water. However, Toomer wrote these remarks six or seven years after *Cane,* and it would be reductive to suggest that he couldn't create a metaphor in a poem that differs from an analogy he used elsewhere. In fact, the passage from "Earth-Being" brings copper and flowers, electricity and showers together in order to assert their differences, not their similarities. He claims to be "a natural poet of man's artifices" (43), thus acknowledging the distinction between nature and technology. It is this distinction that underscores "Her Lips."

According to Tim Armstrong, the first accidental death by electrocution in America occurred in 1881; the first judicial electrocution soon followed in 1890. See Armstrong's "Electrifying the Body" (chapter 1), especially the subsection "Electric Death" (31–36) for a discussion of the public sensation aroused by electrical deaths in the early century.

16. The word "wire" has long-standing associations in amorous lyrics, associations that seem to have been ambivalent all along, most famously in Shakespeare's contrablazon, sonnet 130: "If hairs be wires, then black wires grow on her head."

17. Pound describes three poetic modes: melopoeia, or musicality; phanopoeia, or imagery; and logopoeia, word play and unconventional use of language. He outlines these categories in *How to Read* (25–26) and elsewhere.

18. Innes identifies the "little finger" as an allusion to *Tertium Organum,* where Ouspensky describes our limited perception: "by studying the little finger of man we cannot discover his reason" (315).

19. McKay, Griffin, North, and Whalan ("Technology") read "Seventh Street" as wholly positive, a position that is unresponsive to the ironies and contradictions in the imagery and that ignores the generic differences between the prose, which cannot control the imagery of violence, and poetry, which romanticizes violence as beneficial vitality.

20. The one "who set you flowing" is not the wealthy bootlegger but God, which raises the question: is God just a buzzard in heaven watching the destruction of African Americans in the North as well as in the South? The narration tries to repudiate this possibility: "God would not dare to suck black red blood. A Nigger God! He would duck his head in shame and call for the Judgment Day" (41). Still, something permits the destruction of African Americans, and, if it's not God, then God must not exist: *did he dwell in stars* ("Prayer" 70), he would prevent such violence. Moreover, a God who would have to duck his head in shame is one who cannot protect his people, as he clearly couldn't in "Blood-Burning Moon" and just as clearly

won't be able to in part 2. This tepid defense of God obviously doesn't "answer," and the prose concludes with the question that has become, through repetition, an accusatory refrain: "Who set you flowing?"

21. Darwin Turner, editor of the Norton edition of *Cane*, identifies the Howard Theater as a distinctly African American setting in a note to the text: "A theater in the Afro-American section of Washington, DC; the audiences and the performers were also Afro-American" (52). Scruggs and VanDemarr point out that the Howard "specialized in jazz and 'popular' entertainment" (176) in contrast to the Lincoln Theater, which appealed to more "genteel tastes" (176). The Lincoln Theater is one of the settings in "Box Seat." Scruggs and VanDemarr refer to sociologist William H. Jones, *Recreation and Amusement*, for information about the theater scene in Washington, D.C., at the time *Cane* was written.

22. The *Oxford English Dictionary* dates "snatch" as a slang term for female genitals from 1904.

23. Edmunds provides a fascinating discussion of dancing in *Cane*, arguing for "the radical power of black dance" (157) to transform the lynching plot:

> [Toomer] revises the pattern established in part 1 of *Cane* in which black and white Southerners embody displaced versions of the lynching plot in various forms of hysterical suffering. In part 2, African American characters instead seek to embody the lynching plot in ecstatic acts of aesthetic and cultural self-transformation that simultaneously transform the fabric of everyday life. Deriving the cultural power to overturn the lynching plot from new forms of black working-class music and dance, Toomer neatly undercuts the claims of his black middle-class contemporaries that the culture of respectability offers the only viable route to African Americans' political and social equality. (156)

She and I disagree about the book's attitude toward modern African American popular culture, and especially about dance. But noting the "strain of violence running through the transformative visions of all Toomer's male prophets in *Cane*" (158), Edmunds concludes, as I do, that "the ecstatic transformations of the lynching plot undertaken in part 2 begin to look less like popular blueprints for social and cultural revolution and more like the compensatory fantasies of alienated dreamers" (159).

24. Dan's vision of the mythic progenitor also involves the repeatedly disturbing formulation of part 2: the personification of buildings and streets and the concomitant dehumanization of people.

25. George Hutchinson kindly confirmed my hunch that "Our Poets" refers to those nineteenth-century American poets whose pictures adorned schoolrooms well into the twentieth century: "they'd have a row of portraits above the blackboard or elsewhere, or one framed picture with portraits of each poet and the title 'Our Poets.' Toomer is referring to the pre-'modern' national poetic canon. As opposed, above all, to Walt Whitman. The picture hangs perilously [in "Bona and Paul"] because

of the threat the music implies to the dominance of the Victorian aesthetic" (e-mail to the author, 12 Feb. 2001).

26. Fabre and Feith ("Oracle" 8) and Rice (457) also read "Harvest Song" as a poem about failure.

CHAPTER 4

1. Toomer originally composed "Kabnis" as a play, but Waldo Frank suggested he revise it into a "freer form of narrative in which your dialog, which has no kinship with the theatric, might [thrive] more successfully" (*C* 158). Scruggs and Van-Demarr interpret Frank's advice as a call to abandon "realistic dialogue" in favor of "symbolic or poetic dialogue" (116) since Toomer was more adept at the latter. Even more important, they argue that the "'freer form' allowed him to escape the discursive for the poetic and symbolic, joining this hybrid poetic drama to the patterns of imagery, symbol, and myth that Toomer developed in his other material . . . [pushing] the work toward a modernist form of narration" (117). In my reading, the variegated texture of "Kabnis"—realistic dialogue, theatrical speeches, narrative, stage directions, mythic interludes, and lyrical outbursts—enacts generic tensions that Toomer associates with competing representations of the world. For discussions of the dramatic form in "Kabnis," see Turner ("Failure of a Playwright"), Fabre, Petesch, Reilly, and Mellard.

2. Battenfeld would generalize my thesis about the failure of lyric in *Cane* to the failure of language as a whole. In "'Been Shapin Words T Fit M Soul,'" she argues that Kabnis's desire to be an African American poet-prophet "can only be heard as farcical" because "words in *Cane,* however elegant or eloquent, do not stop racial violence, or inspire action against racial oppression. The novel, and the experience of reading it, prove Toomer's power as a writer, and the power of an African-American cultural heritage. But in the end, words do not liberate the people of *Cane*" (1242).

3. Hajek makes an interesting point that Kabnis's distinction between preachers and orators reveals him to be isolated from the African American community: "As an orator he is, unlike a preacher, no longer dependent on a community that would respond to him and thereby establish his authority" (188–89).

4. Michael North reads the dialect in *Cane* much more positively than I do here, but I certainly agree with him that Toomer explores the possibilities of dialect "not to preserve a particular language but to use the disjunctive strategies of that language to invent new forms" (168). That is, the dialect in "Kabnis" is not a faithful recording of how the rural blacks Toomer heard in Georgia actually spoke but a literary language that captures the disruptive power of nonstandard forms: "When the dialect motive of disarranging and rearranging standard speech patterns is brought to literature, the result is not primitivism but modernism" (168). However, where North senses the creation of a new form, I sense the destruction of the old ("golden-tasting words") without the creation of a new and viable form. Thus, Kabnis falls into silence at the end. Significantly, in noting the distinction between stan-

dard English and dialect, North implies a distinction between poetry and some other kind of language that articulates the deformations of racism in the deformations of speech—that is, a generic distinction between poetry and prose. And *Cane* bears out such an opposition: in all of *Cane* only "Kabnis" is a dialect piece (other parts of *Cane* employ dialect only briefly), though Toomer had written dialect poems as early as 1920 (North 168). While North's immediate subject is not genre, he observes that conventional lyric forms appear to be immune to Toomer's aesthetic of breaks and discontinuities: "the formal structure of most of the poems in the collection—and certainly those in the first section of the book—suggests that Toomer could not imagine how to make the imagist aesthetic of breaks and discontinuities serve" the function of producing a modern literature that honored ancestral voices in avant-garde forms (172). This, for North, is the unresolved conflict in *Cane,* a result of Toomer's "inability to choose when 'modern forms' and 'ancient voices' come into conflict" (173). But if *Cane* chronicles the loss of ancient voices, demonstrating that there will be no blending of the past and the present in a new form, then the failure of the poems to be innovative—especially those in the first section of *Cane*—is a measure of the volume's success.

5. Like the other victims of lynching in *Cane,* Tom Burwell and Bill Burnham, Mame Lamkins's name seems to announce violence: burning, maiming, even perhaps laming. Moreover, she is the "kin" of the sacrificial "lamb." Sam Raymon (90) may be an exception since he chose to leap to his death voluntarily rather than be murdered by the lynch mob.

6. Lewis envisions Carrie K. meeting the same fate as the women in "Face" and "Portrait in Georgia": "His mind flashes images of her life in the southern town. He sees the nascent woman, her flesh already stiffening to cartilage, drying to bone. Her spirit-bloom, even now touched sullen, bitter. Her rich beauty fading" (103).

7. In *Cane* and elsewhere, Toomer employs the figure of impalement not only as an image of lynching/crucifixion but of cultural restraints that effectively destroy one's life. Thus, Kabnis uses this same figure both to express his violent rejection of Father John as the desire to lynch him (114) and to protest his dissatisfaction with being a wheelwright's apprentice (115). I discuss both of these moments in more detail in the text. Moreover, Toomer recurs to this figure in his 1936 "Outline of an Autobiography" when recounting the unrealized lives of the workers in the shipyards, "their spirits crucified in life, up against it and nailed there" (qtd. in Scruggs and VanDemarr 61).

8. For a discussion of the male narrators and characters in *Cane,* especially as they relate to Kabnis, see Gibson.

9. Scruggs has another reading: "The lie that Father John speaks of is the myth that Negroes are the descendants of Cain" ("Mark of Cain" 283). Similarly, Taylor identifies "[t]he biblical lie of the curse of Cain and the curse of Ham [as] an apt symbol for the injuries of slavery and the psychic wounds of its aftermath" (54).

10. For a thorough discussion of how language underwrites racism in the world of *Cane,* see Battenfeld.

11. Griffin makes this point a slightly different way, arguing that Kabnis's soul and its twisted form are "one in the same thing. His soul is the place of beauty and ugliness, pleasure and pain" (152–53). She argues that Kabnis is in a state of fragmentation, alienated from and unable to realize the unity of African American history: "For Kabnis, the history embodied in the ancestor is an ugly history filled with shame and horror. He cannot imagine it as a source that nourishes his artistic imagination" (153).

12. Robert B. Jones views the removal of the robe as a sign that Kabnis is casting off his alienating pretension and accepting his place as a member of the black community: "After a night underground, during which time the depths of his racial consciousness are tested, Kabnis takes off his candidate's robe, symbolizing initiation into the community" (*Prison-House* 54). See also Thornton (275). This interpretation is a first step in claiming that Kabnis is a positive figure at the end. However, the bitterness and dejection with which he removes the robe and the fact that he hangs it on the heavily symbolic nail oblige, as I argue in the text, a much more negative reading.

13. Halsey's home, like his shop, is a shrine to the past. A stopped clock sits on the "old-fashioned mantelpiece" beneath portraits of his ancestors (87). Though he says that "[s]hapin shafts and buildin wagons'll make a man" of Kabnis, the shop has almost no business (97, 99, 104), and Halsey does repairs for white people for free to keep the peace (102).

14. Edmunds also analyzes Toomer's use of lynching imagery to figure forth the unrealized life of African Americans: "Toomer repeatedly links the public torture of terrorized African Americans with the occluded domestic suffering of black and white hysterics. In a final turn of his collection, Toomer presents racial stigma itself as a species of hysteria grounded in the lynching plot" (146).

15. See, for example, McKay (171).

16. Halsey not only works at an old-fashioned job, he holds antiquated notions about race as well. Though he served in Europe in World War I and attended school in the North, he feels more comfortable working in his shop in the South. "Give me th work and fair pay an I aint askin nothin better," he tells Lewis, but he doesn't charge Mr. Ramsay, the white customer, because "[Whites] like y if y work for them" (102). He gets along by being submissive to whites. Carrie, his sister, also submits to Southern codes. She loves Lewis "fearlessly" (103) yet won't allow herself to follow her impulses: "Awkwardly she draws away. The sin-bogies of respectable southern colored folks clamor at her: 'Look out! Be a *good* girl. Look out!' She gropes for her basket that has fallen to the floor. Finds it, and marches with a rigid gravity to her task of feeding the old man" (103). Her care of the old slave, universally read as a positive acceptance of responsibility to ancestors, might also be viewed as indicative of her tending solely to the past and accepting outmoded attitudes. After all, she picks up her fallen basket as Kabnis has just picked up the bucket of dead coals (and these are equally anachronistic props), and her name, Carrie *K.*, hints that she will become Carrie Kabnis, joining Ralph Kabnis in a defeated life.

17. Even when it is first described, the robe bears an oblique resemblance to a lynched body: "A loose something that looks to be a gaudy ball costume dangles from a near-by hook" (106). Here at the end, "hanging" the robe on a "nail" likewise suggests an allusion to the Crucifixion. The association between lynching and crucifying is clear in the image of Mame Lamkins's baby impaled on a tree.

18. The language of the rest of the paragraph is also suggestively autoerotic. Kabnis "strokes" his mustache with one hand and tries to give "squareness and projection" to his chin with the other. Further, the description of his body moves downward, from his mustache to his chin to his armpits, and, by implication, lower. "Moisture gathers in his arm-pits," partly from fear but also, I am suggesting, from sexual arousal. Finally, when a rat runs across the ceiling boards and distracts him, Kabnis "thrusts his head out from the covers," which indicates he hasn't been reading (84).

19. In his autobiographical writings, Toomer associates masturbating with physical and mental weakness. In "The Maturing Years," he describes fits of masturbating that "reduced [him] so low [he] feared [he] was going into decline." He fought back with a discipline of physical training, weight lifting, wrestling, dieting, nature cure, breathing exercises, and careful living (*Wayward* 89–90). Kabnis's desire to join his visionary mind to a "bull-neck and heaving body" is reminiscent of Toomer's attempt to strengthen his mind by building his body. For an excellent study of Toomer's interest in body building as means of creating a new (racial) identity, see Whalan, "'Taking Myself in Hand'": "'self-improvement' through physical culture seemed to offer an identity that was in many ways devoid of history, the chance of a reformation into a 'strong and healthy young man' and the banishment of a history of weakness and 'indulgences'" (604). Whalan does not discuss this scene of Kabnis in bed, but his argument supports my claim that the masturbating Kabnis is one of Toomer's figures for the failed prophet.

20. In his Atlanta Exposition address, delivered in 1895 and widely circulated in *Up From Slavery* (1901), Washington articulates his notion of appropriate progress for blacks. African Americans should "learn to dignify and glorify common labour and put brains and skill into common occupations of life" rather than aspire to intellectual work. Halsey echoes Washington's celebration of manual labor, "there aint no books whats got th feel t them of them there tools," as well as his conviction that African Americans should remain in the South (100). Urging blacks to "learn to draw the line between the superficial and substantial, the ornamental gewgaws in life and the useful," Washington singles out poetry as one of the gewgaws: "No race can prosper till it learns that there is as much dignity in tilling a field as in writing a poem" (100). He tells a story of a ship in need of water that signals to another ship for help. The captain of the second ship signals back that they should cast down their bucket where they are, that is, they should drink the water that's around them, an injunction that appears to be harmful since saltwater is undrinkable. However, when the desperate captain finally casts down his bucket, "it [comes] up full of fresh, sparkling water from the mouth of the Amazon River" (99). Washington

uses this as a parable for African Americans, whom he urges to be satisfied with where and what they are, to seek self-improvement only of the sort Hanby advocates ("to live better, cleaner, more noble lives" [*C* 95]) rather than aspire after what whites have. Hanby is one Booker T. Washington figure in *Cane*, his school modeled after the Tuskegee Institute and his philosophy of model Negroes articulated the night he fires Kabnis: "I cannot hinder the progress of a race simply to indulge a single member" (95). Fabre wonders whether the bucket is an allusion to "Booker T. Washington's famous metaphor" but doesn't speculate about its significance (118).

21. Baker and Ikonné regard the bucket of dead coals as a positive symbol. For Baker, the dead coals represent "past ritual" ("Journey" 43), but this doesn't explain why Kabnis, whom he terms "a new-world creator" (42–43), still carries it at the end. Ikonné asserts that the dead coals "like dry bones to which Ezekial preaches in the valley, are a symbol of rejuvenation" (139).

22. Christ, of course, expresses a human dread of suffering and death in the Garden of Gethsemane (Mark 14:34–36) and just before he dies on the cross (Mark 15:34).

23. Scruggs and VanDemarr give a good summary of the debates over the ending of *Cane* (203). For a range of readings, see Bone (88), Turner (*Minor Chord*), Perry (34, 42), Golding (213), Hutchinson ("Racial Discourse" 243), Caldiera (549), Petesch (211–12), Goede (85), Fisher (509, 513–15), MacKethan (434), and Reilly (323).

24. I read the "gold-glowing child" as an African American. Others specify that he is mulatto, the offspring of a union between whites and blacks. In these readings, Paul's vision of miscegenation as a potentially positive union is the book's antecedent for such a figure: "A Negress chants a lullaby beneath the mate-eyes of a southern planter. Her breasts are ample for the suckling of a song" ("Bona and Paul" 73). Further, Toomer's insistence on positing the "First American," who is raceless because he embodies a blending of races, is another reason critics emphasize the gold-glowing child as an image of interracial harmony. Yet, given the "one drop rule" that designated as black any person with African American ancestors, no matter how remote, the difference between the son/sun being black or mulatto seems slight. The crucial thing, of course, as all readers acknowledge, is that the usurping white child is being superseded by a nonwhite child.

25. The fact that the night winds are "vagrant poets" echoes the song's assertion that whites own the land. The night winds are African American voices ("And cracks between the boards are black. These cracks are the lips the night winds use for whispering" 83), and "vagrant" suggests they are homeless. It is curious that white voices sing the lullaby ("White winds croon [the white child's] sleep-song" 84) since that passage hints that the black mother will eventually let the white child fall.

26. For example, "We raise de wheat" follows this pattern: "We raise de wheat / Dey gib us de corn; / We bake de bread, / Dey gib us de cruss [. . .]" ("We raise de wheat," *American Poetry* 819).

27. Though in my reading it is impossible to take these lyrical flights at face value, readers tend to do so because such moments fulfill cultural expectations for African

American literature, here lyricism and the mythologizing of black women and the Southern landscape. See, for example, Fabre (125–26), whose reading of the opening to section 5 of part 3 is exactly opposite to mine.

28. North's version of this argument is one of the best: "Toomer uses ellipses to suspend ordinary syntax and to mimic the action of splitting or breaking indispensable to creation. Out of these breaks in the ordinary, leaping across them, comes a speech and a poetic, both associated with jazz" (170).

29. Though elsewhere in their analysis Scruggs and VanDemarr view the ending of *Cane* skeptically (see page 203, for instance), they express optimism about the final vision of Carrie K. and Father John: "[W]hen Carrie K. kneels before Father John within a 'soft circle' of morning light, youth embraces age, the present encompasses the past, and the regenerative process begins anew" (186). See also McKay (171) and Martin (18).

30. Several readers who regard Kabnis as a failure are nevertheless persuaded by the concluding lyricism that the dream of the poet-son has not failed. Thus, Griffin imports Toomer as "the true son of the text" (154) to compensate for Kabnis's failure and to account for the closing lyricism and optimism. Scruggs and VanDemarr likewise distinguish between the defeated Kabnis and "the narrator," who turns out to be "the poet of 'Karintha,'" emerging "to restore history" (195). Their notion that the lyrical ending *restores* rather than evades history is unexpected in such an astute book. See also McKay (177), Blake (533), Lieber (50), Bus (69), and MacKethan (433).

31. Scruggs has an interesting account of the word "pauses" here: "Toomer is describing *Cane* in organic terms, and therefore it never really ends. It begins all over again with 'Bona and Paul,' the story that follows 'Harvest Song'" ("Mark of Cain" 279).

32. Charles T. Davis offers a fine reading of the book according to Toomer's retrospective outline, starting from "Bona and Paul" and concluding with "Harvest Song" ("South" 194–96). Byrd also provides a good discussion of the retrospective structure (17–48).

33. Bowen rightly remarks upon the almost synonymous status of "past" and "song" in *Cane*: "If *Cane* is an elegy, it is an elegy for a form; what moved Toomer to write was the sense that the spiritual would soon be lost to us" (16).

CHAPTER 5

1. Toomer was introduced to Gurdjieff's philosophy in 1923 and first traveled to his Institute for the Harmonious Development of Man in Fontainebleau, France, in 1924. He ran his own Gurdjieffian workshops in Harlem (1925) and Chicago (1926–1930). He broke with Gurdjieff in 1935 but never abandoned the master's teachings and attempted to establish his own institute at his Doylestown, Pennsylvania, farm from 1936–1938. In 1938 he began attending Society of Friends meetings, traveled in 1939 to India for spiritual enlightenment, and joined the Friends in 1940. He was active in Quaker ministry from 1941–1954. During this period he had a "physical reading" from psychic Edgar Cayce, entered into Jungian psychoanalysis, and briefly

explored Dianetics (which later became the Church of Scientology). He returned to the Gurdjieffian fold in 1953. See Kerman and Eldridge for a chronology of Toomer's life (1–9) and detailed, sensitive accounts of all these ventures.

2. Nearly all of Toomer's critics express regret about the shift in his writing after *Cane.* See, for example, Nellie McKay (245–46), Turner (30–59), and Gates, who surveys and analyzes both Toomer's remarks on the shift and his critics' responses to it (196–224).

3. In his foreword to Toomer's volume of aphorisms, *Essentials,* Rudolph P. Byrd writes: "Unfortunately, one of the negative consequences of Toomer's immersion in the Gurdjieff work is the disappearance of the lyrical and poetic sensibility that produced *Cane*" (xvi). Jones's chapter on "Art and Gurdjieffian Idealism" provides a detailed, thoughtful, and sympathetic study of the poet as philosopher (*Prison-House* 65–111).

4. See, for example, McKay (212), Turner (30), and Walker (65).

5. In fact, a line from this poem appears in section 57 of *Essentials,* Toomer's book of aphorisms (n. pag.).

6. In addition to Toomer's long-standing suspicion of lyric beauty, expressed most explicitly in "Kabnis," where ugly words and bad poetry are needed to confront modernity, his association with Gurdjieff increased his interest in discordant language. Gurdjieff's style was often crude and shocking, in order to stun people out of their habituated ways, and he coined awkward-sounding words in his own lectures and writings. Toomer emulated these practices, incorporating vulgarity, humor, satire, and grotesque coinages, often character names, into his writings (though he had already demonstrated these tendencies, especially in "Kabnis"). For an excellent discussion of Gurdjieffian aesthetics and their effect on Toomer's writing, see Jon Woodson, especially 30–34. See also Byrd (100–01), Kerman and Eldridge (143, 224, 378–79).

7. Jones says that the poem "[D]evelops in four movements, each beginning with the pronouncement 'It is a new America'" (*Prison-House* 73), while Byrd reads it as "divided into three sections. Each section is introduced by an italicized stanza [the black, white, and blue meridian stanzas] that evokes and establishes the tone and mood for the action that follows it" (158).

8. Byrd offers a succinct account of the four states of consciousness:

[T]he first and most primitive is the sleeping state. In this state we are immersed totally in our dreams. Sensations, sights, sounds may enter the mind, but in the sleeping state we cannot determine their origin and significance, and upon waking we may not even remember them. In this passive, subjective state we cannot be logical or exercise judgment. [. . .] The second state of consciousness is waking consciousness. This is the state in which we work, interact, and exercise. In fine, this is the state in which we fulfill all of our obligations. But [. . .] the effects of sleep remain with us even after we are awake. Plainly, a critical attitude is present in the second state, for our sensory capabilities are fully operable and we are able to engage in complex physical and psychological activities. But the dreams of the night before are still with us[. . . .] Self-consciousness is the [third] state in which we become objective toward ourselves. [. . .] [W]e possess will, that is, the ability to do. We also possess individuality or a permanent, unchangeable 'I.' [. . .] The fourth state [. . .] is objective consciousness or [. . .] 'cosmic consciousness.' In this exalted state we can know the full truth about everything. (80–81)

9. Byrd's detailed analysis of the poem is both generous about the optimism of Toomer's project and exacting about its "disturbing [historical] inaccuracies" (163). See "'The Blue Meridian': Poetry as Development" (152–75), especially 162–75.

10. Since the poem is not lineated, I will give page numbers from *Collected Poems* parenthetically in the text.

11. The entire project of "The Blue Meridian" is Whitmanian in its aspiration to be an American epic and its vision of democratic equality. Rusch details Whitman's influence on the poem, identifying close parallels of phrasing: "Just as Whitman commands, 'Unscrew the locks from the doors! / Unscrew the doors themselves from their jambs!' [. . .], so also does Toomer command, 'Uncase, unpod whatever impedes . . . '" ("Blue Man" 48). Others identify further influences. Bell notes the "harmonious blend of Darwinian evolution and Gurdjieffian mysticism" in the poem ("Poet as Prophet" 78). McKay (214) and Byrd (154–56) discuss Hart Crane's influence as well.

12. See, for example, "White Arrow" (*Collected Poems* 43), where the white arrow represents the "greater" force available to but unused by most people.

13. There is no date for "To Gurdjieff Dying," but he died in 1949.

14. Though Toomer broke with Gurdjieff in 1935, he continued to pursue Gurdjieffian ideas for the rest of his life. In 1930 he claimed, "With certain notable exceptions, every one of my main ideas has a Gurdjieff idea as its parent" (qtd. in Turner, *Minor Chord*, 37, and in Byrd 176). Byrd discusses Gurdjieff's lasting influence on Toomer's work in his conclusion (176–90).

Works Cited

Allan, Lewis. "Strange Fruit." *The Eye of the Storm and Light Verse for Heavy Hearts.* Hastings on Hudson, NY: Peter Piper, 1969. 15.

Alter, Robert. *The Art of Biblical Poetry.* N.p.: Basic, 1985.

Anderson, Sherwood. *Winesburg, Ohio.* 1919. Ed. Charles E. Modlin and Ray Lewis White. New York: Norton, 1996.

Armstrong, Tim. *Modernism, Technology, and the Body: A Cultural Study.* Cambridge: Cambridge UP, 1998.

Baker, Houston A., Jr. *Afro-American Poetics: Revisions of Harlem and the Black Aesthetic.* Madison: U of Wisconsin P, 1988.

———. *The Journey Back: Issues in Black Literature and Criticism.* Chicago: U of Chicago P, 1980.

———. *Modernism and the Harlem Renaissance.* Chicago: U of Chicago P, 1987.

Battenfeld, Mary. "'Been Shapin Words T Fit M Soul': *Cane,* Language, and Social Change." *Callaloo* 25.4 (2002): 1238–49.

Bell, Bernard. *The Afro-American Novel and Its Tradition.* Amherst: U of Massachusetts P, 1987.

———. "Jean Toomer's 'Blue Meridian': The Poet as Prophet of a New Order of Man." *Black American Literature Forum* 14.2 (1980): 77–80.

———. "A Key to the Poems in *Cane.*" *College Literature Association Journal* 14.3 (1971): 251–58.

Benson, Brian Joseph, and Mabel Mayle Dillard. *Jean Toomer.* Twayne's US Authors Ser. 389. Boston: Hall, 1980.

Benston, Kimberly W. "Sterling Brown's After-Song: 'When de Saints Go Ma'ching Home' and the Performance of Afro-American Voice." *Callaloo* 5:14–15 (1982): 33–42.

Blake, Susan L. "The Spectatorial Artist and the Structure of *Cane.*" *College Literature Association Journal* 17.4 (1974): 516–34.

Bond, Kellie Anne. "'All Things Counter': The Argument of Forms in Modern American Poetry." Diss. U of Oregon, 2002.

Bone, Robert. *The Negro Novel in America.* 1965 ed. New Haven: Yale UP, 1958.

Bontemps, Arna. "The Negro Renaissance: Jean Toomer and the Harlem Writers of the 1920's." *Anger and Beyond: The Negro Writer in the United States.* Ed. Herbert Hill. New York: Harper, 1966. 20–36.

Bowen, Barbara E. "Untroubled Voice: Call-and-Response in *Cane.*" *Black American Literature Forum* 16.1 (1982): 12–18.

Boutry, Katherine. "Black and Blue: The Female Body of Blues Writing in Jean Toomer, Toni Morrison, and Gayle Jones." *Black Orpheus: Music in African American Fiction from the Harlem Renaissance to Toni Morrison.* Ed. Saadi A. Simawe. New York: Garland, 2000. 91–118.

Bradley, David. "Looking Behind *Cane.*" *Southern Review* 21.3 (1985): 682–94.

Bus, Heiner. "Jean Toomer and the Black Heritage." *History and Tradition in Afro-American Culture.* Ed. Günter H. Lenz. Frankfurt/New York: Campus Verlag, 1984. 56–83.

Byrd, Rudolph P. *Jean Toomer's Years with Gurdjieff: Portrait of an Artist, 1923–1936.* Athens: U of Georgia P, 1990.

Caldeira, Maria Isabel. "Jean Toomer's *Cane*: The Anxiety of the Modern Artist." *Callaloo* 8.3 (1985): 544–50.

Chase, Patricia. "The Women in *Cane.*" *College Literature Association Journal* 14.3 (1971): 259–73.

Clary, Françoise. "'The Waters of My Heart': Myth and Belonging in Jean Toomer's *Cane.*" *Jean Toomer and the Harlem Renaissance.* Ed. Geneviève Fabre and Michel Feith. New Brunswick: Rutgers UP, 2001. 68–83.

Cooper, Wayne F. Introduction. *The Passion of Claude McKay: Selected Poetry and Prose, 1912–1948.* Ed. Cooper. New York: Schocken, 1973.

Coquet, Cécile. "Feeding the Soul with Words: Preaching and Dreaming in *Cane.*" *Jean Toomer and the Harlem Renaissance.* Ed. Geneviève Fabre and Michel Feith. New Brunswick: Rutgers UP, 2001. 84–95.

Cullen, Countee. Foreword. *Caroling Dusk: An Anthology of Verse by Black Poets of the Twenties.* 1927. Ed. Cullen. New York: Citadel, 1993. ix–xiv.

———. "Yet Do I Marvel." *My Soul's High Song: The Collected Writings of Countee Cullen, Voice of the Harlem Renaissance.* Ed. Gerald Early. New York: Anchor, 1991. 79.

Davis, Arthur P. *From the Dark Tower: Afro-American Writers, 1900–1960.* Washington: Howard UP, 1974.

Davis, Charles T. "Jean Toomer and the South: Region and Race as Elements within a Literary Imagination." *Harlem Renaissance Re-examined.* New York: AMS Research P, 1987. Ed. Victor A. Kramer and Robert A Russ. Troy, NY: Whitson, 1997. 187–99.

"The Day of Judgment." *Slave Songs of the United States.* Comp. William Francis Allen, Charles Peckard Ware, and Lucy McKim Garrison. New York: Simpson, 1867. 53.

"Deep River." *American Poetry: The Nineteenth Century.* Ed. John Hollander. Vol. 2. New York: Library of America, 1993. 765.

Du Boise, W. E. B. *Darkwater: Voices from Within the Veil.* New York, Harcourt, 1920.

——. *The Souls of Black Folk.* 1903. Ed. Nathan Huggins. New York: Library of America, 1986. 357–547.

Duncan, Bowie. "Jean Toomer's *Cane*: A Modern Black Oracle." *College Literature Association Journal* 15.3 (1972): 323–33.

Edmunds, Susan. "The Race Question and the 'Question of Home': Revisiting the Lynching Plot in Jean Toomer's *Cane*." *American Literature* 75.1 (2003): 141–68.

Eldridge, Richard. "The Unifying Images in Part One of Jean Toomer's *Cane*." *Jean Toomer: A Critical Evaluation.* Ed. Therman B. O'Daniel. Washington: Howard UP, 1988. 213–36.

Fabre, Geneviève. "Dramatic and Musical Structure in 'Harvest Song' and 'Kabnis.'" *Jean Toomer and the Harlem Renaissance.* Ed. Geneviève Fabre and Michel Feith. New Brunswick: Rutgers UP, 2001. 109–27.

Fabre, Geneviève and Michel Feith, eds. *Jean Toomer and the Harlem Renaissance.* New Brunswick: Rutgers UP, 2001.

——. "Tight-Lipped 'Oracle': Around and beyond *Cane*." *Jean Toomer and the Harlem Renaissance.* Ed. Geneviève Fabre and Michel Feith. New Brunswick: Rutgers UP, 2001. 1–17.

Fahy, Thomas. "The Enslaving Power of Folksong in Jean Toomer's *Cane*." *Literature and Music.* Ed. Michael J. Meyer. Rodopi Perspectives on Mod. Lit. 25. Amsterdam, New York: Rodopi, 2002. 47–63.

Favor, J. Martin. *Authentic Blackness: The Folk in the New Negro Renaissance.* Durham: Duke UP, 1999.

Fisher, Alice Poindexter. "The Influence of Ouspensky's *Tertium Organum* upon Jean Toomer's *Cane*." *College Literature Association Journal* 17.4 (1974): 504–15.

Ford, Ford Madox. *Thus To Revisit: Some Reminiscences.* 1921. New York: Octagon, 1966.

Frank, Waldo. *City Block.* 1922. New York: Scribner's, 1932.

——. *Holiday.* New York: Boni and Liveright, 1923.

——. *Our America.* New York: Boni and Liveright, 1919.

French, Warren, ed. "Afternote" to Blyden Jackson, "Jean Toomer's *Cane*: An Issue of Genre." *The Twenties: Fiction, Poetry, Drama.* Deland, FL: Everett/Edwards, 1975. 329–33.

Frost, Robert. "To John T. Bartlett." 4 July 1923. *Robert Frost: Collected Poems, Prose, and Plays.* Ed. Richard Poirier and Mark Richardson. New York: Library of America, 1995. 664–66.

Fuss, Diana. *Essentially Speaking: Feminism, Nature and Difference.* New York: Routledge, 1989.

Gates, Henry Louis, Jr. "The Same Difference: Reading Jean Toomer, 1923–1982." *Figures in Black: Words, Signs, and the 'Racial' Self.* Oxford: Oxford UP, 1987. 196–224.

Gibson, Donald B. "Jean Toomer: The Politics of Denial." *The Politics of Literary Expression: A Study of Major Black Writers.* Westport, CT: Greenwood, 1981. 155–81.

Goede, William J. "Jean Toomer's Ralph Kabnis: Portrait of the Negro Artist as a Young Man." *Phylon* 30 (1969): 73–85.

Golding, Alan. "Jean Toomer's *Cane*: The Search for Identity through Form." *Arizona Quarterly* 39.3 (1983): 197–214.

Grandjeat, Charles-Yves. "The Poetics of Passing in Jean Toomer's *Cane*." *Jean Toomer and the Harlem Renaissance*. Ed. Geneviève Fabre and Michel Feith. New Brunswick: Rutgers UP, 2001. 57–67.

Griffin, Farah Jasmine. *"Who Set You Flowin'?": The African-American Migration Narrative*. New York: Oxford UP, 1995.

"Gulp." *Oxford English Dictionary*. 2nd ed. 1989.

Hajek, Friederike. "The Change of Literary Authority in the Harlem Renaissance: Jean Toomer's *Cane*." *The Black Columbiad: Defining Moments in African American Literature and Culture*. Harvard English Studies 19. Ed. Werner Sollers and Maria Diedrich. Cambridge, MA: Harvard UP, 1994. 185–90.

Harmon, Charles. "*Cane*, Race, and 'Neither/Norism.'" *The Southern Literary Journal*. 32.2 (2000): 90–101.

H. D., "Oread." *H. D. Collected Poems 1912–1944*. New York: New Directions, 1983. 55.

Hill, Herbert, Ed. *Anger and Beyond: The Negro Writer in the United States*. New York: Harper, 1966.

Huggins, Nathan Irvin. *Harlem Renaissance*. London: Oxford UP, 1971.

Hughes, Langston. *The Big Sea*. 1940. New York: Thunder's Mouth, 1986.

——. "The Negro Artist and the Racial Mountain." *Nation* 122 (1926): 692–94.

Hutchinson, George B. *The Harlem Renaissance in Black and White*. Cambridge: Belknap-Harvard UP, 1995.

——. "Jean Toomer and American Racial Discourse." *Texas Studies in Language and Literature* 35.2 (1993): 226–50.

——. "Re: A question about *Cane*." E-mail to the author. 12 Feb. 2001.

——. "The Whitman Legacy and the Harlem Renaissance." *Walt Whitman: The Centennial Essays*. Ed. Ed Folsom. Iowa City: U of Iowa P, 1994. 201–16.

Ikonné, Chidi. *From DuBois to Van Vechten: The Early New Negro Literature, 1903–1926*. Contributions in Afro-American and African Studies 60. Westport, CT: Greenwood, 1981.

Innes, Catherine L. "The Unity of Jean Toomer's *Cane*." *College Literature Association Journal* 15.3 (1972): 306–21.

Jackson, Blyden. *The Waiting Years: Essays on American Negro Literature*. Baton Rouge: Louisiana State UP, 1976.

Johnson, James Weldon. Preface to the First Edition. *The Book of American Negro Poetry*. 1922. Rev. ed. New York: Harcourt, 1931. 9–48.

Jones, Robert B. *Jean Toomer and the Prison-House of Thought: A Phenomenology of the Spirit*. Amherst: U of Massachusetts P, 1993.

Jones, Gayl. "Blues Ballad: Jean Toomer's 'Karintha.'" *Liberating Voices: Oral Tradition in African American Literature*. Cambridge: Harvard UP, 1991. 70–78.

Jung, Udo, O. H. "'Spirit-Torsos of Exquisite Strength': The Theme of Individual Weakness vs. Collective Strength in Two of Toomer's Poems." *Jean Toomer: A Critical Evaluation*. Ed. Therman B. O'Daniel. Washington: Howard UP, 1988. 329–35.

Karrer, Wolfgang. "Black Modernism? The Early Poetry of Jean Toomer and Claude McKay." *Jean Toomer and the Harlem Renaissance.* Ed. Geneviève Fabre and Michel Feith. New Brunswick: Rutger UP, 2001. 128–41.

Kerman, Cynthia Earl and Richard Eldridge. *The Lives of Jean Toomer: A Hunger for Wholeness.* Baton Rouge: Louisiana State UP, 1987.

Kodat, Catherine Gunther. "To 'Flash White Light from Ebony': The Problem of Modernism in Jean Toomer's *Cane.*" *Twentieth-Century Literature* 46.1 (2000): 1–17.

Kutzinski, Vera M. "Unseasonal Flowers: Nature and History in Plácido and Jean Toomer." *Yale Journal of Criticism* 3.2 (1990): 153–79.

Larson, Charles R. *Invisible Darkness: Jean Toomer and Nella Larson.* Iowa City: U of Iowa P, 1993.

Lieber, Todd. "Design and Movement in *Cane.*" *College Literature Association Journal* 12.1 (1969): 35–50.

Locke, Alaine. *The New Negro: An Interpretation.* 1925. New York: Atheneum, 1969. 3–16.

MacKethan, Lucinda H. "Jean Toomer's *Cane*: A Pastoral Problem." *Mississippi Quarterly* 28.4 (1975): 423–34.

Margolies, Edward. *Native Sons: A Critical Study of Twentieth-Century Negro American Authors.* Philadelphia: Lippincott, 1968.

Martin, Odette. "*Cane*: Method and Myth." *Obsidian* 2 (1976): 5–20.

McKay, Nellie Y. *Jean Toomer: Artist: A Study of His Literary Life and Work, 1894–1936.* Chapel Hill: U of North Carolina P, 1984.

Mellard, James M. "Solipsism, Symbolism, and Demonism: The Lyrical Mode in Fiction." *Southern Humanities Review* 7 (1973): 37–51.

Michaels, Walter Benn. *Our America: Nativism, Modernism, and Pluralism.* Durham: Duke UP, 1995.

Michlin, Monica. "'Karintha': A Textual Analysis." *Jean Toomer and the Harlem Renaissance.* Ed. Geneviève Fabre and Michel Feith. New Brunswick: Rutgers UP, 2001. 96–108.

"My Lord, What a Morning." *American Poetry of the Nineteenth Century.* Ed. John Hollander. Vol. 2. New York: Library of America, 1993. 794–95.

Nadell, Martha Jane. "Race and the Visual Arts in the Works of Jean Toomer and Georgia O'Keeffe." *Jean Toomer and the Harlem Renaissance.* Ed. Geneviève Fabre and Michel Feith. New Brunswick: Rutgers UP, 2001. 142–61.

Nelson, Cary. *Repression and Recovery: Modern American Poetry and the Politics of Cultural Memory, 1920–1945.* Madison: U of Wisconsin P, 1989.

Nicholls, David G. *Conjuring the Folk: Forms of Modernity in African America.* Ann Arbor: U of Michigan P, 2000.

———. "Jean Toomer's *Cane,* Modernization, and the Spectral Folk." *Modernism, Inc.: Body, Memory, Capital.* Ed. Jani Scandura and Michael Thurston. New York: New York UP, 2001. 151–70.

North, Michael. *The Dialect of Modernism: Race, Language, and Twentieth-Century Literature.* New York: Oxford UP, 1994.

O'Daniel, Therman B., ed. *Jean Toomer: A Critical Evaluation*. Washington: Howard UP, 1988.

———. "Jean Toomer and Mae Wright: An Interview with Mae Wright Peck." *Jean Toomer: A Critical Evaluation*. Ed. Therman B. O'Daniel. Washington: Howard UP, 1988. 25–40.

Oliver, Paul. *Blues Fell This Morning*. New York: Horizon, 1960.

Payne, Ladell. *Black Novelists and the Southern Literary Tradition*. Athens: U of Georgia P, 1981.

Peckham, Joel B. "Jean Toomer's *Cane*: Self as Montage and the Drive toward Integration." *American Literature* 72.2 (2000): 275–90.

Perry, Margaret. *Silence to the Drums: A Survey of the Literature of the Harlem Renaissance*. Contributions in Afro-American and African Studies 18. Westport, CT: Greenwood, 1976.

Petesch, Donald A. "Jean Toomer." *A Spy in the Enemy's Country: The Emergence of Modern Black Literature*. Iowa City: U of Iowa P, 1989. 196–212.

Pound, Ezra. *How to Read*. London: Harmsworth, 1931.

Preminger, Alex and T. V. F. Brogan, eds. "Chorus." *The New Princeton Encyclopedia of Poetry and Poetics*. Princeton: Princeton UP, 1993. 201–02.

Pritchard, William H. *Frost: A Literary Life Reconsidered*. New York: Oxford UP, 1984.

Ramazani, Jahan. *Poetry of Mourning: The Modern Elegy from Hardy to Heaney*. Chicago: U of Chicago P, 1994.

Reilly, John M. "The Search for Black Redemption: Jean Toomer's *Cane*." *Studies in the Novel* 2.3 (1970): 312–24.

Rice, Herbert W. "An Incomplete Circle: Repeated Images in Part Two of *Cane*." *College Literature Association Journal* 29.4 (1986): 442–61.

Rusch, Frederik L. "The Blue Man: Jean Toomer's Solution to His Problems of Identity." *Obsidian: Black Literature in Review* 6.1–2 (1980): 38–54.

Sachheim, Eric, comp. *The Blues Line: A Collection of Blues Lyrics*. New York: Grossman, 1969.

Sanders, Mark A. *Afro-Modernist Aesthetics and the Poetry of Sterling A. Brown*. Athens: U of Georgia P, 1999.

Scruggs, Charles W. "Jean Toomer: Fugitive." *American Literature* 47.1 (1975): 84–96.

———. "The Mark of Cain and the Redemption of Art: A Study in Theme and Structure of Jean Toomer's *Cane*." *American Literature* 44.2 (1972): 276–91.

Scruggs, Charles W. and Lee VanDemarr. *Jean Toomer and the Terrors of American History*. Philadelphia: U of Pennsylvania P, 1998.

"Snatch." *Oxford English Dictionary*. 2nd ed. 1989.

Sollers, Werner. "Jean Toomer's *Cane*: Modernism and Race in Interwar America." *Jean Toomer and the Harlem Renaissance*. Ed. Geneviève Fabre and Michel Feith. New Brunswick: Rutgers UP, 2001. 18–37.

Soto, Michael. "Jean Toomer and Horace Liveright; or, A New Negro Gets 'into the Swing of It.'" *Jean Toomer and the Harlem Renaissance*. Ed. Geneviève Fabre and Michel Feith. New Brunswick: Rutgers UP, 2001. 162–87.

"Stars in the Elements." *Religious Folk Songs of the Negro As Sung on the Plantations.* (New Edition) Arranged by the musical directors of the Hampton Normal and Agricultural Institute from the original edition by Thomas P. Fenner. Hampton, VA: Institute, 1909. 84.

Steele, Timothy. *Missing Measures: Modern Poetry and the Revolt against Meter.* Fayetteville: U of Arkansas P, 1990.

Taft, Michael, ed. *Blues Lyric Poetry: An Anthology.* New York: Garland, 1993.

Taylor, Clyde. "The Second Coming of Jean Toomer." *Obsidian: Black Literature in Review* 1.3 (1975): 37–57.

Thornton, Jerome E. "'Goin on de Muck': The Paradoxical Journey of the Black American Hero." *College Literature Association Journal* 31 (1988): 261–80.

Toomer, Jean. *Cane.* 1923. Ed. Darwin T. Turner. New York: Norton, 1988.

———. *The Collected Poems of Jean Toomer.* Ed. Robert B. Jones and Margery Toomer Latimer. Chapel Hill: U of North Carolina P, 1988.

———. *Essentials.* Ed. Rudolph P. Byrd. Athens: U of Georgia P, 1991.

———. *A Jean Toomer Reader: Selected Unpublished Writings.* Ed. Frederik L. Rusch. New York: Oxford UP, 1993.

———. *Jean Toomer: Selected Essays and Literary Criticism.* Ed. Robert B. Jones. Knoxville: U of Tennessee P, 1996.

———. *The Wayward and the Seeking: A Collection of Writings by Jean Toomer.* Ed. Darwin T. Turner. Washington, D.C.: Howard UP, 1980.

Tracy, Steven C. *Write Me a Few of Your Lines: A Blues Reader.* Amherst: U of Massachusetts P, 1999.

Turner, Darwin T. "The Failure of a Playwright." *College Literature Association Journal* 10.4 (1967): 308–18.

———. *In a Minor Chord: Three Afro-American Writers and Their Search for Identity.* Carbondale: Southern Illinois UP, 1971.

Introduction [to the 1975 Edition of *Cane*]. *Cane.* By Jean Toomer. New York: Norton, 1988. 121–38.

Wagner, Jean. *Black Poets of the United States: From Paul Laurence Dunbar to Langston Hughes.* Trans. Kenneth Douglas. Urbana: U of Illinois P, 1973.

Wagner-Martin, Linda. "Toomer's *Cane* as Narrative Sequence." *Modern American Short Story Sequences: Composite Fictions and Fictive Communities.* Ed. J. Gerald Kennedy. Cambridge: Cambridge UP, 1995.

Walker, Alice. "The Divided Life of Jean Toomer." *In Search of Our Mothers' Gardens: Womanist Prose.* San Diego: Harcourt, 1983. 60–65.

Washington, Booker T. 1901. *Up from Slavery.* Ed. William L. Andrews. New York: Norton, 1996.

"'We raise de wheat.'" *American Poetry: The Nineteenth Century.* Ed. John Hollander. Vol. 2. New York: Library of America, 1993. 819.

Webster, T. B. L. *The Greek Chorus.* London: Methuen, 1970.

Werner, Craig Hansen. *Playing the Changes: From Afro-Modernism to the Jazz Impulse.* Urbana: U of Illinois P, 1994.

Whalan, Mark. "Jean Toomer, Technology, and Race." *Journal of American Studies* 36.3 (2002): 459–72.

———. "'Taking Myself in Hand': Jean Toomer and Physical Culture." *Modernism/modernity* 10.4 (2003): 597–615.

Whitman, Walt. "Song of Myself." *Walt Whitman: Complete Poetry and Collected Prose.* Ed. Justin Kaplan. New York: Library of America, 1982. 188–247.

Williams, William Carlos. *In the American Grain.* New York: New Directions, 1956.

Woodson, Jon. *To Make a New Race: Gurdjieff, Toomer, and the Harlem Renaissance.* Jackson: UP of Mississippi, 1999.

Index